MARCION AND HIS INFLUENCE

MARCION AND HIS INFLUENCE

BY

E. C. BLACKMAN, B.D.

Tutor of Cheshunt College, Cambridge

Wipf & Stock
PUBLISHERS
Eugene, Oregon

Wipf and Stock Publishers
199 West 8th Avenue, Suite 3
Eugene, Oregon 97401

Marcion and His Influence
By Blackman, E.C.

ISBN: 1-59244-731-7
Publication date 6/21/2004
Previously published by SPCK, 1948

CONTENTS

LIST OF ABBREVIATIONS

Harnack = Harnack's monograph, *Marcion: Das Evangelium vom fremden Gott.* 2nd ed., 1924. (Volume 45 of the *Texte und Untersuchungen zur Geschichte der altchristlichen Literatur*, ed. by Harnack and Schmidt.)

Tert. or Tertullian = Tertullian *Adversus Marcionem.* Other works of Tertullian are specifically named when quoted.

Adamantius = The treatise, *De recta in Deum fide*, once attributed to Origen. It consists of five dialogues with heretics, and Adamantius plays the part of the defender of orthodox Christianity. The first two dialogues are the most relevant for our purpose as they are concerned entirely with Marcionite objections.

The edition here quoted is that by Bakhuyzen in *Die griechischen christlichen Schriftsteller.*

J.T.S. = *Journal of Theological Studies.*

Z.N.T.W. = *Zeitschrift für die Neutestamentliche Wissenschaft.*

Z.K.G. = *Zeitschrift für die Kirchengeschichte.*

C.S.E.L. = *Corpus Scriptorum Ecclesiasticorum Latinorum* (1866 ff.).

G.K. = Zahn, *Geschichte des N.T. Kanons.*

FOREWORD

THE practice of this book is, in general, to use a capital C to denote the universal Church and a small c when a local or particular church is meant.

Marcion was a many-sided heretic, and the study of him is rewarding because it introduces so many aspects of Christian theology. I am grateful to Dr. J. S. Whale, now Headmaster of Mill Hill School, who first suggested Marcion to me as a subject of research.

My thanks are also due to Professor C. H. Dodd of Cambridge, for advice at the closing stages of my work ; and to my friends, the Rev. John Wilding of Newbury and the Rev. W. D. Davies of the Independent College, Bradford, for help with the reading of the proofs.

E. C. B.

INTRODUCTION

TO Christian writers at the end of the second and beginning of the third centuries Marcion was the arch-heretic. We learn this from the number of treatises which were written to counteract his influence, and from the intensity with which the controversy was waged. Tertullian thought it necessary to publish five books against Marcion—by far the longest of his writings. Irenaeus had purposed to devote a treatise to the refutation of Marcion, though he never actually carried out this intention.[1] No other single man had called forth such a volume of anxious apologetic from the Church.

For Marcion was a real danger. His was not a semi-philosophical system like those of the Gnostics. Philosophical systems and trends of thought are not in themselves the greatest obstacles to Christianity. The Church has most to fear, not from academic criticisms but from the action of sincere and convinced men. Marcion was such a man. Of his sincerity there is no question; that is why chapters like Tertullian 1. 1 are in such bad taste. He was not primarily interested in abstract speculation, such as the æonic genealogies of Valentinus. But he had passionate convictions, and he founded an organization which rivalled the growing Catholic Church. Justin says that in his time (*c.* A.D. 150—when Marcion was still alive) Marcionites could be found all over the Roman Empire.[2] This is why the leaders of the Church were alarmed. This man was not the head of a school of disciples like Valentinus and Basilides. He was the founder of a Church with a definite organization and a missionary programme.

The organization of the Marcionite Church was parallel to that of the Catholic Church, comprising catechumens, elders and bishops; Marcionites met for worship in their own buildings; they observed the same holy days and the same sacraments as Catholics; most important of all, they had their own canon of Scripture. Tertullian, who of all Christian apologists attacked Marcion most comprehensively and vigorously, did this in spite of some aspects of Marcionitism which we might have expected to moderate his condemnation of it. Tertullian was no friend of the Jews, as is obvious from a glance at his

[1] Irenaeus *Haer.* 1. 27. 4; 3. 12. 12.

[2] κατὰ πᾶν γένος ἀνθρώπων, *Apol.* 1. 26; cf. also Tertullian 5. 19: *Marcionis traditio haeretica totum implevit mundum.*

Adversus Judaeos. Marcion's anti-Judaism might, therefore, have been a merit in Tertullian's eyes. Again, Tertullian himself leaned towards asceticism, and in later life joined the ascetic Montanist community. In Marcionitism he could see an organization which condemned the flesh and all the works of the Creator, and imposed the most rigorous of disciplines. Thirdly, while Marcion was an exclusively Biblical theologian and paid no attention to systematizing his thought in accordance with those schools of philosophy which won most acceptance in his day, Tertullian also had said hard things about the philosophers.[1] And yet, in spite of this which he had in common with Marcion, he denounced him as an enemy of the Church with whom there could be no compromise.

Harnack's comprehensive monograph more than any other book enables us to understand Marcion's thought and to see why he was a danger to the developing Catholic Church. The present essay is a study of Marcion's relation to, and influence on, this development. It considers in turn Marcion's work as the organizer of a Christian church, as Biblical critic, canon-maker and textual emendator, and, finally, as theologian. The attempt has been made throughout to trace the effect of his work in the larger context of Catholic Christianity at that time, and thus to reach some estimate of Marcion's significance in the history of Christianity. Marcion is fortunate to have found such an interpreter as Harnack, whose monograph on him is remarkable not only for erudition and mastery of critical reconstruction, but also for the enthusiasm bestowed on a subject of lifelong interest to the author. The present more modest study, though constantly indebted to that fascinating reconstruction, ventures to protest that Harnack estimated too highly the significance of the great second-century nonconformist.

[1] See *Apol.* 46, *De Praesc.* 7, *Adv. Hermog.* 8, *De Anim.* 1.

1
THE MARCIONITE CHURCH

Habet plane et evangelium Marcionis ecclesias, sed suas, tam posteras quam adulteras, quarum si censum requiras, facilius apostaticum invenias quam apostolicum, Marcione scilicet conditore vel aliquo de Marcionis examine. Faciunt favos et vespae, faciunt ecclesias et Marcionitae.

TERTULLIAN, *Adv. Marc.* 4. 5.

MARCION was the founder not of a school, but of a church. He had in all probability been brought up in the church at Sinope, his Pontic home,[1] and certainly was for a time a member of the Roman Church. Moreover, he had learnt the importance of the Church from his master St. Paul. He retained in his New Testament the Pauline reference to the Church as the Bride of Christ, Eph. 5. 22–32, although a metaphor from marriage can hardly have been to his liking.[2] Stronger than his scruples on this point was his desire to retain a passage describing the closeness of the relation between the Church and Christ. Gal. 4. 24–26 throws further light on Marcion's conception of the Church. Here Marcion altered the text and interpolated Eph. 1. 21 so as to read: ἅτινά ἐστιν ἀλληγορούμενα· αὗται γάρ εἰσιν αἱ δύο ἐπιδείξεις, (*ostensiones* Latin) μία μὲν ἀπὸ ὄρους Σινᾶ εἰς τὴν συναγωγὴν τῶν Ἰουδαίων κατὰ τὸν νόμον γεννῶσα εἰς δουλείαν, ἄλλη δὲ ὑπεράνω πάσης ἀρχῆς γεννῶσα καὶ δυνάμεως καὶ ἐξουσίας καὶ παντὸς ὀνόματος ὀνομαζομένου—οὐ μόνον ἐν τῷ αἰῶνι τούτῳ, ἀλλὰ καὶ ἐν τῷ μέλλοντι—εἰς ἣν ἐπηγγειλάμεθα ἁγίαν ἐκκλησίαν, ἥτις ἐστὶν μητὴρ ἡμῶν.[3] Marcion thus thought of the Church not only as the Bride of Christ, but as the Mother of the redeemed; and as a supernatural creation destined to endure for ever.

A turning-point in Marcion's life came when he openly declared his beliefs in Rome and invited the presbyters of the church to approve them. This was the first Roman synod of which we know. Its outcome was not as Marcion had hoped, for instead of receiving the

[1] According to Hippolytus, his father was bishop there.

[2] Ephraem tells us that the Marcionites actually called the Church the Bride of Christ: cf. Harnack, p. 143, n. 1.

[3] Harnack's reconstruction, p. 76*, from Tertullian's quotation of Marcion's Latin (*Adv. Marc.* 5. 4). The alterations in the text are not certainly the work of Marcion himself, but may be due to a disciple.

official blessing on his theories he was excommunicated.[1] Then began the activity which created the Marcionite Church. Foiled in his attempt to convert the leading church of the West to his doctrine, Marcion addressed himself to the task of building up a church of his own. He seems to have previously advertised his beliefs in Asia Minor, but with little response. We hear of his introducing himself to Polycarp and asking for his recognition, and being rebuffed with the words: "I recognize you—as the first-born of Satan!" This probably took place in Smyrna, where Polycarp was bishop.[2] Possibly Marcion visited Ephesus also.[3] It may be inferred that he left Asia Minor for a twofold reason: he was already suspect there, whereas Rome was the centre of the world, and a doctrine which found acceptance in Rome had more chance of being disseminated than one which found only local acceptance in the provinces. So Marcion came to Rome, doubtless making the journey in one of his own ships. He joined the Christian community there and made it a present of 200,000 sesterces. One wonders if this was meant to allay the suspicions of some brethren who had heard rumours about his heterodoxy.[4] However that may be, he concealed his unorthodox tendencies for a time, until he thought he might commend them to the church at Rome.

[1] Epiphanius, *Panarion* 42. 2 (Holl's edition, vol. ii, pp. 95 f.), and Philastrius, *Haer.* 17 (*C.S.E.L.*, XXXVIII, p. 23), inform us that he enquired of the Roman presbyters the interpretation of Luke 5. 36 and 6. 43, and rejected the interpretation they gave, doubtless indicating the lines his own exegesis would take, i.e., the incompatibility of the Gospel with Judaism, and the doctrine of two gods.

[2] But it may have taken place later in Rome, when Marcion's church was growing. This is perhaps more probable, as Irenaeus relates the story after he has mentioned that Polycarp on a visit to Rome converted many Valentinians and Marcionites. Marcion said to Polycarp: ἐπιγίνωσκε ἡμᾶς. The ἡμᾶς might mean "me and my church". See Irenaeus Haer. 3. 3. 4.

[3] This is in itself probable, but the only actual evidence seems to be Philastrius in his book describing 156 heresies, ch. 17 ad fin. (Harnack's reference on p. 13* is wrong.) Philastrius's testimony is not to be used without caution, for he informs us in this same chapter that Marcion received no Pauline Epistles except the Pastorals! He probably relied on the early evidence in Hippolytus's *Syntagma*, however, and did not merely copy Epiphanius. Bacon (*Studies in Matthew*, pp. 452–466, esp. p. 459) rejects the idea of Marcion's excommunication (? by John) in Ephesus. The Marcionite prologue to St. John might be taken to imply a visit of Marcion to Ephesus, whether it was the Apostle or another who repudiated him there. See below, p. 56.

[4] Some have assumed that Marcion first became a Christian in Rome. For this they rely on Tertullian's words: (Marcion) *pecuniam in primo calore fidei catholicae ecclesiae contulit* (*Adv. Marc.* 4. 4). But Tertullian need not be interpreted literally here. Harnack brings other arguments (p. 17*, n. 2). Elsewhere Tertullian says of Marcion and Valentinus *in catholicae primo doctrinam credidisse apud ecclesiam Romanensem* (*De Praesc.* 30).

The officials of this church rejected them,[1] and in consequence he thought no more of reforming the church from within, but turned rather to the creation of a new church. This was the first "protestant" schism, and it has real affinities with the Lutheran schism of 1519.[2]

Marcion's success as the founder of a church was remarkable, and must have been largely due to an inspiring and energetic personality. Already in the year A.D. 150 Justin could say[3] that his influence extended all over the Empire. A real rival to the growing Catholic Church had sprung into being, and for a few years it must actually have seemed possible that the Marcionite church would become the dominant church.

The danger which the rise of Marcionite churches portended in the eyes of Christian leaders can be inferred from the vigour with which they set about the refutation of Marcion's teaching. Almost every prominent Christian writer in the second half of the second century, from Justin to Tertullian, felt obliged to publish a book against Marcion. Tertullian's five books against Marcion are the longest of all his works. Celsus knows only two Christian Communions of real importance—the Catholic and the Marcionite. The Christian poet and philosopher Bardesanes in Edessa towards the end of the second century composed dialogues against Marcion in Syriac,[4] and these were translated into Greek. The passage of Eusebius shows that Bardesanes treated only secondarily of other heresies, and that, therefore, in Bardesanes' judgement Marcionitism was the great heretical danger in Syria at that time. By the year A.D. 200 Marcionitism had called forth attacks in three languages—Greek, Latin, and Syriac.

The third century saw the decline of Marcionitism in the West, although in the East it continued to hold its own.[5] In the West it is

[1] The date is probably A.D. 144. Tertullian (*Adv. Marc.* I. 19) informs us that the Marcionites reckoned 115 years 6½ months between Christ and Marcion. Bill (*Texte und Untersuchungen*, 38, ii, pp. 66–72) suggests that the day in Marcion's life which they commemorated was the day on which he left Pontus; but Harnack is more persuasive when he suggests that it was the day of Marcion's exclusion from the Roman church, for Marcion's break with the Old Church would be potentially the foundation of the New Church; here is a reason for the commemoration of the day by later Marcionites: cf. Harnack, pp. 21* ff.

Harnack's chronology is disputed by Barnikol in a stimulating essay. For a discussion of this, see Appendix 2 at the end of this chapter.

[2] Harnack sees many parallels between Marcion and Luther: cf. pp. 27, 218 ff., 225. Cf. also Neander's judgement that Marcion was the first Protestant.

[3] *Apol.* I. 26: κατὰ πᾶν γένος ἀνθρώπων.

[4] Eusebius, *H.E.* 4. 30. I.

[5] One reason, if not for the decline, at least for the more moderate increase of Marcionitism was that Marcion relied for the growth of his communities entirely on

noteworthy that as Marcionitism grew weaker, Manichæism grew stronger, and it is a fair assumption, considering certain points of affinity between the teaching of Marcion and that of Mani, that in so far as Marcionites did not die out or become Catholic Christians, many of them joined the Manichæans. Harnack suggests that Western Manichæism was more Christian than Eastern Manichæism. Whether or not this was one of the reasons why Marcionitism had a longer independent life in the East, the fact remains. The oldest church-inscription we possess happens to be the inscription on a Marcionite church.[1] The date is A.D. 318–319. This seems to have been the year in which the church was built, and evidently the Marcionites of that district—Lebaba, near Damascus—took advantage of the imperial edicts of toleration which had recently been promulgated. Thirty years later Cyril of Jerusalem found it necessary to counteract Marcionite beliefs in his Catechisms, and to warn his catechumens against slipping into a Marcionite meeting by mistake. He says that it is not enough to enquire, on entering a strange city, where the church is; one must be careful to ask for the Catholic church: καὶ γὰρ αἱ λοιπαὶ τῶν ἀσεβῶν αἱρέσεις "κυριακὰ" τὰ ἑαυτῶν σπήλαια καλεῖν ἐπιχειροῦσι[2] (Cyril has in mind chiefly Marcionites and Manichæans). Many towns in Cyril's diocese apparently had a Marcionite chapel as well as an orthodox church; and probably some small towns had only a Marcionite building—hence the need for the bishop's warning. Constantine's ban on heretical buildings must, however, have contributed to the decline of Marcionitism. Nevertheless, as late as the middle of the fifth century Theodoret, Bishop of Cyprus, boasts (*Ep.* 113) of "freeing from the disease of Marcion" over a thousand souls; elsewhere (*Ep.* 81) he mentions Marcionite villages, eight of which he had brought back to the true faith. In the same century Esnik of Colb wrote against Marcionites in Armenia, devoting the last of his four books—*Against the Sects*—entirely to them.

The Marcionite methods of church government were, as far as we know, the same as those of the Catholic Church. That the imitation was mutual is quite unlikely.[3] The inscription just referred to bears

---

the winning of new members, not on the birth of numerous and obedient children to Marcionite parents. Strict continence was the rule in the Marcionite church. Doubtless the number of catechumens always far exceeded the number of those who accepted the full discipline, although from the point of view of the orthodox Church all would be heretics.

[1] Le Bas-Waddington, *Inscriptions Grecques et Latines*, III, pp. 582 f.; Harnack, pp. 341* ff.

[2] *Cat.* 18. 26.

[3] Harnack vaguely suggests this (p. 152).

the name of a presbyter who doubtless superintended the building of the church (and perhaps paid for it). As no bishop is named this presbyter must also have been the presiding officer of the church, in which case the church was not a large one. The nearest bishop may have been in Damascus. We know the name of another Marcionite presbyter—Metrodorus, who was crucified at Smyrna during the Decian persecution[1] (for the Marcionite church, as well as the Catholic, produced its martyrs). According to Adamantius[2] there had been a regular succession of Marcionite bishops since the death of Marcion himself. Whether Marcion was called ἐπίσκοπος during his lifetime we cannot say, although the Marcionite Megethius in Adamantius' *Dialogue* is made to say: Μαρκίων ἐπίσκοπός μου ἦν.[2] It is probable that Marcion himself introduced bishops and presbyters, and also the office of deacons[3]—for these, too, are mentioned by St. Paul, Marcion's authority.

A Marcionite innovation was the permission given to women to hold office in a church. This must have rested on a conviction of Marcion's that distinctions of sex mattered naught among the redeemed. Be it noted, too, that Marcion's hatred of marriage was not due to the belief that woman is an inferior vessel. It rested rather on the Pauline principle that in Christ there is neither male nor female.[4] Our evidence for the prominent part played by women is Tertullian's ironical description: *Ipsae mulieres haereticae quam procaces! Quae audeant docere, contendere, exorcismos agere, curationes repromittere, forsitan et tingere.*[5] This is confirmed by the later witness of Epiphanius that women were allowed to baptize.[6]

Tertullian's description of the heretics in this chapter brings information about other church officers and about the conduct of church meetings: "*Imprimis quis catechumenus, quis fidelis incertum est; pariter adeunt, pariter audiunt, pariter orant, etiam ethnici si supervenerint . . . simplicitatem volunt esse prostrationem disciplinae. . . . Ordinationes eorum temerariae, leves, inconstantes, nunc neophytos collocant, nunc saeculo obstrictos,*

[1] Harnack, p. 340*.

[2] 1. 8.

[3] The office of lector as well, cf. Tertullian, *De Praesc.* 41. In all probability Tertullian has Marcionite meetings in mind here.

[4] In 1 Timothy a lower view of the place of woman is expressed, but Marcion rejected the Pastorals, or possibly did not know them.

[5] *De Praesc.* 41. Tertullian does not specify Marcionite women, and may be thinking of Montanism. (This treatise was written before Tertullian himself became a Montanist.) But the passage can hardly be without reference to Marcionites.

[6] But Marcion retained the Pauline prohibition of women speaking in church (1 Cor. 14. 34). Epiphanius, *Haer.* 42. 4 (Holl, p. 100) on women baptizing, copied by Esnik, 4. 16 (Schmid, p. 204).

nunc apostatas nostros . . . itaque alius hodie episcopus, cras alius; hodie diaconus, qui cras lector, hodie presbyter qui cras laicus; nam et laicis sacerdotalia munera iniungunt." After due allowance has been made for Tertullian's misrepresentation, it appears that Marcion more than Catholic leaders favoured democracy in church management. By a frequent re-appointment to offices, as well as by extending to laymen what Catholics would have considered priestly functions, he hindered the growth of a rigid distinction between clergy and laity. How near this comes to the principle of the priesthood of all believers, or how far it is a degradation of that high principle, it is difficult to say. Tertullian's words must not be made the basis of too great inferences, and it is much to be regretted that we have not more detailed information on this point, and that fragments expressing Marcion's own views have not been preserved. There is one passage, quoted by Origen, and copied by Jerome, from Marcion's *Antitheses* which corroborates Tertullian.[1] It is Marcion's interpretation of Gal. 6. 6: *Marcion hunc locum ita interpretatus est, ut putaret fideles et catechumenos simul orare debere, et magistrum communicare in oratione discipulis.* Harnack suggests that Marcion was protesting against the growing conception of special grace given to bishops. Bosshardt[2] sees in Marcion's teaching of the equality of all members and admission of catechumens to the Eucharist a reaction of the laity against the hierarchical tendencies of the Church. He points out affinity with Montanism also, emphasizing the prominent position allowed to women in both Montanism and Marcionitism. Was Marcion protesting against the *disciplina arcani*? The fact that a part of the Christian divine service was carried out in secret gave the heathen an opportunity to fabricate stories of Thyestean banquets and other immorality in Christian assemblies. Marcion may have sought to remove the ground of such accusations. From *De Praescriptione* 41 we gather that in Catholic churches catechumens were separated from the regular service, though we cannot be certain whether they had no admittance at all, or a limited one. According to Justin they were kept out altogether. The *Apostolic Tradition* of Hippolytus agrees with Tertullian on this.[3] Marcion was more tolerant. Even pagans

[1] Harnack, pp. 146 f., 78*.

[2] E. Bosshardt: *Essai sur l'Originalité et la Probité de Tertullien dans son Traité Contre Marcion*, 1921, p. 26.

[3] Dated A.D 217 or a little earlier according to Dix. It can probably be used as evidence of late second-century practice. It prescribes a three-year period of instruction for catechumens, during which they may attend the service of worship, but are not to join in the congregational prayer, nor give the kiss of peace; and they are to be dismissed separately by their teacher. See Dix's edition (1937), pp. 28–39; and for the dating, p. xxxvii.

were welcome at Marcionite meetings. Catholics seem to have been much under the influence of Matt. 6. 5 and 7. 6 (Christ's warnings against praying in public, and giving the holy thing to dogs). But Marcionites did not have these verses in their Bible.[1]

The content of the Marcionite divine service must have been very similar to that of an orthodox one, so much so that orthodox Christians had to be careful not to go into a Marcionite church by mistake (see the quotation from Cyril of Jerusalem on p. 4). The general similarity of Marcionite and Catholic *cultus* is admitted by Tertullian:[2] *Gloriae relatio et benedictio et laus et hymni et signaculum frontium et ecclesiarum sacramenta et munditiae sacrificiorum in te* (i.e., among Marcionites) *quoque deprehenduntur.* The Marcionites used special psalms other than the Davidic ones.[3] They will have held St. Paul in especial reverence, and have given particular attention to the preaching of the Gospel as he interpreted it.

Marcion retained the sacraments of Baptism and the Eucharist. Tertullian says: (Marcion's Christ) *usque nunc nec aquam reprobavit creatoris, qua suos abluit, nec oleum quo suos unguit, nec mellis et lactis societatem qua suos infantat, nec panem, quo ipsum corpus suum repraesentat, etiam in sacramentis propriis egens mendicitatibus creatoris.*[4] Water was used instead of wine at the Eucharist, but otherwise the rite was celebrated in the usual way. Nor was this practice peculiar to Marcion. Marcion's baptismal ritual was also in all probability the same as that of the Catholic Church, for at the time of the Baptismal Controversy in the third century it could be claimed that Marcionite baptism was valid and need not be repeated if a Marcionite sought to enter the Catholic fold.[5]

[1] R. L. Poole, in his *Illustrations of the History of the Mediæval Church*, pp. 92–94, draws an interesting distinction between Marcion and Manes. The main point at which these men's systems diverged was the idea of the Church. While Marcion asserted equal rights for all Christians, Manes inaugurated a priestly caste. The theory of the one was congregational, of the other sacerdotal. Marcion certainly withdrew from that line of development which was represented by Cyprian in the third century.

[2] *Adv. Marc.* 3. 22.

[3] *Muratorian Fragment* 82–84: confirmed by Maruta (see Harnack, p. 363*). According to Ephraem the Syrian Marcionites worshipped toward the sunset: "When the sun comes to the West, they [Manicheans] worship the West, as do the Marcionites their brethren." (C. W. Mitchell, *St. Ephraem's Prose Refutations of Mani, Marcion and Bardaisan*, I. xciv.)

[4] *Adv. Marc.* I. 14. For orthodox baptismal practice and its accompanying unctions, cf. Dix., op. cit., pp. 33–38.

[5] Cyprian, *Ep.* 73. 4; 74. 7. By contrast with Donatist baptism Augustine could defend the Marcionite: cf. his treatise *De Baptismo contra Donatistas*, e.g., 7. 14. 31: *In Marcione agnoscenda est baptismi integritas.* Harnack, p. 390*, n. 4.

It is possible that Marcion used, instead of the Trinitarian formula, simply the words "*in nomine Christi*".[1] If so, he could find support in texts like Rom. 6. 3, and Catholic theologians could hardly contend that his exegesis was wrong. They could only assert that the common practice of their church was different.

Epiphanius[2] informs us that Marcionites allowed the repetition of baptism, in some cases three and more times, their authority for this being Luke 12. 50 (βάπτισμα ἔχω βαπτισθῆναι). This admittedly is hearsay (παρὰ πολλῶν ἀκήκοα, says Epiphanius), but it need not be doubted on that account. Harnack (p. 176) rejects it on somewhat *a priori* grounds: Marcion "the Biblicist" cannot have permitted re-baptism. Harnack also refers to Esnik's statement that Marcionites did penance when they broke their baptismal vows of continence, and argues that Marcionites regarded this as a repetition of baptism, with the result that an outsider might easily conclude that the Marcionites actually did repeat baptism. Elsewhere (*Mission und Ausbreitung des Christentums* i, 402) Harnack calls attention to the fact that no attempts to introduce repeated baptism succeeded (here he admits that the Marcionites attempted it). The purpose of penance is, of course, to restore the grace lost after baptism, so that in effect the permission of penance is equivalent to a repetition of baptism. "Even the Catholic sacrament of penance is nothing but a repetition of baptism" (Harnack, *Marcion*, p. 176).

It is interesting that Esnik[3] mentions a vow which Marcionites made and broke. This must be their baptismal confession. Such a confession will have been introduced by Marcion himself, as we may infer from his interpolation into Gal. 4. 26: εἰς ἣν ἐπηγγειλάμεθα ἁγίαν ἐκκλησίαν. . . .[4]

The creation of the Marcionite church was a great and striking achievement. It marks the founder out as a man of unique impressiveness and organizing capacity. And his success is the more surprising

[1] See further Appendix 3 at the end of this chapter.

[2] *Panarion* 42. 3 (Holl, p. 98).

[3] Schmid's German version, pp. 199 f., quoted in Harnack, p. 379*.

[4] Marcion's baptismal confession then had a clause about the Church. It is tempting to speculate as to whether he influenced the Catholic Confession in this, or whether he was himself copying the confession he had known in the churches of Rome and Sinope. The clause ἁγίαν ἐκκλησίαν seems to be in the Roman Symbol as Tertullian knew it, but how long it had been there before Tertullian's time is uncertain. The existence of a separate *Regula fidei* among Marcionites would give point to Tertullian, *De Praesc.* 42, where he says of heretics: *Mentior si non a regulis suis variant inter se.* Chrysostom relates that Marcionites practised baptism for the dead. See his note on 1 Cor. 15. 29 (quoted by Lietzmann, ad loc.). Harnack, p. 176.

in view of the fact that he made no special claims for himself. He did not come forward as a prophet with " The word of the Lord came unto me, saying . . .". Instead he offered men a book, which, of itself, would teach them what the Gospel was. Believing that the Church in which he had grown up gave men only a perversion of Christianity, he essayed to show what Christianity in essence was. To this end he published his revised New Testament with its commentary, the *Antitheses*, and made plans both for the promulgation of his doctrines and for the fostering of men in the Christian life as he conceived it. He strove to create a church which should be one in faith. Marcionites were to be united by their common belief in the fundamentals of Christianity.

Four reasons may be given for the lasting coherence of the organization which Marcion called into being. There was, in the first place, a deep reverence for the founder himself, exemplified in the belief of some Marcionites that the figure who stood in heaven on the left hand of Christ, while St. Paul stood on the right, was Marcion.[1] Marcion's personal energy, proceeding from a deep conviction that it was given to him to continue the genuine proclamation of the Gospel as begun by St. Paul, but tragically counteracted by the Church since his day, must have contributed largely to the success of his undertaking.[2] In the second place may be indicated the new canonical scriptures which Marcion presented to his followers. Thirdly, there was the common practice of an ascetic life. This does not indeed distinguish Marcionites from the Catholic Church, nor did it have a marked influence upon Catholics, although at that time it probably drew many converts to Marcionitism. Lastly, the comparative simplicity of the means of organization should be stressed. This is emphasized by Harnack (p. 152), who remarks that the Catholic Church required several generations to extend its influence as widely as Marcion extended his after apparently a single generation; and that Marcion succeeded without the institution of synods, which Catholic Christianity found necessary.

It is thus beyond dispute that Marcion played a considerable part in the drama of developing Catholicism. He for his part founded a church which was truly catholic, not merely in the extent of the area over which it spread, but in its pretensions. It was the Bride of Christ and the mother of believers. It professed to restore and teach

[1] So Origen in his commentary on Luke. For the reference, see below, p. 48 n. 3.

[2] Jerome attests a tradition, deriving possibly from Origen, of Marcion's ability: *nullus potest haeresim struere nisi qui ardens ingenii est et habet dona naturae . . . talis fuit Valentinus, talis Marcion, quos doctissimos legimus.* [*Commentary on Hosea*, 2. 10.]

the original Gospel. It was united in its veneration for Paul as the only faithful apostle, and for Marcion, his successor. It had a clearly defined canon of Scripture, and a baptismal creed. And from the beginning it received a simple and definite form of organization—the episcopal.

In contrast with this, the organization from which Marcion separated himself was at that time a loose federation of Christian communities. The Christian mission had spread in Syria and through Asia Minor Greece-wards and Rome-wards; and in another direction it had found its way into Egypt and along the north coast of Africa. As a result there were bands of Christians in many towns, and these were the first churches, meeting regularly for worship and the administration of the sacraments, under the leadership of a body of presbyters. By A.D. 115, as we learn from the seven genuine letters of Ignatius, there was a single bishop elevated above the presbyters as the leader of each local congregation. In some districts a group of churches would hold together, and one of the bishops would acquire an authority extending over the group and not merely over his own congregation—a foreshadowing of the later episcopate. Churches in the larger cities, e.g., Antioch, Corinth, Ephesus, Rome, naturally dominated smaller churches in adjacent towns, and became centres of Christianity. The church in Rome was already advancing to prominence by the end of the first century, as we may judge from the letter written on its behalf by the presbyter Clement to the Corinthian church. But with all this there was no centralized authority and no common plan of action. There were only group loyalties, and a church here and there which looked beyond the limits of the province to which it belonged and maintained contact with churches in other parts of the Empire. Christianity had advanced rapidly, but had not always taken care to secure its conquests behind it and to weld them together. It was not yet " fitly joined together and compacted by that which every joint supplieth ". While conscious of the catholicity of its mission it had not yet given attention to the question of the organization thereby implied. The adequate demonstration of its unity and catholicity in external forms was an urgent need. The relatively sudden appearance of the Marcionite church was thus not merely a challenge, but an example.

Nor was this outward lack of cohesion compensated for by an inner unity of doctrine. The inward faith as well as the outward organization awaited co-ordination and clarification. There was a baptismal confession used—probably—in Asia Minor as well as at Rome.[1] Whether

[1] The Old Roman Symbol, which preserves an older baptismal formula.

this had yet begun to circulate as a statement of the Faith is highly doubtful; in any case its circulation was limited; the *regula fidei* varied, in fact there were several *regulae fidei*. There was no generally accepted basis of doctrine, i.e., no canon of the New Testament. The number of writings recognized as authoritative differed with the leading churches and groups of churches, and even with regard to those which were everywhere accepted there could be a variety of interpretation.[1] For authority in doctrine the churches looked to "apostolical men" like Papias or Polycarp, who had themselves associated with apostles or the disciples of apostles, and remembered what they had taught. In this way it was believed to be still possible to go back to the very source, and these "*viri apostolici*" seem to have played no inconsiderable rôle.

Thus at the beginning of the second century of our era there was no Christian canon beside the Old Testament, no fixed and written creed; and the episcopate was still developing and establishing its authority. At the end of that century the Church is strong in the possession of the treasures of creed, canon and episcopate. There is regrettable lack of precise evidence concerning this century-long evolution from the New Testament period[2] to the time of Irenaeus and Tertullian, whose writings reveal this glorious Church now mature in faith and order. Hence the door is open for a variety of hypotheses, and the novelty and probability of such hypotheses tend to be in inverse proportion.

Our present concern is the place of Marcion and his church in relation to this evolution of the Catholic Church. How far is it true that it was against Marcion that the Church marshalled its ranks and rose to true Catholicity? Had the Catholic Church reached its full stature as a result of its struggle with Marcionitism? Is there a sense in which Marcion may be called the "creator" of the Catholic Church?

This verdict of Harnack's is so challenging that he must be quoted more fully. "It was after Marcion's time that the Church (*die grosse Christenheit*) first began the work of bringing down the Holy Church, the Bride of Christ, the spiritual Eve, the world Beyond (*den jenseitigen Aon*), from heaven, and of welding communities together on earth in real fellowship and unity on the basis of a fixed doctrine derived from the New Testament as Marcion had done. This proves that Marcion, by his activity and by his ideas in organization and theology, gave the decisive impulse in the creation of the old Catholic Church, and left the model."[3] "In order to defend itself against (the Marcionite Church)

[1] Cf. Tertullian, *De Resurrectione* 19, *De Pudicitia* 8–9.

[2] The N.T. communities of Christians cannot be called churches in this sense; although the word *ecclesia* is used in the N.T. in the catholic sense, as well as in the sense of local congregation.

[3] Harnack, *Marcion*, p. 214.

Christianity was obliged to take over from Marcion his entire construction with the exception of the fundamental theology."[1] Harnack states that the Roman Church took the lead in the movement against Marcion. "She was the first to learn from Marcion what could be learnt from him, and she taught the other churches. She then went beyond Marcion in the added support which she devised for the building and strengthening of the new Catholic Church. The conception of the idea of episcopal succession and its connection with the idea of guarantee for the *traditio veritatis* are not Marcion's, even if we do hear at a later period of διαδοχαὶ τῶν ἐπισκόπων in the Marcionite Church."[2]

This judgement is disproportionate. On the one hand, it proceeds from a too intense preoccupation with Marcion. One feels that Harnack became short-sighted through long and detailed attention to Marcion, and in consequence his vision of the background, i.e., the whole of second-century Christianity, was out of focus; his picture of Marcion is in far too exaggerated relief; the general proportions are all wrong. On the other hand, quite apart from the perhaps pardonable over-emphasis due to a lifelong enthusiasm for the Pontic heretic, Harnack's estimate of orthodox Christianity during the second century, and the tendency to make a rigid contrast between the Church of the New Testament period and the Church in the days of Irenaeus and Tertullian, cannot survive thoughtful examination. Moreover, the interpretation placed upon the word "catholic" must be called in question.

It will be the task of later pages in this essay to consider successively Marcion's canon and text of the New Testament, his dualistic creed, his Christology, his attitude to the Old Testament and to Paul. It is advisable to approach this study as a comparison of Marcionitism and Catholicism, or as a consideration of Marcionitism against the background of Catholicism, rather than with an assumption that there must have been mutual influence. The prior question is whether Marcion actually did influence the Catholic faith or practice. If that question permits an affirmative answer, there arises the necessity of assessing the extent of such influence.

But quite apart from deciding whether Harnack's pronouncement that Marcion was the founder of the Catholic Church needs to be modified, i.e., whether the use of "founder" in this connexion is overstatement or sheer misstatement, the usage of the term "catholic" itself raises a question. For Harnack is simply conforming to the custom of some scholars of giving the term "catholic" a sense which

[1] Op. cit., p. 212. [2] Op. cit., p. 212, n. 1.

does not include primitive Christianity, but is even to some extent in contrast to it.[1] The Catholic Church, according to this usage, is the Church as we find it from the time of Irenaeus onwards, the Church of the bishops, conscious of its tradition, its rule of faith and its new canon of sacred scriptures; sure enough of itself to be able to define and ban a heretic; armed spiritually to repel attack; organized to withstand false winds of doctrine; instructed so as to "test the spirits". This Church did not exist in the first century; it came into existence during the course of the second, and we see it clearly at the end of that century.[2] Certainly, if it is agreed to use the epithet "catholic" as a label attaching to the Church from the time of Irenaeus, it is possible to argue that the great second-century movements of Gnosticism, Marcionitism, and Montanism were conditioning factors in the emergence of this new catholic Christianity, and Harnack's opinion will be worth respect if he can show reason for specifying Marcionitism rather than the other movements as the main influence in that development.

So much in criticism of Harnack's main thesis. A final word may be added concerning historical probabilities. Was there a possibility of Marcion's becoming the dominant Christian Church, built up on the foundation of the Apostle Paul? There may indeed have been a few years, between, say, A.D. 160 and 170, during which, to the apprehension of orthodox bishops, the Marcionite church threatened to win more adherents than the remainder of the Christian Church could then boast. But if there was such a time it quickly passed. Compared with pre-existing Christianity Marcionitism was a mushroom growth. Even if it could make a finer show of foliage than the Church of which it was an offshoot, its roots did not strike so deep. Account must also be taken of the fact that converts to Marcionitism were probably drawn in the main not from the pagan world but from the Christian churches,[3] so that Marcion's success was largely at the expense of the orthodox Church, and a slight panic among Church leaders is understandable. By the end of the century, however, the Church had rallied itself after the temporary panic, and was effectively guarding against the ravages of the "Pontic wolf" on its fold. Signs of the decline of Marcionitism were perhaps already in evidence. Its ban on marriage, for instance, meant that it could not hope to augment its numbers from the children

[1] See further Appendix 1 at the end of this chapter.

[2] This point of view is maintained by Barnikol in a booklet which is noticed in Appendix 2. This is a rather arbitrary manipulation of evidence, but in view of its relevance to Marcion could not be ignored in this essay.

[3] Cf. Tertullian, *De Praesc.* 42.

of its members; it must continually bring in converts from outside its borders. The number of converts from the Great Church would dwindle as a result of the writings and oral teaching of bishops and presbyters exposing the inadequacy of Marcionite doctrines. Many were doubtless attracted by the asceticism of the Marcionites, but in the end this must have deterred more than it attracted. Further, as the strength of the Great Church was sapped by the rising Marcionite church, so in its turn was the Marcionite church affected by the spread of Manichæism.

APPENDIX 1

ON THE USE OF THE TERM "CATHOLIC"

There is first a linguistic aspect of this question. If we speak of the Catholic Church emerging as a result of the struggle with Marcion, we are using "catholic" to mean not merely "universal", but "orthodox and apostolic", a sense which the word had acquired by the end of the second century. The author of the *Muratorian Fragment* and Clement of Alexandria[1] are familiar with this sense, but no earlier use of it can be indicated with certainty.[2]

In Ignatius "the catholic church" means the universal as contrasted with the local church; the whole number of Christians, whose head is Christ, as opposed to a particular community with its bishop.[3] On Col. 1. 6, where Paul claims the universal spread of the Gospel as a guarantee of its truth, Lightfoot comments: "Heresies are at best ethnic; truth is essentially catholic." This needs some qualification, for in the case of the Marcionite heresy its catholicity in the sense of breadth of appeal could, on Lightfoot's view, be urged as evidence of its at least partial truth. Modification did come as time went on and the challenge of heresy became more and more formidable, as Lightfoot himself admits: "to the primary idea of extension are superadded the ideas of doctrine and unity. . . . The truth was the same everywhere. . . . Heresies were partial, scattered, localized." This meant for the word catholic a qualitative nuance of meaning in addition to its quantitative sense; a catholic idea in this new sense is one which is not merely held by Christians everywhere, but which is traditional and therefore genuine and therefore true. The word is on the way to becoming synonymous with "orthodox". So much for philology.

To continue with the usage of the term "catholic" in modern

[1] *Muratorian Fragment* 61, 66, 69; Clem. Alex., *Strom.* 7. 17. 106–7.

[2] Since Lightfoot has shown the more probable reading in *Martyrium Polycarpi* 16 to be not καθολικῆς but ἁγίας.

[3] Ignatius, *Ad Smyrn.* 8. 2. See also *Martyrium Polycarpi*, Inscription, 8. 1, 19. 2. Polybius can speak of "catholic" history, i.e., universal history rather than the history of a particular people (Polybius, 8. 4. 11), cf. Lightfoot, *Apostolic Fathers*, II, i, pp. 413 f.; ii, p. 310. Kattenbusch is not convincing with his suggestion that "catholic" in Ignatius is equivalent to *una sola* (*Das Apostolische Symbol* II, pp. 920–927, especially pp. 922 f.). An exhaustive examination of the history and meaning of the word "catholic" is still desiderated.

academic discussion. The usage common among Lutheran scholars has been mentioned. Here are some illustrations. It is an axiom of Sohm's[1] that Catholicism is a decline from genuine primitive Christianity. It is in contrast with it, as Law is in contrast with Spirit. It arises from the (mistaken) identification of the outward visible Church with the company of believers who are the true Church. It represents an institutionalizing which, albeit inevitable, is essentially a corruption of the primitive Gospel.[2] This is an extreme statement of the view we are criticizing, and did not pass without challenge even among Germans, who in many respects agreed with Sohm in their general attitude to Catholicism. It was subjected to careful analysis and criticism by Harnack, for example. But even so it was influential among Lutheran scholars. Catholicism seems to mean for von Dobschütz[3] the organization and officialdom which represents a rejection of the free guidance of the Spirit. More recently Lietzmann has referred to the *1st Epistle of Clement*, particularly chapters 40–44, precisely as Sohm does, as the " birth-hour of Catholic ecclesiastical law " ;[4] and at the end of the same chapter, dealing with the period of Trajan and Hadrian, Lietzmann summarizes the teaching of the writings he has reviewed as " an ethic and liturgy derived from Judaism, a popular sacrament-theology and mysticism derived from Hellenism, with a theology derived from Paul comprising teaching about God and Christ, redemption through Christ's blood and sanctification through the Spirit ", and this he labels " early Catholicism ".[5] Otto discerns " early Catholicism " in Matthew's Gospel, but for him it means simply the interpretation of the Gospel as a new Law offered in place of the Law of Moses.[6]

To come to Harnack, with whom we are chiefly concerned. Harnack

[1] *Kirchenrecht* (1892), esp. pp. 160–164, " Kirchenrecht und Katholizismus ". See the criticism of it in Harnack, *Constitution and Law of the Church*, pp. 175–258.

[2] " Umwandlung des religiösen Wesens des Christentums " . . . " Rechtsordnung für die Ekklesia nach urchristlicher Uberzeugung undenkbar ist " (op. cit., p. 161).

[3] *Christian Life in the Primitive Church*, pp. 277–362.

[4] " Geburtsstunde des katholischen Kirchenrechts " (*Geschichte der alten Kirche*, i. 204). The words are almost a quotation from Sohm's reference (*Kirchenrecht*, p. 160) to *1 Clement 40–44* as " Entstehung des Kirchenrechts ".

[5] Op. cit., p. 234.

[6] *Reich Gottes und Menschensohn*, p. 67. For the influence of this general view of Catholicism, as distinguishable from the most primitive Christianity, see the works of J. V. Bartlet, especially his posthumous *Church Life and Church Order* (ed. Cadoux, 1942) ; e.g., " not only must primitive and catholic be distinguished in a really historical sense and spirit ; but within both of these stages must be discriminated as regards the degree to which the emphasis and elements characteristic of the one tend to prevail over those of the other " (op. cit., p. 4—cf. also pp. 40, 55, 74 f., 167–171).

objects to Sohm[1] that he poses an intolerable dilemma. Law is not incompatible with Christianity.[2] In Sohm's view the Church becomes a mere idea, a sort of disembodied spirit. But it is of the very nature of the Church to have outward form and organization. If there be contradiction here it is inevitable, and is no more to be deplored or avoided than in the case of any other faith or ideal which strives after realization in the world and in human life. Moreover, Sohm gives no satisfactory answer to the question where in primitive Christianity lay the germ from which Catholicism necessarily developed.

This is fair criticism. The Church must be visible; if it is in any real sense a body, that means that it is a human institution. Sohm's distinction of body and community is very artificial and forced. The whole principle of incarnation is involved. It is New Testament teaching that the Church is the extension of the Incarnation of Jesus Christ, his second body, assumed for the purpose of carrying out his will in the world after his first body—a body of flesh and blood and humanity—had been laid aside. Christ himself was not above the need for visible embodiment. On this principle, as applied to the Church, it has been the merit of Catholicism to insist; and probably Protestantism has suffered from the neglect of it. The Church is essentially a society with a life to live and a witness to make in the world. Its head—and heart—must be in heaven; but its feet must be on earth. The Church is indeed *militans in saeculo*, and it is regrettable if the complementary thought of it as *triumphans in caelo* obscures the fact of its necessary earthly embodiment and visibility.

What is Harnack's own view? For all his detailed criticism of Sohm he agrees with him in distinguishing Catholicism and primitive Christianity. There is a point in the development of Christianity at which we can say, as we could not earlier: This is Catholicism. "This point seems to me to occur where the apostles, prophets, and charismatic lay teachers ceased and their place was taken by the norm of the apostolic doctrine, the norm of the canon of Scripture, and subjection to the authority of the apostolic episcopal office."[3] These elements of Catholicity had been present already in embryo, but had not until Tertullian's time received definite form.

This admission that Catholicism is embryonic in the New Testament

[1] *Constitution and Law*, pp. 204–258, a careful examination of Sohm's *Kirchenrecht* and also of his *Wesen und Ursprung des Katholizismus* (1909).

[2] On the danger of pressing this antithesis between Law and Gospel even in the N.T. see W. D. Davies: *Paul and Rabbinic Judaism*, 1948, pp. 145, 221 ff.

[3] Op. cit., p. 245. Cf. "The Catholic Church is the Church of Apostolic Tradition Fixed as Law", p. 246.

is very welcome and significant. Our criticism of Harnack's definition of Catholicism is, in substance, a reiteration and magnification of this admission. For the present we observe how natural it was for Harnack in the light of this opinion of his to ascribe such importance to Marcion. Our ground of divergence from him here must be the acceptance of a different definition of Catholicism.

But Harnack's definition of Catholicism is not yet complete. He thinks of Catholicism as a new theology, made possible by the adoption of Hellenic thought-forms for the interpretation of the earliest preaching. This, in effect, led to an ignoring of the Spirit, a misunderstanding of Faith, the substitution of a philosophic idea of God for the New Testament apprehension of God as the Father of Jesus Christ, and the development of the Logos doctrine. In distinction from Gnostic speculation Catholicism never gave up the belief that its theology was rooted in the historical events of the life and passion of a real man—Jesus Christ.[1]

There is no need to tolerate the antithesis erected between primitive Christianity and Catholicism.[2] As has been pointed out, Harnack, although he speaks of Catholicism emerging during the second century, nevertheless allows that it existed in germ in the New Testament. Indeed, one of his criticisms of Sohm is that he makes no attempt to indicate what motivating force there was in the pure religious life of the earliest Christians which explains the development of Catholicism which Sohm finds so contradictory. To quote Harnack again:[3] "Catholicism is as old as the Church if we include the rudimentary form; there is hardly a single one of its elements which was not present. But . . . the Catholic elements did not constitute the essence of primitive Christianity. It would therefore be misleading to call primitive Christianity Catholic." This is worthy of fuller consideration and emphasis. Is not the essence of catholicity the belief in Christ as Lord—that is, Lord not only of the Church, but of the whole universe? (Col. 1. 15–18; 1 Cor. 8. 6). This is the underlying principle of Ignatius's great saying: "Where Christ Jesus is, there is the Catholic Church."[4] No alien addition is hereby inserted into the primitive *kerygma*; rather is one aspect of that *kerygma* receiving a asisnew emph and formulation. Seeberg [5] points to the consciousness of fellowship with Christ as characteristic of Catholicism: "through

[1] Op. cit., pp. 254 f.

[2] Or between Spirit and Law, as in Sohm. Cf. Seeberg, *Dogmengeschichte*, 1. 101: "Der Geist und die festen Formen, in denen er schafft, dienen beide zur Begründung der Einheit und Katholizität der Kirche."

[3] Op. cit., p. 253, n. [4] Ad Smyrn. 8. 2. [5] Op. cit., i. 232.

this is the Church holy, and through this is the Church catholic". This is equally, if not more true of New Testament Christianity than that of the second century. It was not a bishop of the time of Tertullian, but the Apostle of the Gentiles who wrote: "Ye are all sons of God through faith in Christ Jesus . . . ye are all one in Christ Jesus."

Heiler discerns a characteristic mark of Catholicism not only in the primitive confession of Christ as Lord (dogma), but also in the existence in the Church from the very beginning of sacraments and a hierarchy. "All the institutions of the later Church: dogma, hierarchical order, sacramental worship and liturgy can be shown to be present in their beginnings already in the New Testament. . . . That unmistakable manifoldness which is the proud boast of the fully-developed Catholic Church is not the product of a century-long development, but an essential mark (*Eigentümlichkeit*) of the most primitive Church, and the New Testament is its literary deposit."[1] Heiler goes on very adroitly to quote Harnack[2] in support of this view of Catholicism: "The new religion . . . was from the beginning eminently syncretistic and therefore from the beginning the catholic religion." The New Testament is the foundation-deed (*Urkunde*) of Catholicism, and never to be set in antithesis to it. The essence of Catholicism, viz., the organic connection of Church and Gospel, is already fundamental in the New Testament; and Ignatius's famous saying: "Where Christ Jesus is, there is the Catholic Church," is precisely applicable to New Testament Christianity.[3]

[1] *Urkirche und Ostkirche* (1937), p. 93. Cf. pp. 49–51 of Heiler's earlier book *Katholizismus* (1923), of which *Urkirche und Ostkirche* is a rewriting.

[2] *Marcion*, p. 5. The word syncretistic is used by some, as by Harnack here, in a not very complimentary sense. Heiler evidently thinks it capable of a nobler meaning.

[3] *Urkirche und Ostkirche*, p. 94; cf. also p. 19, where Heiler remarks about modern tendencies: "Protestant Christianity is beginning to realize again that the Church of Christ is essentially and necessarily catholic (*wesensnotwendig katholisch*), and that there neither is nor can be any other church than the Catholic Church."

APPENDIX 2

Die Entstehung der Kirche im zweiten Jahrhundert und die Zeit Marcions. By Ernst Barnikol. (33 pp. 1933.)

Barnikol takes as an axiom that the first Christian Church in the proper sense of the term was the Marcionite church. He then sets himself the task of finding the earliest date at which we can speak of Marcionite and " old Catholic " churches.

The three foundation columns of Harnack's reconstruction of the history of the second century are: (1) The genuineness of the seven Ignatian letters, and a date for their origin before Trajan's death. (2) The year A.D. 144 for the foundation of the Marcionite church. (3) The martyrdom of Polycarp at Smyrna in A.D. 155. The third is not of much importance except for the conference of bishops in Rome. The first and second Barnikol disputes. He endeavours to prove an earlier date for Marcion's activity, and suggests the years 128–144. For this he relies on a Marcionite reckoning preserved in Esnik (given in Harnack, p. 23*, n. 1) according to which 2900 years had elapsed from the Fall till the appearance of Christ, and apparently 3000 years till the entry of Marcion himself upon the world stage, an entry which purported the end of the drama. Obviously a literal interpretation of this yields ± A.D. 129 as the date of the beginning of Marcion's work. Barnikol claims that this agrees better than Harnack's dating with the evidence of Clement, Irenaeus, and Papias; and that it is easier to understand the false chronological statements of Tertullian and Irenaeus, if Marcion's date was earlier, i.e., farther removed from their own time.[1] This eases many problems: it means, for instance, that the Ignatian letters presuppose Marcion; that Marcion found the Fourth Gospel not yet widely circulated; and that he is only ten to fifteen, instead of fifty years, later than *1 Clement*. But in order to establish this position, Barnikol has to argue that the Ignatians belong to a date later than Marcion, and, in fact, attack him as the " first-born of Satan ",[2] and that Justin's *Apology* belongs to the year 138–139 rather than 150–153, as Harnack holds. On neither of these points is Barnikol convincing. There is no reason to call in

[1] The evidence referred to is collected in Harnack, pp. 14*–18*.

[2] Barnikol makes a slip here, for the phrase comes from Polycarp's *Epistle to the Philippians*, ch. 7, where it does not refer solely to Marcion. But see P. N. Harrison, *Polycarp's Two Epistles*, pp. 199 ff.

question Lightfoot's demonstration of the genuineness of the Ignatian Epistles, or his date *c.* 115 for the martyrdom of Ignatius.[1] The reason why Barnikol pleads for an earlier date for Justin's *Apology* is that Justin twice (ch. 26 and ch. 58) says that Marcion is still teaching. There is, indeed, still a case for the date *c.* 138. The fact that Aurelius is addressed (I. 1) as *Verissimus*, not as Cæsar (which title he received in 139), will be decisive to some scholars. But other evidence makes a date *c.* 153 probable. The reference to the Jewish war of 132–135 as recent (ἐν τῷ νῦν γεγενημένῳ χρόνῳ, ch. 31) does not really favour the date 138 as against 153.[2]

Further, in order to establish his thesis, Barnikol has to reject Harnack's date 144 as the foundation-year of the Marcionite church. According to Barnikol Marcion did not found a church at all, but simply restored the apostolic Pauline faith. The day which the Marcionites kept in honour was neither the day of the foundation of their church, nor the day on which their founder turned his back on his Pontic home (Bill's view), but the day of their founder's death. Our evidence does, indeed, as Barnikol contends, leave room for other interpretations beside Harnack's. But Harnack's is still the best reconstruction.

Barnikol passes from the question of the date of the emergence of the Marcionite church to a similar question with regard to the Catholic Church. He finds the " birth-hour " of the Catholic Church in the conference of Polycarp with Anicetus at Rome.[3] The importance of that meeting for Barnikol lies not in the discussions about Fasting and the Eucharist, but in the probability that the two bishops then made a common front against Marcion. This is a highly suggestive proposition, but, in the absence of evidence from other sources to strengthen it, it must remain a proposition and no further hypothesis can safely be built upon it.

Barnikol goes on to specify what the bishops learnt from the already existing Marcionite church. Previously orthodox Christianity had possessed no monarchical episcopate, no New Testament canon, no creed; it had made no parallelism between St. Peter and St. Paul, in fact, it had ignored St. Paul. But all these things are heard of soon after the " conference of bishops ". They must, according to Barnikol, have been copied from the Marcionites.

[1] Cf. Eusebius, *H.E.* 3. 36. Streeter, *Primitive Church*, pp. 273 ff., accepts this.

[2] See the discussion by Blunt in *Cambridge Patristic Texts*, pp. xlviii–lii.

[3] Eusebius, *H.E.* 5. 24. 16–17.

APPENDIX 3

DID MARCION USE THE TRINAL INVOCATION AT BAPTISM ?

According to Cyprian, *Ep.* 73. 4, Marcion baptized " *in nomine Jesu Christi* ", and it might be inferred that he used only this single invocation, in place of the usual Trinitarian formula.

The Pseudo-Cyprianic treatise, *De Rebaptismate*, mentions heretics who baptized " *in nomine Christi* ", and it appears from the description given of them in ch. 13 that these heretics may be Marcionites: *constat haereticum esse qui in alium Deum credat, sive Christum alium accipiat, quam quem Scripturae Novi et Veteris Testamenti manifeste praedicant, quae patrem omnipotentem creatorem omnium et filium eius sine obscuritate annuntiant.* The possibility, however, is not ruled out that Gnostics in general are intended. Rauschen, who edited the treatise in the *Florilegium Patristicum*, thinks the author uses " *in nomine Jesu* " as a regular equivalent for " *in nomine Patris et Filii et Spiritus Sancti* " ; but this is not convincing, in view of the fact that at the beginning of chapter 7 " *invocatio nominis Jesu* " is contrasted with the trinal invocation of Matt. 28. 19.

Burn[1] suggests that the enclosure sent by Jubaianus to Cyprian, which Cyprian answers in *Ep.* 73, was the *De Rebaptismate.* This overlooks the fact that Cyprian declares Marcion to be definitely named in the text to which he is replying, whereas there is no mention at all of Marcion in the *De Rebaptismate.*

On the whole, there is no strong argument for the use of the single invocation alone at Marcionite baptism. Benson[2] writes: " There seem to have been *in Africa* some who understood baptism ' in the name of Christ ' to be sufficient without the Trinal Invocation. This was evidently very rare, if ever it was more than an exception." It may be doubted whether Augustine could have admitted the integrity of Marcionite baptism (p. 7, n. 5) if Marcionites did not use the three-fold formula, because the formula was the essential part of the ceremony, and even if the Marcionite ceremony agreed with the Catholic in every other point, a divergence in the formula used would invalidate it in the judgement of a Catholic bishop. Moreover, in *De Baptismo* 3. 15. 20, Augustine definitely attributes to Marcionites the use of the three-fold formula.

[1] *Introduction to the Creeds*, p. 24.

[2] *Cyprian*, p. 405, cf. also pp. 406–407.

2

MARCION AND THE CANON OF THE NEW TESTAMENT

§ 1. THE MEANING OF CANONICITY

IT has been assumed[1] that the Church already had its canon of the New Testament before the time of Marcion. This, however, has been denied, and there is wide agreement that the first canon was that of Marcion. The protagonist of this latter view is Harnack, who goes so far as to assert not only that Marcion's canon preceded the Catholic in point of time, but that Marcion is to be regarded as " creator " of the Catholic canon.[2]

Clear thinking is imperative here, and, in particular, precision in the use of the term " canon ". It is, in fact, necessary to keep a clear distinction between the *idea* of a canon and the fixation of a canon, i.e., the drawing up of a list of books which are to be accepted as of canonical authority [3] (this would apply both to Marcion's canon of one Gospel and ten Pauline Epistles, and the New Testament canon of twenty-seven writings as commonly used to-day). It is not enough to demonstrate that the writings which we have in our New Testament were known and used by the Churches before Marcion's time. That is indisputable, as any account of the history of the canon shows. The real question is : Had a line already been drawn between writings which are of binding authority on Christians, and those which are only " good and useful to read " ? Were the New Testament writings a definitive collection, side by side with the Old Testament, and, like it, used as Christian Scripture ? When were they elevated to the same level of authoritativeness as the Old Testament and quoted as sacred Scripture ? Marcion denied the authority of the Old Testament and accorded his newly formed New Testament the status in his community which the Old Testament had held among Jews and Christians hitherto. For orthodox Christians the matter was more complex ; but there was less urgency for quick decision and final definition.

The first closed New Testament canon of which we have knowledge was made by Marcion. It consisted of one Gospel and ten Pauline

[1] E.g., by Zahn, *Geschichte des N.T. Kanons*, I, pp. 434 *et passim*.

[2] This view is more recently advocated by J. Knox, *Marcion and the New Testament* (Chicago, 1942). See pp. 38 ff. below.

[3] Cf. Knox's discussion of canonicity (op. cit., p. 25): " a canon is by necessity a closed canon ".

Epistles. It is easy to see the motive which impelled him; and we see at the same time why it was not yet necessary for the Church to take such a step. The Church had as its basic Scripture the Jewish Old Testament, and this was supplemented by the writings of its own Apostles. But Marcion regarded the Old Testament as the law of another God, and as incompatible with the Christian revelation. He was therefore bound to look elsewhere for the record of that revelation, and to invest other writings with that authority in his church which the Old Testament had among other Christians.

To this extent Marcion was a pioneer. Can we go as far as Harnack and say that Marcion was the founder of the Catholic canon? This judgement is a part of Harnack's exaggerated estimate of Marcion's significance in the history of Christianity. It may be remarked in the first place as a general criticism that there were other motives beside the existence of a New Testament canon among the Marcionites, which impelled Catholic leaders to form their own canon. There was a continually increasing number of converts from Hellenism in the Christian Church. These men will have found the Old Testament a strange book, and, even with the aid of allegory, in parts unintelligible. Many of them went after Marcion; but even those who remained in the Catholic Church must have valued more and more highly those writings which arose within the Christian communities, and which were not written specially for Jews. Thus even if there had been no Marcionite collection of Christian Scriptures there would have been sooner or later a fairly clearly defined canon of Scriptures of the New Covenant, as distinct from the Hebrew Scriptures. With the influx of Greek Christians into the Church the soil was prepared for this growth. This argument admittedly must not be pressed too far, for one can point to the philosopher Justin, who after he became a Christian became also an enthusiastic expositor of the Old Testament, and would never have conceded that it was primarily intended for Jews. The *Epistle of Barnabas*, moreover, serves to remind us of the unique authority the Old Testament enjoyed among Christians; for here is a Christian author who found it necessary to allegorize almost everything in the Old Testament in order to maintain its usefulness; and yet he does so allegorize it, and refuses the simpler course of rejecting it, as Marcion did. But there is enough in the argument thus generally stated to weigh down the balance somewhat against Harnack's claim.

To come closer to the problem: before the formation of Marcion's canon the following books were used by the Christian churches: In the first place, the writings taken over from Judaism; and these included not only the Old Testament, but also various Jewish apocalypses which claimed great antiquity and were held to be inspired.[1] Next, there were collections of " words " of the Lord Jesus and narratives of his life and ministry, quotations from which are to be found in the earliest Christian writers, e.g., Acts 20. 35; 1 Cor. 9. 14.[2] Among these records are, of course, our four canonical Gospels. Further, there were epistles believed to be from the hands of Apostles, a number by Paul, at least one from Peter, two from John, one from Jude; an epistle by James the Lord's brother; and a history of the deeds of the Apostles, valued both because of its subject and because it was written by the author of one of the Gospels.[3] Lastly, there were those writings which, though not the work of Apostles, claimed to have been dictated by the Spirit. The fruits of the Spirit were not only prophecy and speaking with tongues; not only the moral graces described in Gal. 5. 22 f.; but also many a written word of comfort and exhortation. This category includes the Johannine and other apocalypses, *1 Clement*, the seven genuine letters of Ignatius, Hermas. Almost all the writings of the so-called Apostolic Fathers are prior in date to Marcion.

Probably no Christian community, not even the Roman, was acquainted with the whole of this literature. Some writings never attained more than a local circulation around the place of their origin; others attained wide circulation only gradually. Some churches will have shown a preference for apocalyptic literature; the bigger churches will have laid stress on obtaining authentic accounts of the life and teaching of the Lord; those churches which had been founded by St. Paul will have shown especial zeal in collecting copies of the Apostle's authentic letters. Thus it is very doubtful whether there was as yet any attempt to classify this growing body of writings, to limit it, or to define its position in relation to the Hebrew Law and Prophets. It is an anachronism to speak of a New Testament canon in this period, at least in the second sense above defined. But the question is not to be so easily decided. Canonicity—the development of the *idea* of a canon—is another matter, and it calls for further consideration.

The conservative view that a New Testament canon existed before Marcion, at the beginning of the second century, was maintained by Zahn in the learned and innumerable pages of his history of the New Testament canon. Against those who dated the origin of the canon at the end of the second century his arguments are not decisive; for they really prove only that the majority of the New Testament writings

[1] Cf. the quotations in 1 Cor. 2. 9; Jude 9 and 14.

[2] Cf. also: 1 Cor. 7. 10; 11. 23; 1 Thess. 4. 15.

[3] A late date for Acts has recently been advocated by Knox, who regards it as published *c.* 150 as part of the Church's protest against Marcionitism. See below, p. 38 ff.

were read and valued throughout the Christian Churches at the earlier date; not that they were recognized as authoritative in the way in which the Old Testament was recognized. When he puts to his critics the question[1] how the canon can have originated at the end of the century—what synod can have authorized it?—the argument can be turned back with even greater force against his own position. For if there was no machinery in the latter half of the century for the official promulgation of a New Testament canon, still less was there in the earlier half. But in fact this is not the main battle. The real problem concerns not the promulgation of an official list of books to be received as canonical, but the concept of canonicity which must have been prior to any definition.

§ 2. THE GRADUAL CANONIZATION OF THE NEW TESTAMENT WRITINGS

The question is: When were the new Christian writings called γραφαί and placed on the same level as the Old Testament? It need not be doubted that for Christians as for Jews the Old Testament had unique authority as a holy book. The New Testament references to it—ἡ γραφὴ λέγει, γέγραπται—are sufficient proof of this. The words of Jesus would have at least equivalent authority; and this applies both to the remembered word and also to its fixation in writing. The influx of Greeks into the Church no doubt strengthened this authority of the words of the Lord, for Greeks would not share that veneration for the Old Testament which was felt by Christians who had formerly been Jews. But when were the writings of Apostles accorded this high status? Concurrently with recognition of their genuineness? Here we are confronted with the fact that a church might so honour the work of one Apostle, but not of others. Ought it to be assumed, for example, that all churches valued equally the epistles of Paul? Again, how much is implied in the request of the Philippians to Polycarp for copies of Ignatius's epistles—a tendency to canonize Ignatius? Examination of the Apostolic Fathers[2] reveals acquaintance with various books of the New Testament, but this is not all we want to know. The desideratum is the degree of authority with which they are quoted; for example, does *1 Clement's* acquaintance with Hebrews mean that Hebrews is credited with the same authority which the Law had for a Jew?

[1] *G.K.* I., p. 438.

[2] Cf. *The N.T. in the Apostolic Fathers*, by a Committee of the Oxford Society of Historical Theology, 1905.

To consider this with reference to writings earlier than and contemporary with Marcion. Already before the end of the first century the Sayings of Jesus must have been regarded as of equal authority with the Old Testament, though comparison and precise definition had not yet been thought out. This is clear from the way in which St. Paul appeals to the authority of the Lord in settling disputed points with his converts.[1] From the more tentative way in which he offers his own opinion it is also clear that apostolic authority was on a different level.[2] Thus, as soon as there was a collection of Sayings of the Lord, there was an embryonic canon of Christian Scripture and its components were twofold, viz., Old Testament and λόγια τοῦ Κυρίου. The well-known reference of Justin to the reading of "memoirs of the Apostles" and "scriptures of the prophets" at Christian worship is somewhat belated evidence in this connection. There can hardly be any doubt that memoirs of the Apostles means Gospels and that the usage Justin refers to places them on a par with the Old Testament prophets.[3] A passage of 2 *Clement* (7. 2) calls for consideration here.[4] After speaking of the Old Testament (citing Gen. 1. 27) as ἡ γραφή it then refers to "the books and the apostles". Is it justifiable to take "books" as equal to Gospels and "apostles" as equal to Epistles? This is at least a possible interpretation; but other views are held. Knopf[5] suggests that βίβλια here means prophetic books, possibly including Gospels; in this case apostles are not regarded as on the same level of authority or canonicity. Another view is that of McNeile[6] who takes βίβλια to mean the Old Testament and apostles to mean the New Testament, including Gospels and Epistles, but considered as not quite in the same high category of sacred Scripture as the Old Testament. This accords with the opinion of Westcott.[7] One must not be too confident here; the nature of the evidence does not permit it.

[1] Cf. 1 Thess. 4. 13; 1 Cor. 7.; *1 Clement* 13 calls the words of Jesus "commandment" and "orders" (ἐντολή, παραγγέλματα).

[2] Cf. 1 Cor. 7.

[3] McNeile, *Introduction to N.T.*, p. 300, disagrees.

[4] Lightfoot dates this work A.D. 120–140.

[5] *Handbuch zum N.T.* (Ergänzungs-Band) ad loc. The Syriac version actually reads "books *of the prophets*". Knopf is here repeating the conclusion of Zahn, *G.K.* II, pp. 942–945.

[6] Op. cit., p. 297, following Lightfoot.

[7] *The Canon of the N.T.*[3], p. 163: "Still . . . the N.T. had no certain and defined existence as co-ordinate with the Old . . . though the Gospel at least was quoted as 'Scripture'" and "the scriptures of the Lord were formed into a collection and distinguished from other writings". The quotation of the Gospel as Scripture occurs in ch. 2, where Mark 2. 17 (= Mt. 9. 13) is so quoted.

If *1 Clement* is considered, for example, there is a noticeable contrast between the inexact way in which the New Testament is quoted and the authority ascribed to the Old Testament; clearly the New Testament is not regarded by this author as Scripture in the same sense as the Old Testament. But even those who take this as typical of the general attitude at the end of the first century, have to admit that one generation later when *2 Clement* was written we are a stage further on. For here the allusions to words of the Lord, though not given with precise wording and not—apart from the reference in chapter 2 to Mark 2. 17—quotations from our four Gospels, are certainly treated as Scripture.[1] The *Didache* and Hermas are indecisive on this point; nor does Polycarp's Epistle yield much help, at any rate as regards the place of the Gospels. The *Epistle of Barnabas*[2] introduces one of its two solitary Gospel quotations with the phrase "as it has been written", which suggests that the Gospel is equivalent to the Old Testament in authoritativeness as Scripture. One passage of Ignatius is relevant:[3] "I heard certain people say: If I find it not in the archives, I believe not in the Gospel." These critics seem to be Jewish Christians who refuse to accept any Christian dogma which cannot be justified by appeal to the Old Testament. In that case we have an opposition between the Old Testament (archives, ἀρχεῖα) and the Gospel, and when Ignatius goes on to assert "For me archives mean Jesus Christ", he clearly ranks the Gospel as more than equivalent to the Old Testament in authority.

Speaking of the Apostolic Fathers generally we may accept the verdict of Westcott:[4] "The words of Scripture are inwrought into the texture of the books, and not parcelled out into formal quotations . . . exactness of quotation was foreign to the spirit of their writing." But this lack of explicit quotation should not blind us to the significance

[1] The formula of introduction is: "The Lord saith" (λέγει, φησί). Knopf on *2 Clement* 2. 4 points out the significance for the history of the canon that here Gospel tradition is cited side by side with O.T. passages.

[2] 4. 14, quoting Mt. 20. 16 (= 22. 14). That Barnabas is really quoting Matthew is doubted by Bartlet in *The N.T. in the Apostolic Fathers*, pp. 2 f., 18. Also by Jülicher, *Einleitung* [5 and 6], p. 428; Knopf, *Einführung* [2], p. 154.

[3] *Philad.* 8. 2. The interpretation given above follows Lightfoot. The alternative interpretation of Zahn (*G.K.* II, pp. 945–948) punctuates so as to put archives and Gospel in apposition thus: "If I do not find it in the archives, that is the Gospel, I do not believe", and the dispute is regarded as concerning the true interpretation of the Gospel. Both Zahn and Lightfoot take Gospel to mean a document, and so even if we follow Zahn we have a recognition by both Ignatius and his opponents of a written Gospel as the supreme authority for Christians.

[4] Op. cit., pp. 47 f.

attached, not only to the Old Testament, but to the apostolic writings also, by this group of writers. They are conscious that they are not themselves the first age of the Church, the fount of inspiration and authority; they are very clear as to the distinction between apostolic writings and their own. To quote Westcott again: "Without having any exact sense of the completeness of the Christian Scriptures, they still drew a line between them and their own writings. . . . The fact is most significant: for it shows in what way the formation of the Canon was an act of the intuition of the Church, derived from no reasoning, but realized in the course of its natural growth as one of the first results of its self-consciousness." [1]

But when and how were apostolic writings placed with the Gospels as part of the new Christian supplement to the old-established Scriptures inherited from Judaism? Was the example of Marcion's canon creative in this respect, and is Harnack's judgement to that extent justified? The first thing to note about Marcion's Bible is not that it contained only one Gospel and the writings of only one Apostle, each emended in the interest of his theories; but that it had this twofold content, viz., Gospel and Apostle, not Gospel only. The question then arises: Had the common mind of Christians not already perceived that a collection of writings of the New Covenant would necessarily have these two components; or did Marcion introduce such a precedent?

A passage of Ignatius [2] has been appealed to by Westcott as implying a Christian collection, side by side with the prophets (i.e., the Old Testament), which included apostolic writings as well as Gospels. Ignatius speaks of himself "taking refuge in the Gospel as the flesh of Jesus, and in the apostles as the presbytery of the Church; the prophets also we love because they proclaimed the Gospel and hoped in it." The inference is hardly justified.[3] But it is beyond doubt that we

[1] Op. cit., p. 53. Westcott, of course, illustrates this differentiation of themselves from the Apostles on the part of the Apostolic Fathers. Cf. also Zahn, *G.K.* I, pp. 820 f. "Even if the extent of the post-apostolic literature were three times as great as it actually is, it would be a mistake to try to decide the precise date at which the Church included the letters of Paul and other N.T. writings in the concept of holy scriptures." Further (p. 847) Zahn argues that already in Ignatius the Gospel is on the same level of authority for Christians as the O.T. Cf. also his *Grundriss*, p. 41.

[2] *Philad.* 5, referred to in Westcott, op. cit., p. 54, n. 4.

[3] Cf. McNeile, *Introduction to the N.T.*, p. 304, who finds no reference to Christian books on a par with the prophets, but simply to Christian truth confirming prophetic hopes. So Bauer (*Handbuch zum N.T.* ad loc.). Lightfoot, while agreeing that authoritative *writings* of the N.T. are implied in the passage, nevertheless feels that in this context εὐαγγέλιον does not mean written documents, and thus makes ἀπόστολοι

have here well before Marcion's time a Christian conception of the Word of God spoken in old time culminating in recent testimony, if not actual writings, which naturally groups itself as "Gospel" and "Apostles". A late passage of the New Testament (2 Peter 3. 15–16) implies that the Epistles of Paul were recognized as Scripture, together with other writings (ὡς καὶ τὰς λοιπὰς γραφάς). The *Epistle of Barnabas* seems to rank Paul as Scripture like the Old Testament, and this is definitely so in one passage of the *Letter of Polycarp*.[1] The more extensive evidence of Justin does not permit a sure judgement on this point.[2] According to Clement of Alexandria, Valentinus cited Ephesians as ἡ γραφή.[3] Basilides uses the phrase ὡς γέγραπται with reference to 1 Corinthians, and ἡ γραφή with reference to Ephesians.[4] An example of an admittedly later date in the *Acts of the Scillitan Martyrs* (*c.* 180) is also worth notice. The contents of the satchel of the martyr Speratus were "books and epistles of Paul a just man". Presumably these documents were the most precious possessions of Speratus. It may be doubted whether "books" here signifies Gospels or Gospels and the Old Testament, but in either case the main thing to note for our present purpose is that the supplementary books which that martyr group chose as their vade-mecum to martyrdom were "Apostle", the Apostle being Paul. Dare we pronounce this Marcionite influence? Or is it not a safer inference that still at that date in this district of Africa Paul's Epistles had not been combined with other apostolic writings, but that here as elsewhere in Christendom the *communis sensus* of the Church had adopted Gospels and apostolic writings as the proper Christian complement of the Old Testament Scriptures, since before Marcion's time and without being indebted

---

include Gospels as well as Epistles (he would interpret similarly the famous phrase "apostles' memoirs" in Justin, 1st *Apology* 67). The distinction of Gospel and Apostle is later than Ignatius, Lightfoot thinks. Zahn (*G.K.* I, p. 844) holds that neither Gospel nor Apostles here refers to documents, although his general view is that Ignatius did use written Gospels and Epistles and regard at any rate the Gospel as of authority at least equal to that of the O.T. (*G.K.* I, p. 847).

[1] Ch. 12, quoting Eph. 4. 26. This is not noticed by Westcott.

[2] Zahn (*G.K.* I, p. 585) holds that Justin ranked Paul as well as the Gospels on the same level as the O.T. Westcott denies this (op. cit., p. 154).

[3] Quoted by Westcott, op. cit., p. 270, from *Strom.* 6. 34.

[4] The evidence is in Hippolytus, *Refutatio* 7, 13–14. Zahn is unduly sceptical about the value of the testimony of Hippolytus (*G.K.* I, p. 765, n. 4). Nor does the fact that Basilides was a heretic invalidate his testimony in this connection (*pace* Westcott, op. cit., p. 263). The date of Basilides is before A.D. 138; Clement of Alexandria places him in the reign of Hadrian. Indeed, he is probably the earliest to quote N.T. writings in the same way as books of the O.T.

to any suggestion of his?[1] The intuition of the Church—to borrow Westcott's phrase—was already classifying its new documents into two groups, and needed no prompting or pushing from Marcion. The sound assumption is that he followed precedent rather than created it, and the burden of proof of Marcion's creativity remains on Harnack.

A brief glance at Irenaeus is not out of place here, although his date is later than Marcion's, because of the extent of his writings and his general importance at that time. Irenaeus is familiar enough with the idea of Gospel and Apostle, which as Christian authorities have ranked themselves with the Old Testament Scriptures.[2] But this does not mean that for him Apostle was in the same category of authoritativeness as Gospel and Old Testament. This has been pointed out in a careful study by Werner.[3] Among Werner's strong arguments is the fact that none of Irenaeus's 206 quotations from Paul is introduced with *scriptura ait*[4] or any comparable formula. The general conclusion is that Irenaeus witnesses to the Pauline Epistles as on the way to becoming canonized, but as not yet having completely attained that dignity. This would apply to the passage already quoted from the *Acts of the Scillitan Martyrs*, though it is not the only possible explanation of that passage. The canonical value of the Gospel, as on an equality with the Old Testament, or as even higher in authority, in Irenaeus is patent.[5] In view of this reluctance by Irenaeus to equate them in canonical status it would be possible,[6] though far from necessary, to

[1] An interesting collocation of phrases in the *Epistle to Diognetus* (11. 6) lends some support to this argument. The author, who at the beginning of the chapter styles himself a "disciple of apostles", is speaking of the work of the eternal Logos who is now enriching the Church and causing grace to abound: "Then fear of the Law is sung and the grace of the prophets is recognized and the faith of the gospels is established and the tradition of the apostles is guarded." Clearly Law and Prophecy, Gospel and Apostle together constitute the foundation documents of the Church; and even if it be argued that "tradition of the apostles" may equally well mean oral as written tradition here, the main point is that the new and distinctively Christian counterpart of the older Law and Prophecy is not Gospel alone but Gospel plus Apostle. It must be admitted that this writing can hardly be dated before A.D. 150, and the last two chapters, from which the quotation above comes, are generally regarded as a late addition to it made at the end of the second century.

[2] Cf. *Haer.* 3. 17. 4: "As the Lord himself testifies, and the Apostles confess, and the prophets announce."

[3] *Der Paulinismus des Irenaeus* (1889), pp. 21–46.

[4] Op. cit., pp. 37 f. (against Hitchcock, *Irenaeus of Lugdunum*, p. 228, who makes too many assumptions).

[5] Cf. *Haer.* 1. 3. 6; 3. 11. 4.

[6] Cf. Knox, op. cit., p. 31.

argue that Marcion's association of Apostle with Gospel was influential toward the eventual canonization of Paul by the Church as a whole. But we cannot really be sure that Marcion actually equated his Gospel and Apostle in this sense, and all that it is safe to assume is that Marcion made up his mind about the canonical authority of Paul before the Church as a whole did.[1]

§ 3. MARCION'S INFLUENCE

Our inference from the foregoing is that Marcion introduced the first fixed canon of Christian Scriptures; but this is to be regarded as a published selection of books by an advocate of sectarian ideas, and by no means as the source of the notion of authoritative Scripture. Harnack's estimation of Marcion's influence in this field is an over-statement due to failure to distinguish the fundamental notion of canonicity from the actual drawing up of a list of canonical books. The idea of canonicity was as familiar in the Church as that of revelation, and it is superfluous to speak of Marcion's influence in this regard. "The canon of Marcion may have been the first which was publicly proposed, but the general consent of earlier Catholic writers proves that within the Church there had been no need for pronouncing a judgement on a point which had not been brought into dispute. The formation of the canon may have been gradual, but it was certainly undisturbed. It was a growth, and not a series of contests."[2] So Westcott. More positively, with regard to the actual effect of Marcion's canon among non-Marcionite Christians, the following judgement of Zahn's is probably nearer to the truth than the over-estimate of Harnack's which we have been considering: "Marcion formed his Bible in declared opposition to the holy scriptures of the Church from which he had separated; it was in opposition to his criticism that the Church in its turn first became rightly conscious of its inheritance of apostolic writings."[3]

§ 4. OTHER INFLUENTIAL FACTORS

Having rejected the view that Marcion is to be regarded as the creator of the Catholic Canon of the New Testament, we may go on to indicate other factors which contributed to the actual delimiting

[1] Cf. Harnack, *Briefsammlung des Apostels Paulus*, p. 21: "Marcion ist der erste gewesen, der der Paulinischen Briefsammlung die Autorität der litera scripta gegeben hat, indem er sie seinem ' Evangelium ' völlig gleichstellte und beide an die Stelle des A.T.s setzte."

[2] Westcott, op. cit., pp. 297 f.

[3] *G.K.* I, p. 586.

of a New Testament Canon. Marcion was not the founder of the New Testament in the sense that without him no New Testament would have been formed. Even Harnack does not mean that. There were in the Church growing collections of writings, and sooner or later order would have been imposed on them; some would have been credited with more, some with less authority; and some would have dropped out of use altogether, as was actually the case after the New Testament as we know it was formed. The only question was, what sort of collection would receive the highest authority, and here there were several possibilities. As we have seen, there is reason to assume that the common mind of the Church was already before Marcion's time moving towards canonization of Gospels and apostolic writings, in addition to the Old Testament. To attribute creativity to Marcion in this regard is to go far beyond the mark. It need not be denied, however, that the example of his canon of the New Testament was not without effect upon Christianity at large, beyond the circle of his own adherents. For example, if we enquire why the Epistles are to such a large extent Pauline, we must take some account of the fact that Marcion's New Testament contained only Pauline Epistles, beside its Gospel. Dared the orthodox Church appear to value the writings of the great Apostle of the Gentiles less highly than did a heretic? Marcion's influence may be described as provocative. But even so his was not the only provocative influence. He was not the only heretic.

In particular, the significance of Montanism for the growth of the New Testament Canon must not be forgotten. In the midst of a Church which was tending to look back to the age of the Apostles as the time when God had come especially close to mankind, and when his will was directly revealed in the preaching and writing of his chosen messengers, Montanism arose and declared that the Spirit was not the prerogative of a past generation, but was now once again active among men. To counteract this movement the Church reiterated that the New Covenant was completed by Christ and the Apostles: the age of enthusiasm was past, and the Spirit now spoke with final authority only through a book, viz., the collection of writings which originated in the age of the Apostles. Against the pretensions of these new spirit-filled persons the leaders of the Church made the greatest possible use of those writings which had apostolic authority; and the desire to state unambiguously in which books the Spirit authoritatively spoke led to the completion of a New Testament Canon. Now for the first time the New Testament becomes a closed collection.[1]

[1] For the distinction between the apostolic age, as the only age when the Spirit was

It was long, of course, before the closed canon was in every detail complete. East and West clung tenaciously to minor peculiarities, and in the East there was further division between Greek and Syrian churches over the question whether this or that writing should belong to the canon or not; and as late as the sixth century complete and final unity had not been reached. But, in principle, the limits of the canon were fixed by about A.D. 180. The struggle with Montanism rather than the struggle with Marcionitism was the decisive factor in producing the conception of a closed, " apostolic " canon. Montanism could never have made the claims it did make if a closed canon of the New Testament already existed. It was instrumental in a negative way in bringing the fixed canon into existence.[1]

It was not altogether fortunate that it was pressure from heretics which accelerated and conditioned the delimiting of the Church's canon. Inevitably in those circumstances there was an element of compulsion in its origin, and it is indeed possible that if the ecclesiastical atmosphere of the second century had been less troubled, and some of the books (e.g., the Apocalypse) could have had a longer trial, the contents of the New Testament would have been slightly different. Harnack's judgement[2] that " the New Testament was composed as a weapon not of attack but of defence " has much

---

given in full measure, and all subsequent ages, cf. Clement, *Strom.* 4. 21. 135: Ἕκαστος ἴδιον ἔχει χάρισμα ἀπὸ θεοῦ, ὁ μὲν οὕτως, ὁ δὲ οὕτως, οἱ ἀπόστολοι δὲ ἐν πᾶσι πεπληρωμένοι. Even Tertullian, who became a Montanist, wrote (*De Exhortatione* 4): *Spiritum quidem dei etiam fideles habent, sed non omnes fideles apostoli—proprie enim apostoli spiritum sanctum habent . . . non ex parte quod ceteri.* The date of the *De Exhortatione* is probably A.D. 204–206. Tertullian was acquainted with Montanism then, but his definite break with the Church did not come till slightly later, A.D. 206–207. See Harnack, *Die Chronologie der altchristlichen Literatur* (1904), p. 296.

[1] Eusebius (*H.E.* 5. 16. 3) preserves some significant words of an anti-Montanist writing in the year 192–193: ἐξευλαβούμενος μὴ πῃ δόξω τισὶν ἐπισυγγράφειν ἢ ἐπιδιατάσσεσθαι τῷ τῆς τοῦ εὐαγγελίου καινῆς διαθήκης λόγῳ, ᾧ μήτε προσθεῖναι μήτε ἀφελεῖν δυνατόν. This presupposes an already closed N.T.

The *Muratorian Fragment* excludes the *Shepherd* of Hermas from the canon on the ground that it was composed " *nuperrime temporibus nostris* ". This is significant: the criterion was whether a book was old enough, i.e., whether it was apostolic.

The expression " Books of the Old Covenant " seems to be first found in Melito of Sardis, an opponent of Montanism *c.* A.D. 170–180 (Eusebius, *H.E.* 4. 26. 12–14). It may be assumed that Melito knew also books of the New Covenant.

[2] *Die Entstehung des Neuen Testaments*, p. 22, n. 3. A sentence of W. F. Howard's is worth considering in this connection: " To the mistaken critical judgement of the ancient Church we owe the presence in the N.T. of not a few books. The most striking instance is Hebrews, which was certainly not written by Paul. O felix culpa! " (*The Bible in its Ancient and English Versions*, ed. by H. W. Robinson, p. 68).

justification. When he goes on, "Were it other than an anti-gnostic apostolic–catholic collection, the Acts of the Apostles and the Apocalypse would hardly stand in it; and the Pauline Epistles would stand in an appendix", he is guilty of overstatement.

One effect of the newly canonized Scripture can be seen in Tertullian's *De Praescriptione*. Tertullian in polemic against heretics is faced with the difficulty of excluding false interpretations of the Scriptures. Not only must there be an authorized collection of books and an authorized text, but an authorized exegesis is also needed. Here is the place for tradition as well as Scripture. Tertullian lays great weight on the *regula fidei* as the embodiment of the oldest and best tradition.

On the whole, then, Marcion can only in a restricted sense be called the founder of the New Testament Canon. He made the first closed canon; that is certain. One gets the impression from Harnack's book that the Catholic Church merely adopted Marcion's canon and made certain enlargements and corrections. But this is to magnify the importance of Marcion, and to lose sight of the variety of motives which prompted the formation of the canon. When one considers the large number of Christian writings, many claiming apostolic authorship, which were in use in the latter half of the second century A.D., the real question becomes: why was the Catholic canon limited so much? For a collection of sacred scriptures the New Testament is by no means a big book, and the Church had a precedent for a larger collection in the Old Testament. The answer is that the Catholic New Testament is the result of a process of selection rather than of collection. It was not intended to be a mere new edition of the Marcionite canon, "revised and in large part rewritten" to meet the needs of non-Marcionite Christians. The Catholic New Testament was to be the foundation document of Christianity, in the sense that it contained only "apostolic" writings. The only books which were not reported to be of apostolic authorship were Acts, and the Gospels of Mark and Luke. But the two latter had already established themselves in Church usage, and, moreover, were supposed to contain the preaching and teaching of Peter and Paul respectively; and the inclusion of a book describing the deeds of the Apostles is not difficult to understand.[1]

Previously Christians had been content to derive authority from the

[1] See below, p. 37. The *Muratorian Fragment* (line 34) refers to it as *Acta omnium apostolorum*. Hebrews also nearly failed to obtain a place in the canon. It was not recognized as Pauline at Rome and in the West till the end of the fourth century. In the East it was recognized earlier, but Origen doubted its Pauline authorship. (Cf. Eusebius, *H.E.* 3. 3. 5; 6. 14. 2.)

Old Testament and to claim that their religion originated at the very beginning of things. Christianity was " as old as creation " ! Marcion and the Gnostics, on the other hand, maintained that Christianity originated with Christ. The assertion of this need not have made the appeal to the Old Testament irrelevant; but if the Church was successfully to guard itself against these heretics it had to give more attention to writings inspired by the new revelation in Christ. Marcion and the Gnostics appealed to Paul. The Greater Church laid claim to every apostolic writing. Having appropriated everything apostolic, it was secure against the charge of not perceiving and preserving the Gospel in all its newness, and yet it could continue to believe in the consonance of the new with the old revelation.[1]

The acceptance of the four Gospels and a collection of Pauline Epistles was probably almost automatic. Marcion reduced the number of Gospels to one, and he seems not to have been alone in feeling that the existence of four Gospels was an embarrassment. It has been suggested[2] (but with little probability) that the Fourth Gospel was intended to replace the Synoptics. A more certain witness of an attempt to emphasize the unity of the Gospel by suppressing the four independent records of it is Tatian's *Diatessaron*. But neither Tatian nor Marcion succeeded in influencing permanently the whole Church. In spite of difficulties arising from the use of different records, the Church abode by those four Gospels which had already won for themselves the highest place. We have Irenaeus explaining why there can be no more and no less than four Gospels.[3]

The generally recognized Pauline Epistles were not only those retained by Marcion, but also the Pastorals. In the East Hebrews was also recognized as Pauline, but the West was not convinced of this; Tertullian, for example, regarded it as the work of Barnabas. A further advance on Marcion was the general acceptance of other epistles than the Pauline as of apostolic authorship—an assertion

[1] In defining the canon the Church appealed to the traditions of the apostolic sees, and the books it admitted were not those which were merely reputed to be apostolic, but those *which the apostolic sees accepted* as apostolic. Cf. Streeter, *The Four Gospels*, pp. 501 f.

[2] E.g., by Hans Windisch, *Johannes und die Synoptiker* (1926).

[3] *Haer.* 3. 11. 8: ὁ λόγος . . . ἔδωκεν ἡμῖν τετράμορφον τὸ εὐαγγέλιον, ἑνὶ δὲ πνεύματι συνεχόμενον. The Gospels are the four pillars of the Church, just as there are four quarters of the earth, four main winds, four beasts attached to the divine chariot (Ezekiel 1), and four divine covenants (viz., with Adam, Noah, Moses, and Christ). Knox considers that there is no adequate evidence for the existence of this fourfold Gospel of Irenaeus before A.D. 150. See Knox, *Marcion and the N.T.* pp. 149–152.

that St. Paul was not the only Apostle, and that Christianity was not built solely on Pauline foundations. It is clear that canonicity was equivalent to apostolicity.

At the end of the second century we find in the canon of most churches, beside the Gospels and thirteen letters of St. Paul: 1 Peter, 1 John, the Apocalypse (nearly everywhere believed to be the work of the Apostle John), and probably Jude and 2 John. The second part of the canon, i.e., the Ἀποστολικόν as distinguished from the Εὐαγγέλιον, is not yet clearly limited. Hovering on the borders of it are James, 3 John, Hebrews, and also a number of writings which still retained some authoritativeness, but which were gradually being excluded from the highest rank because not really apostolic, e.g., *Didache*, *1 Clement*, *The Shepherd of Hermas*, the *Apocalypse of Peter*.[1]

There remains Acts. How is its inclusion in the canon to be explained, when it was not regarded as the work of an Apostle? Probably the need was felt for a history of the Apostolic Church. Perhaps, also, there was wanted a work written not by one Apostle only, but in the name of all the Apostles. Acts, indeed, made no claim to speak on behalf of the Apostles as a body, but it contained the testimony of the original eleven Apostles in the speeches of Peter. It was therefore better fitted than any other of the *Acta Apostolorum* to supplement in the canon works written by, or representative of individual Apostles. This may be the intention of the *Muratorian Fragment*, when it definitely refers to it as *Acta omnium apostolorum*. Its Lucan authorship gave it a strong claim, for Luke was already accepted as *vir apostolicus*.[2] Another motive for its inclusion in the canon, and particularly for its place at the head of the Pauline Epistles, may have been the desire to ratify for St. Paul authority as an Apostle which otherwise would depend solely on his own testimony (Gal. 1. 1–2), and to justify the inclusion of so many Pauline writings as compared with writings of other Apostles.

A novel theory about the inclusion of Acts in the New Testament—that it was provoked by the Marcionite over-valuation of Paul and was intended to define his relation to the other Apostles—has been recently put forward by J. Knox in a book of which separate notice must now be given.

[1] Clement of Alexandria used these four still as Holy Scripture.

[2] Hardly anything is known of Acts before its emergence in the canon of the N.T.

§ 5. J. KNOX, MARCION AND THE NEW TESTAMENT

Marcion and the New Testament. An Essay in the Early History of the Canon. By John Knox, University of Chicago, 1942.

Knox argues, following Harnack, that Marcionism served as the decisive occasion for the creation of our New Testament. The pattern of the Marcionite canon (Gospel–Apostle) provided the scheme for the Church's canon. " The structural principle of Marcion's canon became the organizing idea of the catholic New Testament. Here is the fundamental fact in the relation of Marcion and the canon. Here is the principal ground for holding that it was Marcion's distinction between Scriptures ' false ' and ' true ' which forced the Church, almost against its will, to distinguish between Scriptures ' old ' and ' new '. Marcion is primarily responsible for the idea of the New Testament " (p. 31). " This does not mean . . . that opposition to Marcionism was the only factor contributing to the creation of a distinctively Christian canon of Scriptures. Many other factors were at work which would eventually have produced a New Testament of some kind. I am merely urging that Marcion's canon served as the decisive occasion of its creation, just as the addition of a single element to a highly complex chemical solution often produces the precipitate " (p. 161).

The predominance of Pauline letters in the Catholic New Testament is accounted for by Marcion's view of Paul as the only Apostle: apart from this the general estimation of Paul before A.D. 150 would not have ranked his writings so high. " Marcion forced the issue for the canon-makers: either more of Paul or all of Paul " (p. 36). Orthodox Christians extended the " Apostle " section of the canon by the addition of epistles by other Apostles (the Catholic Epistles); and of Acts, a main motive of which was to show that Paul, so far from being the sole Apostle, or working against the opposition of the Apostles (false apostles and Judaisers, according to Marcion), actually worked in collaboration with the Twelve. Here Knox introduces his own theory about Acts, viz., that it was published as part of a two-volume work, the first part of which—our present Luke—was a re-writing of an earlier and shorter Luke which was the Gospel Marcion used and emended in the interest of his own doctrines. This publication of Luke–Acts was part of the Church's reaction against Marcion and is dated *c.* A.D. 150. " I regard Luke–Acts as being under one of its aspects an early apologetic response to Marcionism. The ' Gospel and Apostle ' of ' Luke ' follow the ' Gospel and Apostle ' of Marcion, as they also anticipate the ' Gospel and Apostle ' of the official canon. The author of Luke–Acts sought to reclaim both a Gospel and Paul from the Marcionites " (p. 139). The general implication of Knox's work is that it was not Marcion who abridged so much as the Church which added to the original Gospel and Pauline *corpus*.

So much for the thesis of this freshly argued and stimulating book. But probability points the other way. The " idea of the New Testament " (Knox's phrase) was not Marcionite in origin, but was in the Church before him. Certain events of the second century, if taken in isolation from the whole of the literature and history of that century, can be made to support Knox's thesis ; but the weight of probability is on the side of orthodox Christianity having moved toward canonization under the impulse of its own convictions. What heretics contributed was a certain acceleration. It may sometimes happen that a traveller, after allowing ample time to reach his destination, arrives ahead of his schedule by the use of a new by-pass road which he had not expected to find. On this analogy Marcion may be given credit for providing a sort of by-pass ; but no more credit than that.

Knox's argument (pp. 84–88) is strong against the assumption that it was our Luke which Marcion abridged. He suggests that Marcion had a Luke shorter than the canonical one, and emended this to suit his theories. This original Luke was enlarged to the canonical Luke in the interest of anti-Marcionite apologetic (e.g., the inclusion of the first two chapters would indicate that the Church was rooted in Judaism). Thus would Knox explain the apparent omission by Marcion of such passages as 15. 11–32, which are not antipathetic to Marcionite doctrine. Harnack and others attribute this to a lack of consistency in Marcion, but Knox suggests more simply that Marcion never knew those passages, since they are Catholic additions made after Marcion's time. The argumentation is based on linguistic considerations, with full recognition of the fact that what we know of Marcion's Gospel comes to us from his opponents and that their failure to mention a passage as being part of Marcion's text is no proof that it was absent from Marcion's text. Care must be taken lest arguments based upon a reconstructed text of Marcion are given greater weight than they are capable of bearing. Thus, with regard to the relation of Marcion's Gospel to the canonical Luke " our knowledge of Marcion's Gospel is too scant to justify any confidence in its literary homogeneity with, and thus its dependence upon, Luke–Acts " (p. 97).

Knox argues (pp. 99–106) that the complete work Luke–Acts is distinct from Marcion's Luke—its distinctive characteristics, as often pointed out, e.g., by Cadbury, are missing from Marcion's Luke—

D

and from the compiler of the source of Marcion's Luke. This argument is not really convincing, because any book might be split up and the characteristics of it as a whole would not necessarily be found in all the detached parts.

Knox makes much of the fact that verses lacking in Marcion are mainly from passages peculiar to Luke; and on this he bases the suggestion that these peculiarly Lucan passages were added to the Gospel subsequently, by the compiler of Luke–Acts.

The assumption is made—it is no more—that without Marcion's canon the Church would not have canonized "Apostle" as well as "Gospel" at all (pp. 114–117). The emphasis on the possibility of Paul being "lost" to the heretics is quite exaggerated (p. 115). But Knox is more plausible in his argument that Acts was placed in the Catholic "Apostle" in order to bring Paul into proper subordinate relationship to the other Apostles. "The book of Acts serves the double purpose of exalting and idealizing Paul and at the same time definitely subordinating him to the leaders at Jerusalem" (p. 120). But this cannot be proved from our present almost non-existent external evidence, and the case for the publication of Acts as late as A.D. 150 needs more proof than Knox offers. He considers the evidence of the use of Luke and Acts before A.D. 150 and thinks it negligible. Such traces of this use as are generally allowed (e.g., in the cautious statements of the *New Testament in the Apostolic Fathers*, Oxford, 1905) Knox counters with the suggestion that it may just as well be a source of Luke or Acts that is quoted. To resort to that suggestion cannot be ruled out of order, but it is hardly convincing.

Such a summary as has been given does less than justice to the detailed reasoning of this book. Chapters 4 and 5, for example, which deal with Marcion's Gospel and our Luke and the relation of Luke–Acts to Marcion, go into considerable detail and make use of statistics and, therefore, demand something more than a précis. And this is the strongest part of the book. It is the general axioms that are not convincing. Indeed, one is left wondering whether Knox has not, despite his demurrer,[1] succumbed to the influence of P. L. Couchoud, who propounded the theory that Luke was dependent on Marcion rather than Marcion on Luke (Marcion's Gospel being a sort of Proto-Luke), and that the Synoptic Gospels were all produced subsequently to Marcion and within a very short space of time, *c.* A.D. 135–145.[2] This theory was promptly subjected to devastating

[1] P. 107.

[2] "Is Marcion's Gospel one of the Synoptics?" (*Hibbert Journal*, XXXIV, pp. 265–277). Loisy's answer is in the same volume of the *Hibbert Journal*, pp. 378–387.

criticism by Loisy. Knox does not really claim more for his thesis than " a rational consistency which gives it a certain *a priori* probability " (p. 166). He admits that the " textual evidence prevents our saying that Luke simply added to Marcion ", but screens himself with the counter-assertion that " it does not establish the opposite view that Marcion simply abridged our Luke " (p. 167). There is truth in this last contention. The safest course, however, is not to adopt Knox's theories, but to remember that both our reconstruction of Marcion's text and our information about his methods are after all fragmentary and therefore not capable of bearing too solid a superstructure of deduction and theory. They are sufficient foundation for a modest house, but not for a skyscraper !

Knox refers to this (p. 106, n.). Couchoud had a similarly mistaken theory about Marcion's *Apostolicum*, which he held to be the earliest edition of Paul (*Revue de l'Histoire des Religions*, 1926).

3

MARCION AND THE TEXT OF THE NEW TESTAMENT

§ 1. MARCION'S METHOD

MARCION'S criticism of the Gospels and Pauline Epistles—"with a knife", as Tertullian bitingly describes it—arose from his conviction that they contained not the genuine Gospel, but a Jewish contamination of it.[1] It was an axiom with Marcion that very soon after the ascension of Jesus "Judaizers" began a kind of conspiracy against the truth of the Gospel. The success of this conspiracy was so great that the Apostles themselves were deceived,[2] and Christ had to appoint another apostle—Paul—to begin afresh the preaching of the Gospel. The Judaizers strove their hardest against Paul during his lifetime, and after his death succeeded in falsifying his writings so that his message was obscured. The new wine was once more poured into old wineskins. Marcion believed himself to have the new bottles which had been prepared for it, and he essayed the task of pouring the wine back into these bottles. On that new wine so preserved he would nourish the true believers.

He made no claim to special gifts of the Spirit, nor to a special revelation which he alone had received. No prophet he, nor a prophet's son. He appealed to no secret tradition, but simply took his stand on his interpretation of the Pauline Epistles. He probably had no more information than we have to-day about the results of Paul's struggle with Jewish and Jewish–Christian opponents, or about the historical development of Christianity between Paul's and his own time. His whole conception of the early days of Christianity was governed by the idea of Jewish opposition to the true, i.e., Pauline, Gospel.

He seems to have derived these convictions primarily from his reading of the Epistle to the Galatians. This Epistle stood first in his collection of Paul's writings, probably because it was for him the most important. From Galatians Marcion made two deductions: that there

[1] Pp. 42–47 are based on Harnack, pp. 35 ff.

[2] For Marcion's views of the Apostles' culpability we have the early evidence of Tertullian: *Apostolos praevaricationis et simulationis suspectos . . . usque ad evangelii depravationem* (*Adv. Marc.* 4. 3); *Petrus legis homo* (4. 11); and earlier still Irenaeus: *Apostolos admiscuisse ea quae sunt legalia salvatoris verbis* (*Haer.* 3. 2. 2.); *Non cognoverunt veritatem* (*sc. apostoli*) (op. cit., 3. 13. 2).

is only one Gospel, namely, that given to Paul δι' ἀποκαλύψεως Ἰησοῦ Χριστοῦ (1. 12); and that others had preached a false Judaistic Gospel. Marcion, as the follower of Paul, had to continue Paul's struggle against Judaizers. This meant that he must rediscover the original teaching of his master; that is, he must become a textual reviser, and eject from the text of the Pauline Epistles every interpolation; further, he must restore the true Gospel out of those Gospel records which were most read by Christians.

This was no easy task. He might, indeed, have prepared his own version of the Gospel, making use of a licence not uncommon at that time. He chose instead a more prosaic path. Where was the one Gospel of which Galatians 1. 8–9 speaks? Which of the then current Gospel records was it?[1] Marcion decided on Luke, but we are unfortunately not well informed as to the motives which led him to this choice. He was doubtless influenced by the tradition that Luke was the companion of Paul. Harnack (p. 42) suggests that Luke was the first Gospel which Marcion knew, and that in any case only accidental circumstances made him fix upon Luke rather than Mark. As for Matthew and John, the general Judaic character of the former, and in the latter the Prologue (" He came to his own "), the marriage at Cana, the importance attached to John the Baptist, were to Marcion obvious stumbling-blocks. The Gospel which Marcion eventually selected was, of course, falsified, so that the reviser still had much to do; the first two chapters, for instance, were intolerable; even the name Luke must have been appended by the falsifiers, for the Apostle asserts that he received the Gospel direct from Christ, and it can therefore have no human name at its head. But the task was at least clearly defined, and Marcion could now turn the searchlight of his critical mind straight upon it.

Harnack suggests that Marcion began with expurgation of the Epistles, and thence obtained a criterion by which to judge the Gospel itself.

We now come to the question of Marcion's method in dealing with the texts before him. The Marcionite Gospel and Apostle have been carefully restored by Harnack, and all subsequent students of Marcion and of the New Testament Canon will use Harnack's restoration. Nothing more remains to be done except a revision of the critical

[1] Harnack seems to overlook the probability that Marcion had more than our four canonical Gospels to choose from.

It has been suggested that Marcion was the first to call a book Ἐυαγγέλιον. Instances of the use of εὐαγγέλιον for a written Gospel, however, are pointed out by Souter in the *Didache* and Ignatius (cf. Souter, *Text and Canon of N.T.*, pp. 160 f.).

apparatus.[1] For all purposes, except those of detailed study of the New Testament, Harnack's work is amply sufficient. It cannot be reproduced here, but we must consider Marcion's motives and the most significant of his alterations.

As instances of Marcion's corrections the following may be selected:

In the first verse of the Epistle to Galatians he struck out καὶ θεοῦ πατρός in order to make the verse say that Christ raised himself from the dead.[2]

In Chapter 3 of this epistle the references to Abraham were omitted; in fact, as a general rule, Marcion rejected all quotations from the Old Testament, i.e., all passages introduced by γέγραπται.[3]

In Gal. 4. 8–9 Marcion read τοῖς ἐν τῇ φύσει οὖσι θεοῖς instead of τοῖς μὴ φύσει οὖσι θεοῖς, because it was integral to his theory that heathen gods were real beings; they were nature gods and angels of the Demiurge.

In Gal. 5. 14 after ὁ νόμος πεπλήρωται Marcion added ἐν ὑμῖν (i.e., "in you", with the implication "not in the Jews").[4]

In 1 Cor. 3. 17 φθερεῖ τοῦτον ὁ θεός was displaced by φθαρήσεται: the God who is *pura benignitas* cannot destroy anyone! In Chapter 15 of this epistle v. 3 f. ὃ καὶ παρέλαβον and κατὰ τὰς γραφάς disappeared, and v. 20 ἐγήγερται became κηρύσσεται ἀναστῆναι.

2 Cor. 2. 15 lacked τῷ θεῷ: Marcion's God did not, like the Creator, delight in εὐωδία. In 3. 14 (ἐπωρώθη τὰ νοήματα αὐτῶν)

[1] A. Pott in *Z.K.G.* xlii, pp. 202–223, adduces witnesses out of Tischendorf's and von Soden's Apparatus for readings which Harnack gives as unattested. This indicates that Marcion's text was even more closely related to the pre-canonical text than Harnack showed. Pott's criticism, however, does not affect Harnack's main contention, viz., that the text used by Marcion was a Western text. Harnack relied on Tischendorf for all questions of the text and variant readings. Textual discoveries subsequent to Tischendorf of which Tischendorf had no knowledge are also ignored by Harnack; e.g., the readings of the Old Latin versions r and r_2 (edited by T. K. Abbott, *Evangeliorum Versio Ante-Hieronymiana*, 1884).

[2] This verse is indicative of Marcion's modalistic Christology. It also gives expression to his theory that Christ raised himself from the dead, and depended for nothing on the Creator.

[3] There are exceptions, e.g., 4. 22 ff., for Marcion was not always consistent. Tertullian in considering Marcion's handling of these verses (*Adv. Marc.* 5. 4) says: *Ut furibus solet aliquid excidere de praeda in indicium ita credo et Marcionem novissimam Abrahae mentionem dereliquisse.*

[4] It is possible that Marcion found this reading already in the text he used, as it is attested by D G d g. But it fits in so well with Marcion's doctrines that it is perhaps more likely to be a tendencious alteration of his, and an instance of his text actually influencing the Western text. So Harnack, p. 154*. See also Appendix 7.

Marcion substituted τοῦ κόσμου for αὐτῶν, and meant by it the Creator-God. This identification of the Creator and the world occurs also elsewhere in Marcion's work.

In Rom. 1. 16 Marcion removed πρῶτον after Ἰουδαίῳ, and 1. 18 θεοῦ after ὀργή—the good God cannot be angry! the rest of this chapter was omitted *in toto*, doubtless because God is said to have given men over to crimes as a punishment. The passage 3. 31–4. 25 was also omitted, for the thought of "establishing the Law" and the references to Abraham were alike intolerable to Marcion. A similar motive prompted the rejection of all but a few verses in Chapters 9–11. The verses which describe how Nature as well as mankind awaits redemption were probably inexplicable to Marcion, and omitted on that ground. In 6. 9 we meet the familiar substitution of ἀναστάς for ἐγερθείς. At 11. 33 ἀνεξερεύνητα τὰ κρίματα αὐτοῦ fell out—Marcion's God does not judge.

Eph. 2. 14 f. Marcion left out αὐτοῦ after ἐν σαρκί and ἐν before δόγμασι. He could then preclude the thought of Christ having in his *flesh* destroyed the enmity, and proceed to interpret: God has annulled the Jewish Law by introducing the new Christian δόγματα.

Eph. 2. 20 lost καὶ προφητῶν: the prophets could not be understood as being a part of the foundation of the new Christian building.

Eph. 3. 9 is perhaps the most notorious of Marcion's tamperings. By leaving out ἐν before τῷ θεῷ τῷ τὰ πάντα κτίσαντι he obtained a valuable proof-text for his theory that the Creator had been from the beginning entirely ignorant of the Redeemer-God's plans.[1]

Eph. 4. 6. Marcion wrote ἐν πᾶσιν ἡμῖν instead of simply ἐν πᾶσιν, in order to exclude the possibility of his God being thought of as pervading the universe.[2]

From Colossians may be noted the shortening of 1. 15–17 to ὅς ἐστιν εἰκὼν τοῦ θεοῦ τοῦ ἀοράτου, καὶ αὐτός ἐστι πρὸ πάντων, for Christ could not be thought of as having any part in the creation of the world.

The famous κένωσις passage in Philippians 2 was suited to Marcion's Christology by the omission of γενόμενος and ὡς in v. 7.

We pass to Marcion's treatment of the Gospel. For obvious reasons the Birth and Pre-Birth stories, and the Jewish genealogy could not be allowed to stand. The Baptism and Temptation of Christ were also left out, and His connection with Nazareth was obscured. Marcion himself struck Ναζαρηνέ out of 4. 34, and later Marcionites actually substituted Bethsaida for Nazareth.

[1] ἐν is missing also in ℵ*, but no importance can be attached to this.

[2] ἡμῖν is also found D G d g Vulgate K L etc. But Harnack thinks this is an instance of Marcion's corrections creeping into the Western text (p. 154*).

5. 39 ὁ παλαιὸς (οἶνος) χρηστός ἐστι was unacceptable because it referred to the Old Testament and the dispensation of the Creator.

8. 19 (the mother and brothers of Jesus try to reach him) likewise had to be removed: Jesus was not born in earthly wise, therefore he had no earthly kinsfolk.

The Thanksgiving-Prayer of Jesus: Ἐξομολογοῦμαί σοι, Πάτερ, Κύριε τοῦ οὐρανοῦ καὶ τῆς γῆς (10. 21 ff.) was considerably tampered with. Most noticeable is the omission of Πάτερ, and καὶ τῆς γῆς. Verse 24 was weakened so as to read only: λέγω γὰρ ὑμῖν, ὅτι προφῆται οὐκ ἴδαν, ἃ ὑμεῖς βλέπετε.

10. 25 lost αἰώνιον after ζωήν in accordance with Marcion's regular interpretation of the promises of the God of the Old Testament as referring only to this life.

The passage about God's care for sparrows and the higher worth of mankind (12. 6 f.) was omitted.

15. 10. "There shall be joy in the presence of the angels of God over one sinner that repenteth" lost "the angels of". Only the Creator God had angels. In the same chapter the parable of the Prodigal Son was rejected *in toto*. One might have expected this to be retained, as a worthy illustration of just that attribute of the Divine Nature which for Marcion was first and last, namely, compassion for mankind. But if the parable was fully to satisfy Marcion's doctrine the elder son would need to have been cast out; moreover, the suggestion of a return to the father's house was unacceptable to Marcion.[1]

Christ's announcement to the Twelve of his Passion and Resurrection, as the fulfilment of prophecy, was struck out (18. 31–33).

The story of Zaccheus was retained, but with the significant omission of καθότι καὶ αὐτὸς υἱὸς Ἀβραάμ ἐστι (19. 9).

22. 20 lacked καινὴ before διαθήκη. The "old" covenant was made by the God of the Old Testament, whereas Marcion's God had made no previous covenant with men.

24. 27. Jesus expounds to the two disciples on the road to Emmaus the Old Testament prophecies which referred to himself. Marcion could not retain this, as he referred the Messianic prophecies to an earthly Jewish Messiah who was yet to come. 24. 44–46 were rejected for the same reason.

24. 39–40. Jesus showed the disciples his hands and feet—ψηλαφήσετέ με καὶ ἴδετε. This conflicted with Marcion's Docetic Christology. Marcion also left out the last five verses of the Gospel. He did not like the declaration that the preaching about Jesus should

[1] For an alternative explanation of the absence of this parable in Marcion's Luke, see p. 39 above.

begin from Jerusalem, nor the promise of the Spirit to the Eleven. Why he omitted the Ascension is not so clear.

These are the most striking of Marcion's omissions and alterations, and those of which there can be no doubt. When one goes through Tertullian and the other sources it is often difficult to decide whether they pass over a passage because it was not in Marcion's text or because they had nothing in particular to say about it; e.g., it is uncertain whether Marcion's text contained the parable of the Good Samaritan and the story of Martha and Mary (10. 29–42), because Tertullian goes straight from 10. 28 to 11. 1 (*Adv. Marc.* 4. 25 f.). There is no apparent reason why Marcion should have taken offence at anything in these verses, and it may well be that Tertullian is silent because he had nothing convincing to say against Marcion's exegesis here. At the same time it must be remembered that Marcion was not always consistent, as we may judge from passages which he allowed to remain, but which are distinctly unfavourable to his position.[1]

Marcion's emendations consisted mainly of omissions. Additions, substitutions and transpositions by him are, however, also attested. He believed the Judaizers to have corrupted the text not only by spurious insertions, but also by every kind of alteration. Marcion seems to have been more confident in striking out what he took to be Judaistic interpolations, than in re-inserting what he supposed to be omitted, as his additions are few. The most notable are κατὰ τὸ εὐαγγέλιόν μου in Gal. 1. 7 and καὶ καταλύοντα τὸν νόμον καὶ τοὺς προφήτας . . . καὶ ἀποστρέφοντα τὰς γυναῖκας καὶ τὰ τέκνα in Luke 23. 2. To Marcion's credit be it said that he brought in no apocryphal material.

His transposition of words, i.e., restoration of them to what he conceived to be their right position before Judaizers misplaced them, is often subtle, though sometimes the motive is not apparent. But we may infer how far-reaching he imagined the tamperings to have been. We note especially Marcion's substitution of ἀγοράσαντος for ἀγαπήσαντος, Gal. 2. 20, to recover what he thought a lost emphasis; τὴν κλῆσιν for τὴν κρίσιν Luke 11. 42; σοῦ for ἡμῶν after τὸν ἄρτον in the Lord's Prayer; διὰ τῆς φιλοσοφίας ὡς κενῆς ἀπάτης instead of δ. τ. φ. καὶ κενῆς ἀπάτης Col. 2. 8; ἐπιδείξεις for διαθῆκαι Gal. 4. 24; κηρύσσεται ἀναστῆναι for ἐγήγερται 1 Cor. 15. 20; ὁ Χριστὸς for ὁ βασιλεὺς τῶν Ἰουδαίων Luke 23. 3. For the full list see Harnack, pp. 62 f. It is not necessary to see in Marcion an " expert philologian " as Harnack does.

[1] E.g., 1 Cor. 6. 14 (Harnack, p. 84* f., with Tertullian's comment): cf. also n. 3 to p. 44 above.

A consideration of these textual alterations suggests the following as Marcion's leading motives: The good God must not be spoken of as ruler of the world. He had nothing to do with the world, and was entirely unknown to the Creator of the world, until his appearance in Christ. His redemption refers to the eternal life, not to life in this world. He is not a Judge who punishes men for their evil deeds. The Creator-God, on the other hand, is the ruler of this world. All his promises refer to this world, and are valid only for the Jewish race. The Old Testament is his book, and cannot have prophesied that which is fulfilled in Christ. It is to be understood literally. It cannot have been quoted as authoritative by Christ or Paul. The Creator must not appear as the Father of Jesus Christ. Lastly, with regard to Christ, he is the son of the good God, in a modalistic sense. He cannot have had a body of flesh and blood, for these are earthly elements. As he is himself independent of the World-Creator and all his works, so he demands that men also shall free themselves from the Creator and from this world. Christ brought to light the contrast between Law and Gospel. His earliest Apostles proved failures, but he raised up Paul after them, and Paul proclaimed the true Gospel. Christ will not appear to judge the world, but will at the last day declare the great division of men (into those who have worshipped the Creator-God and those who have sought the redemption of the good God).

Marcion's work as a Biblical critic was carried on by his disciples.[1] Seeing that he himself claimed no special inspiration for his alterations of the text he could hardly expect others to feel themselves unworthy of this task. Indeed, it is probable that he laid express commands upon his followers to continue his efforts to free the text of the Gospel and the Apostle from all corruptions. To these scholars are probably to be ascribed the composition of the Marcionite Prologues, and the admission of the Pastoral Epistles to the Marcionite canon.

It is probable that later Marcionites also admitted into their Bible verses from the Gospels according to Matthew, Mark, and John. They undoubtedly adopted Mt. 5. 17, after inverting the order of the clauses so as to give exactly an opposite sense, that is to say, they read Οὐκ ἦλθον πληρῶσαι τὸν νόμον, ἀλλὰ καταλῦσαι.[2] Origen [3] informs

[1] Cf. *Adamantius* 2. 18 (Bakhuyzen, p. 96): ὁ γὰρ σχέτλιος Μαρκίων, ῥαδιουργήσας τὰ κατὰ τὸν 'απόστολον, οὐ παντάπασιν ἀπήλειψε, καὶ οὗτοι (i.e., Marcionites) μέχρι τοῦ δεῦρο περιαιροῦσιν ὅσα ἂν μὴ συντρέχῃ τῇ αὐτῶν γνώμῃ. Cf. also Tertullian, *Adv. Marc.* 4. 5: *Cotidie reformant evangelium, prout a nobis cotidie revincuntur.*

[2] *Adamantius* 2. 15.

[3] *Hom.* 25 on Luke (vol. 9 of Origen's Works in *Die Griechischen Christlichen Schriftsteller*, p. 162).

us that Marcionites thought of Paul seated in Heaven on the right hand of God, while Marcion sat on the left; they must then have accepted Mark 10. 35 ff. or Mt. 20. 20 ff. and have put this interpretation upon it. Ephraem Syrus[1] says that the Marcionites had not rejected Mt. 23. 8. John 13. 34, 15. 19 are quoted by the Marcionite Marcus in Adamantius' *Dialogue*,[2] and may be presumed to have stood in some Marcionite Bibles. The same dialogue brings evidence of the substitution of πνεῦμα for σῶμα at 1 Cor. 15. 38. Esnik of Colb in his work *Against the Sects*[3] witnesses for the casting of 1 Cor. 15. 25 into a passive form so that Christ should not be presented as a warrior. Moreover, part at least of the alterations quoted by Tertullian and Epiphanius as Marcion's own work will be in reality the work of his disciples. The Chronicle called the Fihrist[4] records that Marcion wrote a book which he called " Gospel ", and that his disciples composed a number of other books " which God alone is able to find " !

Harnack thinks the Doxology (Rom. 16. 25–27) was added by Marcionites. It is certain that Marcion did not know these verses, for his copy of Romans ended at 14. 23. But according to Harnack they are strongly Marcionite, and only very clumsily " Catholicized " by the insertion of καὶ τὸ κήρυγμα Ιησοῦ Χριστοῦ, διά τε γραφῶν προφητικῶν, γνωρισθέντος. Harnack's arguments (pp. 165* f.), however, do not amount to scientific proof, and we may not take this as a certain example of Marcionite influence on the Catholic New Testament. It is an interesting possibility, no more. Lietzmann ad loc., referring to Corssen's work, explains how the textual variants arose. The original text ended at 16. 23. Then Chapters 15 and 16 dropped out—this is the form which Marcion knew. But now there was no conclusion at all, and so our verses 16. 25–27 were added (perhaps in Marcionite circles, adds Lietzmann). They are of a liturgical character and probably the Doxology used at the close of Divine service; this explains their quite un-Pauline language.

Marcion justified his criticism of the Scriptures and the formation of his Canon in his book *Antitheses*. We have many quotations from this work, but unfortunately not enough to make possible any reconstruction of it. Tertullian calls it a kind of dowry for Marcion's Gospel: *ut fidem instrueret (suo evangelio) dotem quandam commentatus est illi.*[5] In reality it was much more than an introduction to Marcion's New Testament;

[1] *Song* 24, 1 ff.

[2] Op. cit., 2. ch. 16 and 20: for 1 Cor. 15. 38, see ch. 25.

[3] Book 4, p. 190. (J. M. Schmid's German translation.)

[4] Quoted by Harnack, p. 384*.

[5] *Adv. Marc.* 4. 1.

it was an exposition of Marcion's whole system—his systematic as well as his Biblical theology—the *summum instrumentum* for the Marcionite Church.[1] What Tertullian quotes in his fourth and fifth books against Marcion as Marcion's exegesis of passages in his Gospel and epistles must come from the *Antitheses*. And it seems that Marcion discussed there not only passages which he accepted, i.e., Luke and the ten Pauline Epistles, but also passages from the other Gospels, e.g., Mt. 5. 17.[2]

§ 2. THE INFLUENCE OF MARCION'S TEXT

We come to the question of the actual text. Harnack has established beyond the possibility of doubt that the text Marcion used was a Western text. Its readings frequently agree with the chief Western authorities, D and the Old Latin, in their distinctive variations from the rest of the MSS.[3] Pott, after comparing the Apparatus Criticus of Harnack's restored text of Marcion's Gospel with von Soden's and Tischendorf's Apparatus, shows that Marcion's text was even more closely related to the pre-canonical Western text than Harnack had shown.[4] Pott also points out the affinity between Marcion's text and the texts used by Tatian and by the Curetonian and Sinaitic Syriac. Marcion and Tatian are, in fact, with Justin the oldest representatives of this pre-canonical text.

Once it is realized that Marcion used a Western text two important questions present themselves. Does Marcion represent a distinct type of text within the Western group? And did his text influence other members of that group? The first question cannot be answered affirmatively. After Marcion's conformities with Western readings have been set aside his text still offers no certainly attested readings which are unknown to the Western text and differ from it more widely than the other witnesses of it differ from one another; and which also cannot be taken as tendentious alterations of Marcion's.

The answer to the second question is also in the negative.[5] The

[1] *Adv. Marc.* I. 19.

[2] Origen in his commentary on Mt. 19. 12 quotes an interpretation of Marcion's. Where should he have found this except in the *Antitheses*?

[3] It may be assumed that the Roman Church shortly before the middle of the second century used texts of this type, and Harnack thinks Marcion prepared his text of the N.T. in Rome, rather than in Pontus or Asia. Of course, the circulation of the Western text was not confined to the West.

[4] *Z.K.G.*, xlii, pp. 202–223.

[5] With a few exceptions. Harnack allows the possibility of Marcionite readings creeping in at Luke 5. 39; 9. 54 ff.; 22. 43 f.; 23, 2; 23. 34; 24, 12; 24 40; and Gal. 5. 14; Rom. I. 16; I Cor. 15. 3; I Thess. 2. 15; Eph. 4. 6; 5. 31.

main result of Harnack's study of this problem is to have proved that the great majority of readings which were formerly held to be Marcionite corruptions are not Marcionite at all, but simply come from the Western text as Marcion found it. Harnack does not follow Zahn in denying that Marcionite readings influenced the Catholic texts, but he argues that their influence was very limited.[1] "The agreements of Marcion's text with the Western text are with few exceptions to be considered as stylistic peculiarities of the Western text which Marcion's text shares. Subsequent influence of Marcion's text on the Western text and on the textual tradition in general was not entirely absent, but, so far as the material at our disposal permits of a judgement, it was small."[2]

There remain still about one hundred readings peculiar to Marcion, but which are dogmatically neutral, i.e., not introduced by Marcion in the interest of his doctrines. They consist of alterations of the place of words, differences of tense or number, use of a different preposition or participle, exchange of a word for its synonym, e.g., κύριος for θεός, logical improvements, e.g., Gal. 2. 2 Marcion offers ἔδραμον ἢ τρέχω instead of τρέχω ἢ ἔδραμον. Such variations are common among manuscripts and in general have no special significance. Moreover, it is difficult always to be certain that the variant reading really stood in Marcion's text; the sources, Tertullian, *Adamantius*, or Epiphanius may have quoted incorrectly. It may well be that many of these readings are not peculiar to Marcion, but either belonged to the Western text, or are carried over by Marcion from the original text, when all other witnesses of the Western type deviated from the original. This latter possibility should not be overlooked, although no proof can be adduced for it. Harnack suggests that Marcion's addition at the close of 1 Cor. 6. 13 (ὡς ὁ ναὸς τῷ θεῷ καὶ ὁ θεὸς τῷ ναῷ) may be a preservation of the original text. Pott, in the article already referred to, thinks that the text of Luke which lay before Marcion came very near to the original text of the Gospel. Pott criticizes Harnack's dating of the composition of the Gospels as too early, on the ground that Harnack is tempted to it by his desire

[1] Von Soden in *Z.K.G.* xl, p. 197, attributes even less to that influence, and holds that those readings which Harnack regards as tendentious corrections of Marcion's may not be so, but can still be Western: cf. Harnack, p. 247*.

[2] Harnack, pp. 154* f. He reaches a similar conclusion after his examination of Marcion's Gospel text, pp. 247* f. He notes, however, that Marcion's text (of the Gospel) found an immediate entry into the Western text and was propagated with it to some extent. Beside the seven passages of Luke where Harnack demonstrates Marcionite influence on the Western text (see above p. 50, n. 5), there is also the Marcionite reading φάντασμα for πνεῦμα, Luke 24. 37, preserved in D alone.

to allow ample time for the emergence of those corruptions of the Western text which Marcion shared.

§ 3. MARCIONITE PROLOGUES

Something must be said about the influence of the Marcionite prologues. These are Latin prologues to the thirteen Epistles of Paul (i.e., Marcion's ten plus the Pastorals).[1] They have been handed down to us in the majority of the best MSS. of the Vulgate. The sixth-century codex *Fuldensis* contains them. Their style shows them to be a translation from the Greek, but we no longer have them in Greek. The hypothesis of their Marcionite origin rests on the following observations.[2] They are governed by the supposition of an attack by false Apostles upon the word of truth (*verbum veritatis*) and the Epistles are considered as either St. Paul's method of winning the Church back to the true Gospel (*veram evangelicam fidem*), or as congratulation because they had stood firm. St. Paul is referred to as "*apostolus*". The false Apostles wished to draw St. Paul's converts back "*in legem et circumcisionem*" (Galatians), "*in legem et prophetas*" (Romans); those mentioned in the prologue to Corinthians were "*quidam a philosophiae verbosa eloquentia, alii a secta legis Judaicae inducti*".[3]

De Bruyne, from an examination of the inner relations of the first ten prologues (i.e., all except those to the Pastorals), perceived that the

[1] They can be conveniently referred to in Harnack, pp. 127*–129*, or in Souter, *Text and Canon of the N.T.*, pp. 205–207.

[2] It has been called in question by W. Mundle (*Z.N.T.W.*, 1925, pp. 83–91), and R. P. Lagrange (*Revue Biblique*, 1926, pp. 161–173). Lagrange does no more than repeat Mundle, but it would have been surprising if Mundle's careful statements had found no agreement. The theory that the prologues (with the possible exception of those to the Pastorals) are Marcionite was first stated by de Bruyne (*Revue Bénédictine*, Jan. 1907, pp. 1–16, 257 ff.) and Corssen (*Z.N.T.W.*, 1909, pp. 36 ff., 97 ff.), and since then has received the assent of Harnack, Wordsworth and White, Rendel Harris, Burkitt and Souter. Mundle, after pointing out parallels between these prologues and those of Ambrosiaster, goes so far as to say they are actually dependent on Ambrosiaster (op. cit., p. 72).

[3] It is not so certain that the prologues to the Pastorals are also from a Marcionite hand. Harnack was converted by Corssen to the belief that they are, but de Bruyne held the other view. See Harnack, p. 132*. It is not enough to say that these prologues are similar both in form and content to the others. For Harnack the decisive factor is the expression "*de haereticis vitandis qui in scripturis Judaicis credunt*" in the prologue to Titus. He goes on to infer that the text of this Epistle must have read "*scripturis*" instead of "*fabulis*" at I. 14, and that some Marcionites must have received the Pastorals into their canon. Mundle (op. cit., p. 61) uses the fact that there are prologues to the Pastorals as a chain in his argument that none of the prologues are from Marcionite hands.

original order of the Epistles was the Marcionite order. This is a further indication of the Marcionite authorship of the prologues.[1]

Wordsworth and White suggest Marcion himself as the author, but if this is so, it is difficult to see why Tertullian says nothing about them. Nevertheless, the supposition of an early origin is necessary to explain the wide dissemination of the prologues in the West. It is one of the paradoxes of history that these prologues were taken up into the Catholic New Testament and their motif unrecognized. Harnack infers the poverty of churches in texts and in aids to the elucidation of the Scriptures.

The prologues can hardly have been written in Italy, or otherwise the prologue to Romans would not begin : *Romani sunt in partibus Italiae.* That the Pastoral Epistles were at some date after Marcion's death admitted to the Marcionite Bible is a possible inference from the words "*de haereticis vitandis qui in scripturis Judaicis credunt*" in the prologue to Titus. It is supported by a passage of Chrysostom[2] which says Marcionites used 2 Tim. 1. 18 as evidence for their doctrine of two lords or gods. There is a bare possibility that Marcion himself had never seen the Pastorals, but that later Marcionites, finding collections of thirteen Pauline Epistles, and seeing no reason to doubt the Paulinicity of any of them, readily enlarged their canon from ten to thirteen. Against this must be set the probability that the whole *Corpus Paulinum* including the Pastorals goes back to the first century.[3]

Harnack makes much of the wide circulation of the prologues in the West, and argues from this that they must have been composed before the end of the second century. He claims[4] that they were actually contained in the Bible used by the author of the *Muratorian Fragment* ; and, moreover, so closely bound up with the Epistles as to be indistinguishable from the text. For this theory Harnack relies on lines 39–41 of the Fragment : "*epistulae Pauli quae, a quo loco, vel qua ex causa directae sint . . . ipsae declarant*". In actual fact the Epistles themselves do not yield this information as to their origin and purpose (*a quo loco vel qua ex causa*) or as to the state of affairs in the churches to which they are addressed (*quae*). But the prologues do. Therefore they must have been already connected with the Epistles. This theory

[1] Mundle (op. cit., pp. 58 f.) denies this, adducing evidence that the Syrian Church had the epistles in the same order as Marcion.

[2] Quoted in Harnack, p. 368*, whose reference, however, is not very clear. It should be: Montfaucon, revised edition, 1838, vol. xi, p. 727.

[3] For evidence of this, see Harnack's pamphlet: *Die Briefsammlung des Apostels Paulus*, 1926.

[4] *Z.N.T.W.*, 1926, pp. 160–163.

is interesting and may be true, but the historical student must leave it as a supposition. It can be accepted as fact only by those who, like Harnack, are so much in love with Marcion that they accept with enthusiasm any theory which magnifies his importance.

The prologues were originally in Greek (this is obvious from the character of the Latin) but are preserved to us only in Latin. The fact that Pelagius is the first who mentions them[1] and that no MS. of the Old Latin versions contains them forbids the assumption that the Church admitted them as *Argumenta* to the Epistles before the end of the fourth century, i.e., at a time when only a few Marcionites were left and Marcionitism was no longer a danger. Even then they can only have been admitted because of the scarcity of introductory aids to the Scriptures. It is, of course, possible that they found their way here and there into earlier MSS.

Harnack seems to assume that when Catholic churches adopted these prologues they must have found with them the Marcionite text of the New Testament, and have taken that as well, so great was the need of Latin translations of the Pauline writings. Harnack quotes Wordsworth and White's opinion[2] that Marcion's *Apostolicon* circulated in Latin and was commonly used in the West. It is not quite certain, however, that the prologues were attached to the Epistles and circulated in the same MS. Harnack himself (p. 131*) suggests that they were originally not written in connection with each separate Epistle, but stood together, possibly as part of some larger work. They may, therefore, have continued to circulate as a separate collection—one of the first Introductions to St. Paul.

§ 4. ANTI-MARCIONITE PROLOGUES

What of prologues to the Gospels? Two groups of these are known. The group of better known, longer prologues was formerly regarded as Monarchian and as dating from the second century, but the prevalent view now is that they are as late as the fourth century, and of Priscillianist origin.[3] These prologues are in Latin.

The other group of shorter prologues—also in Latin—to the Gospels of Mark, Luke, and John, was little noticed until de Bruyne examined them, searched until he found thirty-eight MSS. in which they were

[1] They are used in the prologue to Pelagius' *Epistles of St. Paul.*

[2] *N.T. Latine,* 1913, p. 41.

[3] Cf. Dom Chapman, *Notes on the Early History of the Vulgate Gospels,* 1908, pp. 217–288. F.L. Cross in *Expository Times,* Jan. 1937, p. 188, where references to other authoritative studies are given.

extant, and submitted them to a careful study.[1] He came to the conclusion that they were originally composed in Greek (the Greek form of the Lucan—the most detailed—prologue is extant); that the Monarchian or Priscillianist group are a later expansion of them; that they were composed in order to counteract Marcionitism and their Greek originals date from soon after Marcion's death and probably before Irenaeus wrote his *Adversus Haereses*, probably in Rome, the Latin translations being made about a century later in Africa. These arguments were immediately welcomed and supported by Harnack,[2] with small variations of opinion, e.g., Harnack ventures to date these prologues between A.D. 160 and 180; and is inclined to allow Asia or Achaea as alternative possibilities for the place of origin.[3]

At first reading there appears small suggestion of anti-Marcionite intention. The strongest argument is the statement of the Johannine prologue that "*Marcion haereticus, cum ab eo* (= Papias) *fuisset improbatus eo quod contraria sentiebat, abiectus est ab Johanne. Is vero scripta vel epistulas ad eum pertulerat a fratribus qui in Ponto fuerunt.*" The connection of Marcion with John the Apostle (assumed by this prologue to be the author of the Gospel) raises doubts. If we could assume that the John here mentioned as author of the Gospel was not that Apostle but another John (? the so-called Elder), then the statement would gain in verisimilitude.[4] But de Bruyne and Harnack concur in rejecting this solution. Whatever difficulties there may be on historical grounds about this reference to an excommunication of Marcion by the Apostle, after a previous expostulation and exposure of his heretical views by the faithful Papias, there can be no doubt that the prologue-writer regarded Marcion as a dangerous deceiver who had to be dealt with peremptorily. But is it necessary to infer from this brief prologue that he believed the Gospel to have been written with Marcion mainly in mind, or that he himself had Marcion solely in view?

Moreover, does this anti-Marcionite tendency underlie all three prologues? Are we to agree with de Bruyne that "Luc et Jean ont une tendance anti-marcionite commune, explicite dans Jean, implicite mais certaine dans Luc"?[5] For evidence of this de Bruyne points to the reference to "*haereticae fabulae*" in the Lucan prologue, and also

[1] *Revue Bénédictine*, July 1928, pp. 193–214.

[2] *Sitzungsberichte der preussischen Akademie*, 1928, pp. 322–341.

[3] These prologues can most conveniently be found in an article by W. F. Howard discussing the work of de Bruyne and Harnack just mentioned, *Expository Times*, Sept. 1936, pp. 534–538.

[4] See Dr. Cross's letter to *The Times*, Feb. 10, 1936.

[5] Op. cit., p. 201; cf. also p. 206.

to that prologue's emphasis on the importance which the Gospel of Luke attaches to the birth and work of John the Baptist; this feature of the prologue de Bruyne thinks must be determined by the omission of the birth of John the Baptist in Marcion's Luke. Harnack discerns other indications of anti-Marcionite intention: τὸ πᾶν τοῦτο εὐαγγέλιον—a hit at Marcion's omissions;[1] the emphasis on the accuracy of Luke;[2] the strikingly high appreciation of the Baptist and the mention of his work as prophesied in the Old Testament.[3]

De Bruyne suggests that the man who, according to the Johannine prologue, excommunicated Marcion was some authority in the Roman Church, for whose name that of the Apostle John has been substituted. This was subsequent to the stigmatizing of Marcion as a heretic by Papias in Asia. The difficulty remains, as de Bruyne admits, of explaining why this mention of Marcion occurs in a prologue to John if John was not concerned in the excommunication. This suggestion of de Bruyne's might be taken a little further: suppose, for example, that the Roman authority was actually named John, and that the prologue-writer in ignorance of chronology mistakenly took this John to be the Apostle and Gospel-writer. But there is no need at all to think of Rome as the place of the excommunication. All that we know about the circumstances of the origin of the Fourth Gospel suggests rather Ephesus or somewhere else in Asia Minor, and therefore it is better to follow Harnack, who would simply delete the words *ab Johanne*, and interpret the whole passage as a rejection of Marcion following denunciation of his heretical beliefs by Papias in Phrygia. We then have a kind of parallel to the rejection of Marcion by Polycarp (in Asia?).[4] There is no reason to doubt the statement of the prologue that Marcion set out from Pontus with some sort of commendatory letters from Pontic Christians, and if we accept this it is altogether reasonable to suppose that he tried to get recognition in the leading churches of Asia Minor before proceeding to Rome.[5]

[1] The Latin has simply *hoc evangelium*, but this is probably due to the Latin version having been made when the influence of Marcion's truncated Gospel was no longer feared.

[2] But this is no more than Luke himself promises in his preface, and Marcion was not then on the scene!

[3] Too much should not be made of this, in view of the fact that Marcion apparently did have a high opinion of John the Baptist; he certainly allowed verses which praise him to remain in his Gospel, e.g., 7. 27 f.; 16. 16.

[4] Irenaeus, *Haer.* 3. 3. 4.

[5] Bacon denies the historicity of the incident and regards the statement of the prologue as a mistaken inference from Tertullian. He questions de Bruyne's reconstruction of the Latin text and his excision of *ab Iohanne*. (*Journal of Biblical Lit.*, XLIX, pp. 43–54.)

If the general thesis of de Bruyne and Harnack concerning these prologues be correct, it strengthens the view that the Catholic New Testament was formed in opposition to Marcion. De Bruyne and Harnack both think that the prologues were composed—doubtless there was originally a prologue for Matthew—for the earliest Catholic edition of the four Gospels. This must have been accompanied by a series of prologues to the Pauline Epistles. But here the Catholic canon-makers actually adopted the Marcionite Pauline prologues, which de Bruyne thinks were written by Marcion himself. It remained to add prologues to the Pastorals. Of these de Bruyne's view is that they are the work of Catholics, not of Marcionites. Harnack disagrees.[1]

No other prologues are known, and de Bruyne suggests that the earliest Catholic New Testament contained no more than four Gospels and thirteen Pauline Epistles; the immediate need being to make Marcion's truncated New Testament as harmless as possible, and to eclipse it as soon as possible. " Le but n'était pas d'éditer tout le Nouveau Testament mais de répondre a l'édition tronquée et faussée " (op. cit., 214). Harnack would add Acts and Apocalypse to this rudimentary catholic New Testament on the ground that Irenaeus reckoned these books canonical, and the *Muratorian* so reckoned Acts.

§ 5. THE LATIN MARCIONITE NEW TESTAMENT

We turn to the question whether the Marcionite Latin text preceded the orthodox Latin. Was Marcion's the first translation into Latin of the Gospel of Luke and the Pauline Epistles? Moreover—a different question—did it influence the orthodox translations? In that case the Latin New Testament of the Catholic Church was no more than an enlargement of Marcion's! It is antecedently improbable that the Catholic Church simply corrected Marcion's version of Luke and Paul and added its own translation of the other canonical writings. That would have been a laborious piece of work, and all probability is against it. It could have taken place only when the struggle with Marcionites had died away and been forgotten. But we know (*pace* Zahn) that the Church possessed a Latin New Testament by A.D. 200.[2]

[1] Op. cit., p. 340, n. 1. He says he would be inclined to agree with de Bruyne but for the phrase in the prologue to Titus " *de haereticis vitandis qui in scripturis iudaicis credunt* ". Harnack thinks only a Marcionite could thus see a reference to the O.T. in the " Jewish fables " of Titus 1. 14.

[2] For the evidence see Harnack, *Geschichte der altchristlichen Literatur*, II, 2, pp. 296–302; von Soden in the *Festgabe für Jülicher*, 1927, p. 240, n. 1; Corssen in the *Jahresbericht über die Fortschritte der classischen Altertumswissenschaft*, 1899, pp. 8–15. In a review of Corssen's article in *J.T.S.*, July 1900, Burkitt doubted whether a Latin

Lietzmann[1] has suggested that the earliest Latin version of Paul was made by the first generation of Marcionites in Rome through their desire to win converts among the illiterate who knew only Latin.[2] Marcionites did no doubt have a Latin translation of their Scriptures very early, and it is probable that in point of time this preceded Catholic translations. Lietzmann's hypothesis thus has a certain persuasiveness. But when he goes on to suggest that the Catholic Church adopted this Marcionite version he passes from the possible to the unlikely. He was not without support in high places, however. De Bruyne, for example, expressed the opinion:[3] "depuis plusieurs années je soupçonne que notre texte latin n'est que l'Apostolicum marcionite corrigé et completé. Quant à l'Évangile, plusieurs changements marcionites se sont infiltrés (ou sont restés) dans nos anciens manuscrits latins: 6 dans e, 5 dans b et c, 4 dans a." Vogels[4] also allowed the possibility that the Marcionite Latin both preceded and influenced the Catholic Latin. Salvatorelli[5] considered the theory worth mentioning: "*v'è chi sostiene che in parte la Latina Vetus cattolica possa non esserne che il rimaneggiamento* (del N.T. del Marcione)".

As Harnack admitted, this question could not be finally decided until the Latin of those parts of the New Testament which were common to Marcion and the Catholics had been carefully compared with the Latin of the rest of the New Testament. This still remains to be done. But von Soden has already provided most of the material required in his essay on the Latin text of Paul in Marcion and Tertullian.[6] In this careful piece of work von Soden compares Marcion's Latin text, as reconstructed from Tertullian's quotations in his fifth book against Marcion, with the text used by Tertullian himself, as revealed in the multitude of quotations throughout his writings. Von Soden reaches the following results: Marcion's Latin and Tertullian's Latin are not dependent upon one another (p. 259). Marcion's Latin is not an African translation, but stands relatively near to the European text.

---

version existed before the time of Cyprian. For the view that as late as Novatian no Latin version of the Bible was current in the Roman Church, see Haussleiter's three articles on *Zwanzig Predigten Novatians* in *Theologisches Literaturblatt*, April 1900.

1 *Handbuch zum N. T., Römer*, 1919, pp. 14 f. In his 4th edition (1933) Lietzmann admitted that this is very doubtful.

2 It must be remembered that the Roman Church used Greek writings till the end of the second century, and to a large extent spoke Greek.

3 *Bulletin d'ancienne littérature chrétienne latine*, Oct. 1921, pp. 13–15.

4 In the article on "*Evangelium Palatinum*" in *N.T. Abhandlungen* (ed. by Meinertz), vol. 12, 1926, p. 97.

5 *Storia della Letteratura Latina Cristiana*, 1936, p. 7.

6 *Festgabe für Jülicher*, pp. 228–276.

It was probably made in Rome, at the same time as some forms of the European Old Latin, and was exported to Africa with the rest of the Marcionite propaganda. It is "the independent translation of a different Greek text (i.e., the Marcionite Greek). It had no previous Catholic Paul to work upon, nor can it itself be the foundation of such a version. We have no longer any knowledge of a translation from which Marcion's was an excerpt, or which was the result of a supplementation (*Ausfüllung*) of Marcion's Latin. There is neither an *a priori* nor an empirical ground for doubting the original unity of the Catholic-European translation of the Pauline Epistles" (p. 273). Von Soden's general conclusion is that "Comparison of the Marcionite translation as such with the Catholic texts of the Latin Paul leads necessarily to the perception of the independence of the translations, and probably of the priority of the oldest Catholic text-forms" (p. 230).

A. d'Alès[1] agrees with Harnack that Tertullian had the Marcionite Scriptures before him in Latin, and suggests that Marcion was the first to conceive the idea of a Latin Bible. But he denies that the Marcionite Latin influenced the Catholic Latin.[2] In a further article[3] d'Alès compares Marcionite readings with those of Novatian and reaches the conclusion that all the actual evidence we possess for Marcion's Latin on the one hand, and, on the other hand, the oldest Roman Latin text as discoverable from Novatian (together with a few other writings of third-century Roman provenance) and the oldest African as discoverable in Cyprian, testifies against the hypothesis of Marcionite influence on the Catholic texts.

The Marcionite Latin prologues hardly come into consideration here, as it is doubtful whether they belong to the second century. They are found only in Vulgate MSS., not in MSS. of any of the Old Latin Versions.

The only way of discovering whether the Catholic Latin text was affected by Marcion's Latin is to compare, as von Soden has done, the earliest Catholic Latin text of which we have any knowledge with Marcion's Latin. Harnack's section[4] in which he professes to deal with this problem in reality does not touch it, but is relevant only for the question of the relation between Marcion's Greek text and the Catholic Greek text. The necessary comparison has been made at length by the present writer,[5] and its results are as follows:

[1] In *Recherches de Science Religieuse*, 1922, pp. 137–168.

[2] Op. cit., pp. 166 ff.

[3] *Biblica*, 1923, pp. 87–90.

[4] Pp. 160*–170*.

[5] See Appendix 7.

A. *Gospel of Luke.*

(1) The majority of the agreements between Marcion and the Old Latin are not tendentious and did not originate with Marcion, but were drawn by him from the Greek text of his day with which he was most familiar (i.e., a " Western " text).

(2) There is, however, a small class of tendentious alterations by Marcion which crept into the Old Latin tradition at certain points. The following passages may be listed in evidence: 10. 21, 10. 25, 11. 29–32, 11. 42, 13. 28, 16. 12, 21. 27, 21. 32, 23. 2, 23. 5, 24. 12; and with less probability 5. 39, 6. 35, 17. 10b, 23. 34a, 24. 6.

The influence of Marcion on Catholic texts was on the whole greater than Harnack allowed, but it was, nevertheless, very limited. The more palpable Marcionite alterations did not insinuate themselves.

(3) No connection of Marcion's text with any Old Latin MS. or group of Old Latin can be established. The coincidences between Marcion and *Evangelium Palatinum* (e), an African MS., are not sufficient to prove any special influence of Marcion on the African text of the Gospel; and we should continue to assume the contrary with von Soden.

B. *Paul.*

Similar results are yielded when the comparison is extended to the Pauline Epistles. The question of Marcionite tendentious emendations affecting non-Marcionite texts arises only with reference to the five passages: Rom, 1. 16; 6. 9; 1 Cor. 10. 9; 15. 3; Eph. 5. 28 (*pace* Harnack, p. 153*, who would add: Gal. 5. 14; Eph. 4. 6; and probably Gal. 1. 6).[1]

[1] Similar comparison of Marcion with the *Diatessaron* and Old Syriac Gospels corroborates the inferences drawn from this examination of the Old Latin in relation to Marcion. There is no case of a tendentious Marcionite alteration affecting these texts.

APPENDIX 4

THE EPISTLE TO THE LAODICEANS

The *Muratorian Fragment* informs us that Marcionites forged in St. Paul's name epistles to the Laodiceans and Alexandrians.[1] Of the Alexandrian Epistle nothing more is known, and we are left to suppose that it was similar to the Laodicean, i.e., a patchwork of selections from genuine epistles of Paul.[2] A letter to the Laodiceans is still preserved, however, and Harnack believed (pp. 141* ff.) that this is a Marcionite forgery, and therefore the writing to which the *Muratorian Fragment* refers. It was finally ejected from the Canon in the sixteenth century alike by Reformers and by the Council of Trent, but previously it had enjoyed a wide circulation among the Pauline Epistles. It was known to Jerome, who rejected it; thus its origin was in the fourth century or earlier. If we identify it with the epistle mentioned in the *Muratorian Fragment* we must date it before A.D. 190.

The epistle is almost entirely a compilation of extracts from the Pauline Epistles. It is printed and commented on by Lightfoot, *Colossians and Philemon*, 1904, pp. 272 ff. The excuse for its compilation is Col. 4. 16: ὅταν ἀναγνωσθῇ πὰρ' ὑμῖν ἡ ἐπιστολή, ποιήσατε ἵνα καὶ ἐν τῇ Λαοδικέων ἐκκλησίᾳ ἀναγνωσθῇ, καὶ τὴν ἐκ Λαοδικίας ἵνα καὶ ὑμεῖς ἀναγνῶτε. Availing himself of this excuse some scholar of Marcion's may have forged the letter in the hope of disseminating Marcionite doctrine. The author can hardly be Marcion himself, because Marcion called our Ephesians Laodiceans. But according to Harnack some later Marcionites adopted the Catholic title Ephesians, and the address: "To the Laodiceans" was then, so to speak, in the air, and waiting for the forger to make use of it. This man stopped short of an altogether new composition according to his master's teaching; he doubtless realized that that would only have betrayed the forgery. The method he chose was the safer one of first patching together what were obvious Pauline sentences and then interweaving a few Marcionite threads. He hoped thus to secure that the Marcionite—i.e., for him the true—interpretation should be the only possible one. For example, the first verse is copied from Gal. 1. 1, but it is Gal. 1. 1 with the significant Marcionite omission of καὶ θεοῦ

[1] Line 63 f. *Fertur ad Laudicenses, alia ad Alexandrinos, Pauli nomine finctae ad haeresim Marcionis.*

[2] B. W. Bacon, *Studies in Matthew*, p. 464, throws out the suggestion that it was Hebrews.

Πατρός; in verse 3 *Gratias ago Christo* is copied from Phil. 1. 3, but with the Marcionite substitution of Χριστῷ for τῷ θεῷ μου; verse 4, *ut vos avertant a veritate evangelii quod a me praedicatur* is a further Marcionite touch, emphasizing the one true Gospel which Paul alone preached.—So runs the theory. It falls short of demonstration, and the Marcionite touches in the letter will not be so clear to everyone as they were to Harnack. It might be argued from the reproductions of Marcionite readings in Gal. 1. 1 and Phil. 1. 3 that the forger used Marcionite texts, but was himself orthodox, and made his compilation at a time when the Marcionite danger was past. *Veritas evangelii* was indeed a favourite phrase of Marcion's, but he had no monopoly of it. Its occurrence in Laodiceans is by no means so strong an indication of Marcionite origin as its occurrence in the prologues.

Lightfoot rightly believed in a Greek original for the Epistle to the Laodiceans. Harnack thinks it was issued in both Latin and Greek. He declares dogmatically that a Latin edition is presupposed by the *Muratorian Fragment* and the Marcionite prologues, which are themselves in Latin.

Harnack is persuaded that the Epistle to the Laodiceans and the Marcionite prologues belong together and were forged on the same anvil. Both claim *Codex Fuldensis* as their oldest witness. The tendency of both is the same. Both manifest the emphasis on Paul as the true Apostle, on the truth of the Gospel, on the false teachers. Here again Harnack is in the realm of supposition, but the theory is illuminating when applied to the question of the influence of these Marcionite writings in the Catholic Church. Harnack further holds that the author of the prologues knew the letter to the Laodiceans and had it in his canon as well as Ephesians, for we have a separate prologue to Ephesians,[1] and the prologue to Laodiceans can be reconstructed from that to Colossians, which begins "*Colossenses et hi sicut Laudicenses* . . .". It could be objected that the *Laudicenses* mentioned in the prologue to Colossians are Marcion's *Laudicenses*, i.e., Ephesians; but the reconstructed prologue is not at all applicable to the Epistle to the Ephesians, while it is applicable to Laodiceans. Moreover, the Marcionite prologue to Ephesians is found in the MSS. in its proper (i.e., in Marcion's New Testament) place before Colossians.

[1] With the substitution of *Laudicenses* for *Ephesii* at the beginning, this stands as the prologue to the Laodiceans in the MS. containing this epistle (Wordsworth and White, *N.T. Latine* II; Romans (1913), p. 41). Marcion himself called Ephesians Laodiceans, but the disciple here has departed from his master, and adopted the title used in the Catholic Church. Harnack, pp. 146*–148*.

APPENDIX 5

TATIAN AND MARCION

It may be asked what was the relation of Tatian's *Diatessaron* to Marcion's work. Tatian's object in producing his harmony of the four Gospels seems to have been to emphasize the fact that the Gospel was *one*.[1] Possibly some thought it unfortunate that four[2] records of the Gospel were in use, each under a different name; and Tatian may have sought to obviate this difficulty. It is suggested that a secondary motive with Tatian may have been to counteract Marcion's adulterated edition of a single Gospel by publishing the full[3] text of the four authentic Gospel records.[4] Here again the answer must be that all too insufficient information about this period has come down to us. If the *Diatessaron* was composed in Rome, that is perhaps an extra link in the chain of this hypothesis. But even so, the chain has far too few links. The only evidence for Rome as the birthplace of the work is that it shows no trace of heresy (Tatian became an Encratite after the death of his master Justin), and that its text is closely akin to the Old Latin versions. Harnack (p. 73)—curiously—remarks that the hypothesis that Tatian's *Diatessaron* was directed against Marcion "is in the historical situation *a priori* certain" although he admits, to be sure, that *a posteriori* no proof can be brought.

In any case the publishing of the *Diatessaron* was not an official act of the Church, either in Rome or in Syria.

For the possibility that Marcionite readings influenced the text of the *Diatessaron* see Appendix 8 (pp. 169–171) below.

[1] In the first century and probably far into the second εὐαγγέλιον did not mean a book, but the good news brought by Christ; and in this sense there could be only one Gospel. We find the word used in the plural, however, by Justin, *c.* A.D. 150 (*Apol.* 1. 67) to mean the Gospel records, and the earliest use of the word in this sense seems to be *Didache* 8. 2.

[2] At least four.

[3] Tatian excised the genealogies of Jesus—or used a text which did not contain them.

[4] This is on the supposition that the *Diatessaron* first appeared in Greek (so Harnack and Pott). Plooij, however, holds that it was first issued in Syriac, and very soon translated into Latin. See D. Plooij, *A Primitive Text of the Diatessaron*, 1923; *A Further Study of the Liége Diatessaron*, 1925; *The Liége Diatessaron, edited with critical apparatus*, 1929–1935.

APPENDIX 6

MARCIONITE PSALMS

The work *De Sancta Synodo Nicaena* by Maruta, Bishop of Maipherkat, contains a catalogue of heresies, and this catalogue yields the information that the Marcionites had in place of the Acts a book of their own called *Summa*,[1] and that they had composed psalms of their own for use instead of the Davidic psalms in their meetings for worship. This refers primarily to Marcionites in Mesopotamia at the beginning of the fifth century. With regard to these Marcionite psalms, we may compare an obscure reference at the end of the *Muratorian*: *Arsinoi seu Valentini vel Mitiadis nihil in totum recipimus, qui etiam novum psalmorum librum Marcioni conscripserunt*. The author of the *Fragment* also knows that the Marcionites used psalms other than those in the Old Testament which were the hymn-book of the Catholic Church, though he denies that they were written by Marcionites. No certainty is possible on this point. One object of the author of the *Fragment* may have been to discredit Valentinus and the others by associating them with the arch-heretic Marcion, so that the early date of his evidence need not be decisive against Maruta. Moreover, if Valentinus is the well-known Gnostic, it is highly improbable that he would have helped to compose a book of hymns for Marcion. Arsinous and Mitiades are otherwise unknown, but are evidently not Marcionites. Perhaps Zahn is right in taking *Marcioni* as a corruption of μακρόν, and translating: long book of psalms. If Marcionites used a different hymn-book from that used in the Catholic worship it was natural for Maruta to suppose that the hymns were their own composition. But most hymn-books are compilations of hymns from various sources, and it is possible that if Arsinous and Mitiades and Valentinus had written hymns Marcionites might adopt them when they made their collection.

The other Marcionite work mentioned by Maruta, the *Summa* or *Liber propositi finis*, must also remain a mystery. Harnack identifies it with Marcion's *Antitheses*, on the ground that the *Antitheses* served among Marcionites a corresponding purpose, viz., explanation of the divergence between the Old and New Covenants, to that achieved for Catholics by the Acts, viz., the concordance between the two Covenants

[1] This is the title according to the Syrian MS., which uses the word *saka*. The Arabic MS. says "*Liber propositi finis*".

and between Paul and the original Apostles. Harnack here gives a somewhat strained significance to the Acts, and in any case his argument gives no more than an interesting possibility. He suggests that *Summa* was not the title of the book, but a description of its contents, in which case it can be referred to the *Antitheses*.

4
MARCION'S DUALISM

§ 1. THE NATURE OF MARCION'S DUALISM

MARCION brought his conviction of the fundamental contrast between Law and Grace to clearest expression in his doctrine of two gods. Considered as an intellectual theory this dualism is grotesque and Christian apologists may well have felt that their own doctrine had nothing to fear from it. Monism is ultimately always more satisfying to the intellect than dualism. Tertullian makes a strong point of this (1. 3. 6–7) with reasoning which amounts to a form of the famous Ontological Argument: God is *ex hypothesi* perfect (*summus*), and this carries with it oneness as an essential attribute. Tertullian is ahead of his time, for this essential oneness was not so axiomatic to the men of his day as it is to us. The argument for Monism which Tertullian develops, however, is so academic that it overreaches itself and hardly satisfies those who, like Marcion, are concerned with the anomalies of human existence. There is weight as well as irony in Tertullian's further demonstration that dualism is logically bound up with polytheism and open to the same objections. The Christian Church had not advanced very far in the direction of a Christian philosophy, but at least it was monotheistic, and a dualism philosophically so crude as that of Marcion was no danger.

Concerning the precise nature of Marcion's contrasted gods or principles there has been some dispute. Irenaeus appears to regard the dualism as a simple one of good and evil principles: a creator (κοσμοκράτωρ), who is *malorum factor et bellorum concupiscens et inconstans quoque sententia et contrarius sibi ipse*, and the Father of Jesus Christ, whose purpose is to abolish the creator together with all his works, including the law and prophets who testified to him (Irenaeus 1. 25. 1, Harvey, and 3. 12. 15). Elsewhere, however (3. 40. 2), Irenaeus distinguishes the two Marcionite deities not as good and evil, but as good and judicial (*judicialis*), and the question is raised whether the creator in Marcion's view was entirely bad. Some—notably Bousset in *Hauptprobleme der Gnosis*—say yes, and explain Irenaeus 3. 40. 2 as due to a confusion of Marcion with Cerdo, to whom Irenaeus ascribes a similar distinction of a god proclaimed by law and prophets and a god who is Father of Jesus Christ, the former, however, being regarded not as evil, but as righteous (*justus*).

It is assumed by Bousset that the distinctively Marcionite creator was evil. This ignores the whole evidence of Tertullian, who, though later than Irenaeus, had set himself the task of composing a full-length refutation of Marcion—which Irenaeus had intended but not carried out—and did so with Marcion's *Antitheses* and canonical books before him for constant reference. Tertullian certainly believed Marcion to have explicitly taught a just creator (5. 13), though it appears from what Tertullian says on Ephesians 6. 11–12 that Marcion also called the creator a devil (5. 18). If it be objected that Tertullian is self-contradictory we may reply that he is only reflecting contradictions in Marcion; and Marcion himself might reply that it is the Old Testament god who is self-contradictory—this is precisely what Irenaeus says about Marcion's view of the god of law and prophets (*contrarius sibi ipse*).

Tertullian's first precise statement about Marcion's two gods (1. 6) contrasts them as "*alterum judicem, ferum, bellipotentem, alterum mitem, placidum et tantummodo bonum atque optimum*". A straightforward distinction of good and evil gods is also ascribed to Marcion by Hippolytus (*Refutatio* 17–19), who attributes the introduction of a third principle, mediating between good and evil, to Prepon, a follower of Marcion (otherwise unknown, but mentioned by Theodoret). Hippolytus unfortunately is not very reliable. He arbitrarily derives Marcion's system from Empedocles and appears to believe that Marcion's canonical Gospel was Mark. In another treatise (*Contra Noetum* 11) he argues that even Marcion has to admit an ultimate Monism: τὸ πᾶν εἰς ἕνα ἀνατρέχει . . . εἷς αἴτιος τῶν πάντων. But here it is difficult to believe in Hippolytus's accuracy; he is clearly lumping Marcion with Valentinus and Cerinthus without bothering to notice what was distinctive of each. His account of the teaching of Apelles (*Refutatio* 26) should be read with caution in view of what has been said: Two superior gods, one of whom is ἀγαθός (this is Marcion's supreme god), and the other of whom is creator and δίκαιος; and two inferior deities, also called angels, one of whom is the Old Testament god, and the other κακῶν αἴτιος. This perhaps justifies the view that Apelles attempted to clarify contradictions in the system of his master Marcion. With regard to the original teaching of Marcion, however, Hippolytus can hardly be taken to support Bousset's view.

May it not have been that Marcion indeed started with a plain contrast of good and bad gods, but later accepted Cerdo's teaching that the creator was not altogether evil, but in some respects just? After all, Irenaeus does connect Marcion with Cerdo, and all our evidence agrees that Cerdo influenced Marcion, and that Marcion was in some sense his successor. Is there any reason to doubt this? Only if, like Harnack, one is committed to the attempt to maintain Marcion's originality at every point. Harnack greatly minimizes Cerdo's influence on Marcion, in the teeth of all the ancient evidence. He would restrict it to docetism and the ascetic attitude derived from a negative view of the flesh.

§ 2. THE INFLUENCE OF CERDO

Some take the view that Marcion derived not merely the qualifications of his teaching about the Demiurge, but the contrast itself between Demiurge and God of Love, from Cerdo.[1] According to Irenaeus, our earliest witness, Cerdo did not teach a contrast of good and evil gods; his inferior deity, the creator proclaimed in the Old Testament, was δίκαιος, not κακός. Hippolytus agrees, though it is doubtful whether he had any authority besides Irenaeus. Tertullian is silent on this point. His four references to Cerdo amount to little more than the mention of his name in connection with Marcion. The first of these is in a passage where he discusses the origin of Marcion's dualism (1. 2). It gives the impression that Marcion reached a dualistic view independently through reflection on the problem of evil, and this was a straightforward contrast of an evil creator and a kind stranger god. Cerdo helped Marcion to form this opinion—*habuit et Cerdonem quendam informatorem*[2] *scandali huius*, but it was not due entirely to him; probably it was the more precise formulation which Marcion owed to Cerdo. Tertullian presumably accepts Irenaeus's statement about Cerdo. The remaining evidence about Cerdo, which is much later, speaks of his subordinate god as evil (Pseudo-Tertullian: *saevus*; Epiphanius: πονηρός; Philastrius: *malus*).[3] Harnack holds that this goes back to an early source which is to be preferred to Irenaeus; and that Irenaeus has mistakenly attributed Marcion's distinctive teaching about the Demiurge to Cerdo. Harnack himself is unwilling to allow any influence of Cerdo on Marcion in the formulation of his dualism. P. N. Harrison, accepting Harnack's treatment of our evidence about Cerdo's teaching, ascribes to Cerdo the common dualism of good and evil principles, and retains for Marcion alone the peculiar doctrine of a Demiurge who is not simply κακός or πονηρός, but δίκαιος. Thus

[1] Cf. P. N. Harrison, *Polycarp's Two Epistles to the Philippians*, pp. 184–196.

[2] Moses is called *informator populi*, i.e., teacher, leader (4. 22).

[3] The evidence is set out in Harnack, pp. 31–34, to which must be added a reference in Gennadius of Marseilles' *Liber Ecclesiasticorum Dogmatum* (*c.* A.D. 500), ch. 21: *duo principia sibi ignota introducunt, ut Cerdo et Marcion* (C. H. Turner's edition in *J.T.S.*, Oct. 1905, p. 94).

room is made both for the distinctive genius of Marcion, and for the consentience of all ancient authorities about Cerdo's influence on Marcion. Dr. Harrison's treatment of the sources is fairer than that of Harnack.[1] It does, however, with Harnack reject Irenaeus's succinct statement of Cerdo's doctrines. Feeling this perhaps as a weakness in his theory, Dr. Harrison throws out the suggestion that Marcion made a sort of bargain with Cerdo: I will take over your dualism if you will modify it according to my ideas (p. 196, n. 1). A rather desperate expedient for saving Irenaeus's reputation!

If, as Irenaeus (1. 27) says, Cerdo was at Rome during the bishopric of Hyginus (136–140 is given by F. X. Funk as the approximate date of this bishopric), there is no difficulty in supposing that Marcion met him soon after his own arrival (probably in 139). And if we may suppose that Marcion had not yet fully elaborated his system it is more than likely that the influence of Cerdo guided him to the completion of it. It is possible that when Marcion left Asia for Rome he was still questing, still open to correction, or rather hoping to find not only adherents, but some teacher who would help him to cement more firmly together what convictions he already had. May not Cerdo have been such a teacher? If Marcion came to Rome already having learnt from Paul the distinction of Law and Grace, and already having rejected the Old Testament under a conviction of the absolute newness of the revelation in Christ, Cerdo's doctrine of two gods may well have been that complement which he needed, and Cerdo's lecture-room may have provided him with a stimulus to the clear expression of his theories. Thus it will have been in Rome that Marcion first entered the arena as a heretic with a definite system,[2] and in Rome that on the basis of a system at last articulate and complete he set himself to "criticize the Gospels with a knife" and prepare his own book of Scriptures. This theory by no means attributes Marcion's main teaching to Cerdo. It does justice to the evidence which declares that Marcion was influenced by Cerdo, but it does not at all deny his originality. The emphasis on the newness of the Gospel remains Marcion's, but it is an exaggerated emphasis because it overlooks the fact that "*nihil a deo subitum, quia nihil a deo non dispositum*" (Tertullian 3. 2). Tertullian here lays down a sound canon of criticism relevant to all assertions of the novelty and uniqueness of Christianity: the work of Christ is intelligible only when acknowledged to rest on the "*fundamenta dispositionis et praedicationis*", i.e., as part of God's

[1] I am not convinced by his distinction of κακός and πονηρός (op. cit., p. 188).

[2] The anti-Marcionite prologue to John might be taken as unfavourable to this assumption. See above p. 56.

eternal purpose which had been proclaimed already by antecedent prophecy.[1]

The origin of the belief in two ultimate principles, opposed as good and evil, is no doubt the Iranian dualism. That is a question which cannot be taken up here. It is interesting, however, to note its appearance in Plutarch in the form of belief in a good and bad soul of the world.[2] Plutarch bases this on a passage in Plato's *Laws*, and is mistaken in thinking he can claim Plato's authority. But it is significant in connexion with the present study that Plutarch gave credence to the idea only a few decades before Marcion. How much Plutarch helped to spread the idea is hard to say. It need not be assumed that Marcion had read Plutarch.

There was no doubt a danger during the second century that Christianity might evolve for itself a dualistic philosophy. But this would not have been a dualism like Marcion's, between God the creator of the world and God the redeemer of mankind. It would have been a dualism either between God the Father and God the Son, the Eternal Spirit and Christ the revealer; or a dualism between God and a Prince of darkness or evil. But Christianity was too deeply rooted in Hebrew monotheism for its theology to take a frankly dualistic form. Whatever antithesis there may be among the functions and attributes of God, it is *within* the Godhead itself; there can be no other divine power distinct from, and alien to, God.[3] The very centrality of Christ in the new religion was bound to create difficulties for thought as soon as men began to systematize their beliefs concerning him and to define his relation to the Father. There is an apparent dualism at the heart of the Christian faith. Men could not but worship Christ when the message about his Cross and Resurrection claimed them and they began to experience in the Church new mental and moral power; yet in thus honouring Christ they were not conscious of apostatizing from the worship of the Father. Such religious feeling might conceivably have expressed itself as a modified dualism or bitheism. But Chris-

[1] Cf. Irenaeus, *Haer.* 4. 34. 1, an argument that retention of the O.T. is still consistent with the conviction that something quite new and unprecedented entered the world in Christ.

[2] Plutarch, *De Animae Procreatione in Timaeo Platonis* 1015e (Vol. VI of the Teubner text of the *Moralia*); Plato, *Laws* 896e. Plato's argument strictly is that there must be *at least two* "souls" responsible for the "motions" of the world and of human life in their totality of orderliness and disorderliness, good and evil; the "best soul"—i.e., God—is not the cause of them all. Cf. Taylor's *Plato*, pp. 491 f., and also his translation of the *Laws*, p. 289, n. I owe this reference to Plutarch to Dr. J. B. Skemp.

[3] On this cf. Irenaeus, *Haer.* 3. 25; 4. 28, 40; Tertullian 1. 16; 2. 12–13. 29. Origen, *De Principiis* 2. 5.

tianity consistently refused to confess itself dualistic. It evolved a theology and honestly attempted to give philosophic expression to its creed, and in the end rather than become avowedly dualistic it left its central paradox unsolved. Its inheritance of Hebrew monotheism was too precious to surrender; nevertheless, Christ Crucified continued to be the central object of its worship.

§ 3. MARCION'S DUALISM NOT METAPHYSICAL

But Marcion's doctrine of two gods could not simply be dismissed as crude philosophy. Philosophical criticisms did not touch Marcion.[1] His dualism was not offered as a new theory of the universe nor as a contribution to the philosophy of religion. It was the expression of what were to him the fundamental facts of human life. We might in more modern terms express Marcion's thought somewhat as follows. Marcion saw two principles at work in the universe. The first is the principle of Justice or Law, inherent in the universe and in fact the originator of it; not entirely regardless of man, but responsible for "Nature red in tooth and claw"; responsible for human nature as well, particularly for the sense of obligation which causes man to see certain actions as duties without supplying always the power to perform them. The second principle intervenes and overrules Justice; we may call it Grace or Redeeming Love. Man can come under the dominion of this second principle and then he is delivered from the bondage of the first. So stated, Marcion's theory appears as more than a piece of mythology. It is seen to be dealing with the moral problem of all men. It is inadequate, but at least the problem, which is its starting-point, is not a fanciful one.[2] Nor is the solution fanciful. For evidence of the principle of Justice Marcion could point to the outside world and the human soul. Had he lived in the eighteenth century and been more of a philosopher he might have spoken of a categorical imperative; had he lived in the nineteenth century he might have found kindred spirits in those who drew attention to the ruthlessness of Nature or the universal reign of Law. As it was, he lived in the second century, and was not enough of a philosopher to make the best use even of the philosophic forms then current. He found it easier to speak of gods than of ἀρχαί, principles. Beliefs developed by men of other civilizations—in Fate, Destiny, Schicksal, Natural Law,

[1] For this reason some of Tertullian's reasoning hardly touches Marcion's case; e.g., the argument that the goodness of Marcion's god is irrational (I. 23).

[2] A more serious objection is that Marcion's theology lacks a proper sense of sin. Something is said about this below, in the section on Marcion's Paulinism.

Evolution—in so far as they are derived from observation of the Kosmos and of the Microkosmos, Man, are analogous to Marcion's conception of the Just God.[1]

Marcion's dualism, then, is to be appreciated not as an adaptation of philosophic ideas, but as an inference from everyday experience, and the appeal to experience justifies his case equally with that of his Catholic opponents. Tertullian, for example, roundly asserts (*De Resurrectione* 9): *Bonum Deum novimus; solum, optimum, a Christo eius addiscimus.* But from Marcion's point of view this begs the whole question. He would say experience does not teach that God is *bonus*; only an arbitrary selection from it yields that inference. (I assume that *novimus* means knowledge by experience as contrasted with revealed knowledge which is implied in "*a Christo addiscimus*".) Tertullian's solution of the problem (*De Resurrectione* 14), though somewhat doctrinaire, found a much longer acceptance: God is *deus optimus, de nostro* (i.e., because of human sin) *justus. Nisi enim homo deliquisset, optimum solummodo deum nosset, ex naturae proprietate; at nunc etiam justum eum patitur, ex causae necessitate.* By this means Tertullian avoided dualism, but he saw no more deeply into the problem of evil than did Marcion. An argument like that of Irenaeus (*Haer.* 2. 3. 1) is quite ineffective as criticism of Marcion. When faced by the dilemma: either the supreme God is limited in knowledge, or he is creator of all things, including this world, Marcion could reply: Yes, but I cannot ignore the implications for the character of God of the belief that he is responsible for this sorry world. Tertullian foresaw this Marcionite objection and strove to counter it. In one place he almost starts to outline a teleological argument (1. 14 init., refers to the activities of bee and ant, rather than gnats and the more annoying things of which Marcion apparently made much), but he breaks off and merely taunts Marcion with inconsistency: what right has he to admire a rose? Why does he not cut himself off from the Creator's world altogether? This is not very convincing. More powerful artillery is used by Tertullian when he raises the question (1. 22): If Marcion's god is good and kind, why

[1] This paragraph is partly suggested by Burkitt's stimulating re-interpretation of Marcion's main ideas in *The Gospel History and its Transmission*, pp. 294 ff. The dualism of Marcion is regarded by Jonas (*Gnosis und Spätantiker Geist*, i. 172–178) as a contest between Fate and Providence. Stoic monotheism or pantheism identified these powers, but Marcion set them in strict opposition, his creator with his law being an expression of Fate (εἱμαρμένη), and the benevolence of his Supreme deity being an expression of Providence (πρόνοια). In general, Jonas follows Harnack rather than Bousset in his estimate of Marcion's gods; i.e., he takes Marcion's creator as equivalent to the World or Spirit of the world rather than as evil Matter or the Devil.

did he ignore human suffering for so many centuries? thereby showing that the problem of evil still exists for Marcion.[1]

Thus it may be allowed that Marcion's subordinate god is not a creature of fancy, but a hypothesis sensibly based on real evidence. But what evidence could Marcion adduce for the existence of his superior deity, that august being who is pure benevolence? It might be said that belief in a power which produced man and the universe is credible enough, but that belief in a god whose sole activity is redeeming love is supported by no evidence and therefore a precarious assumption. In answer to such objections Marcion would say that the warrant for belief in the redeemer-god is given in the message of the Gospel and confirmed by study of the Christian Scriptures. Its sole, but adequate, justification was in the fact that "In the 15th year of Tiberius Christ Jesus deigned to descend from heaven" (Tertullian 1. 19); a fact which was, be it noted, an event of human history. Here Marcion is on firm ground, for there is much of essential Christian affirmation in this. Christ is self-authenticating. His credentials are his own words and works. His virtues are his *documenta* (Tertullian 3. 13).[2]

§4. TERTULLIAN'S CRITICISMS

Tertullian's discussion of this is not really serious. He does not consider the weight of Marcion's assertion "*deus noster, etsi non ab initio, etsi non per conditionem, sed per semetipsum revelatus est in Christo Jesu*", but takes refuge in the witticism that it actually amounts only to a revelation in Marcion, 115 years after the coming of Christ in the reign of Tiberius. We must look elsewhere in Tertullian for convincing argument. In 3. 3 Tertullian denies that Christ's mighty acts are in themselves sufficient authentication; there must be antecedent prophecy as well. But in *De Carne* 5 he does attach full weight to Christ's miracles, and so inadvertently gives Marcion his point: *virtutes spiritus dei deum, passiones carnem hominis probaverunt.* According to Marcion the creator is γνωστός, κατονόμαστος; and the other god is ὁ ἄγνωστος Θεός. Tertullian directs his sarcasm against this weak

[1] Tertullian's logic is not irreproachable. He occasionally lays himself open to the charge of dualism, cf. 2. 10, where he is dealing with a Marcionite view of the Devil; *n.b.* how Tertullian avoids himself discussing the origin of the Devil. Cf. also *Adv. Praxean* 23.

[2] Cf. the quotation from Origen's *Commentary on John* printed in Harnack, p. 285*: (referred to by Origen as the opinion of certain heretics): μὴ δεῖσθαι μαρτύρων τὸν υἱὸν τοῦ Θεοῦ ἔχοντα τὸ τοῦ πιστεύεσθαι ἄξιον ἔν τε οἷς κατήγγειλε σωτηρίοις λόγοις . . . καὶ ἐν τεραστίοις ἔργοις. (Brooke's edition of Origen's *Commentary on St. John*, vol. 1, p. 100.)

point, as in the closing words of his third book: *ante omnia est ut, quem caelestia praedicas repromittere, aliquod caelum probes eius: at nunc vocas ad caenam nec domum ostendis!* This objection was no doubt constantly made against Marcionites. The stranger god ought to have given at least some evidence of his existence and his power. Surely he could have made a pea or two: *unam saltem cicerculam deus Marcionis propriam protulisse debuerat!* (1. 11). He has let the creator get away with it, instead of outdoing him with superior acts of creation: *etiam insigniora et superbiora opera debuisset condidisse, ut et deus ex operibus cognosceretur secundum creatorem, et ex honestioribus potior et generosior creatore* (1. 11).

To Marcion's thinking it followed logically that if the superior god was *tantummodo et perfecte bonus* (Tertullian 1. 24) he must be entirely removed from this universe which is so full of imperfection. Thus he was referred to as ὁ ξένος, ὁ ἀλλότριος. Among the Syrian Marcionites the commonest title for him was simply " the Stranger ".[1]

From the point of view of epistemology Marcion would perhaps have said he relied on the faculty of intuition for his confidence in the reality of this kind stranger god. One passage of Tertullian suggests a special Marcionite use of the Latin word *agnitio* in this connection: *Scio quidem quo sensu novum deum iactitent, agnitione utique* (1. 9).[2] But more probably *agnitio* is Tertullian's term. In the *Clementine Recogni-*

[1] See the three dialogues against Marcion in C. W. Mitchell, *St. Ephraim's Prose Refutations of Mani, Marcion and Bardaisan*, 1921, vol. ii: especially the Marcionite saying, not in Harnack, quoted on p. lvii: " In his law our Lord was a stranger, but in his action one of the household ". Jesus' action in healing sick human bodies marks him out as akin to the creation, not alien to it, even if the laws which he proclaimed were utterly new: " Instead of bestowing strange eyes that it might be known that he was a stranger, he restored to health those former ones, that it might be known that he is that being who existed in former times " (op. cit., lviii—see esp. lvii–lxiii).

[2] *Agnitio* is rare in classical Latin, but came into more frequent usage in the second century A.D. Whether it then acquired a distinctive meaning as compared with the more usual *scientia* and *cognitio* may be doubted. Tertullian seems to be fond of it, e.g., in 5. 20 he quoted Phil. 3. 8, γνῶσις χριστοῦ 'Ιησοῦ as *agnitio*, where the Old Latin, Lucifer, Ambrose, Ambrosiaster, Augustine, and Vulgate all agree in reading *scientia*. He has *agnitio dei* twice (*de Pudic.* 9, *De Pat.* 4). The Latin *Thesaurus* quotes other authors for this phrase, though it does not give the reference quoted in our text above. Tertullian uses *agnitio* for knowledge of the tree of good and evil (*De Jejunio* 3), and with *veritatis* (*Apology* 21) quoting Col. 1. 9, where Ambrosiaster and Vulgate agree with him; Old Latin here have *scientia*, Ambrose *cognitio* (I quote these pre-Vulgate readings from Sabatier). Later, Jerome regards *agnitio* as equivalent to ἐπίγνωσις and defines it as recognition of things we know but had forgotten; he distinguishes it from *notio* (= γνῶσις), which means knowledge of new truths. See *Thesaurus*.

tions (2. 50 and 60) the suggestion is made that the Supreme Unknown God ought to have bestowed on man a new sense by which man might recognize him.

Burkitt suggests that Marcion might have made his conception of a divine Stranger more acceptable had he been able to make use of our modern idea of a fourth dimension, arguing perhaps that the supreme God is a stranger to man because he exists in a dimension of existence of which man is normally unaware. But the conception needs more than a mathematical analogy to make it living and give it religious value.

Had he lived to-day Marcion might have found a vehicle for his thought in the conception of God as altogether *Jenseits*, Beyond, separated from man by a great gulf which no human effort of will or speculation can cross, but who does himself cross the gulf and come face to face with man; the Beyond is in some sense akin. Marcion would doubtless have been sympathetic with this notion. But a god who is wholly other is far from being identical with the stranger deity of Marcion. For Marcion was led to belief in this being by a conviction of the utter newness of the Gospel. "O wealth of riches! Folly, power and ecstasy! seeing that there can be nothing to say about it, or to imagine about it; or to compare it to!" This is Burkitt's translation of what Harnack holds to be the opening words of Marcion's *Antitheses*.[1] It is a cry of joy over the newness, the unprecedentedness, the given-ness, the uniqueness of the Gospel. Alike in content and in form of expression the Gospel is new. Hence Marcion's inference of the existence of a god who is entirely separate from the creator. In Harnack's words: "The God who accomplished this work of redemption cannot have created anything else, i.e., cannot have created this world whose being and significance are characterized by loathsome vermin, sexuality, and reproduction. Tertullian hands down the Marcionite words: *Sufficit unum hoc opus deo nostro, quod hominem liberavit summa et praecipua bonitate sua et omnibus locustis anteponenda.* The world could not be rejected with greater disdain than in the words

[1] Burkitt in *J.T.S.*, 1929, pp. 279 f. The words are quoted from the Pro-evangelium of Marcion by an old Syrian (Anti-Marcionite) exegesis of the Lord's parables. Rendel Harris in his work *Marcion's Book of Contradictions* takes Pro-evangelium literally as a prologue to Marcion's Gospel, but Harnack takes it to mean the *Antitheses*. On referring to the original Armenian Burkitt found that the four opening words are key-words of Marcion's Bible. See Harnack, pp. 354* f. With the ecstatic utterance itself cf. *Epistle to Diognetus* 9. 5: ὢ τῆς γλυκείας ἀνταλλαγῆς, ὢ τῆς ἀνεξιχνιάστου δημιουργίας, ὢ τῶν ἀπροσδοκήτων εὐεργεσιῶν, an outburst of gratitude over Christ's justification of the ungodly; also Ignatius, *Eph.* 19. 2: ξενισμὸν παρεῖχεν ἡ καινότης αὐτοῦ.

'*et omnibus locustis anteponenda*'. The redemption is redemption not only from the world, but also from its creator and lord."[1]

Admittedly this conception of a god who is a stranger to the universe and who yet intervenes once, catastrophically, in Christ, to redeem mankind, is a conspicuous weakness in Marcion's system. Tertullian is only making the obvious criticism when he jibes at this Being for his inactivity in remaining unrevealed till so late in the history of the world![2] Marcion could indeed assert that in Jesus is revealed a God of love and compassion, but he could not fairly trace in the pages of even his expurgated Gospel a god who was thus ἄγνωστος, ἀποκεκρυμμένος, ἀλλότριος. Irenaeus pertinently asks (2. 4. 2 ad fin.): Why did not the Supreme Being extend his benignity to the Demiurge? Marcion's theory is that a new religion of redemption is suddenly proclaimed by the emissary of a new god; we may add that the emissary comes from nowhere! This makes nonsense of history; and in religion leaves no place for the idea of development. It is an emphasis on the newness of the Christian revelation carried to such extravagant lengths that it becomes impossible to believe in the revelation as so proclaimed. Tertullian and Catholic theology, with four Gospels to read and a truer understanding of the Old Testament witness to God's revelation of His purpose "in divers portions and manners", had no difficulty in proving that Marcion's statement of Christian truth was an impossible one.

As a modification of Marcion's dualism it must be remembered that in one sense the creator-god is not a god at all, for he is not eternal; at the end of this age he is to disappear with the world which he has made. We have no explicit teaching of Marcion on this point, but the inference is almost certain. Marcion frequently identified the creator and the world (2 Cor. 3. 14, reading τοῦ κόσμου for αὐτῶν, 1 Cor. 3. 10, Gal. 6. 14, Eph. 2. 2), and he undoubtedly taught that the world was to pass away. There is also the fifth-century testimony of Esnik the Armenian, who devoted the last of his four books *Against the Sects* exclusively to the Marcionites: "The Lord of the world destroys himself and his world eternally."[3] (This was the Marcionite exegesis of 1 Cor. 15. 24 f. ὅταν καταργήσῃ πᾶσαν ἀρχὴν καὶ πᾶσαν ἐξουσίαν καὶ δύναμιν. δεῖ γὰρ αὐτὸν βασιλεύειν ἄχρι οὗ θῇ πάντας τοὺς ἐχθροὺς ὑπὸ τοὺς πόδας αὐτοῦ.) Thus at the consummation of the age the Good God is alone supreme, and we may claim that

[1] Harnack, p. 96.

[2] As Esnik puts it: Why did the Stranger not take pity on mankind till twenty-nine generations were in Hell? (J. M. Schmid's translation, p. 184).

[3] J. M. Schmid's translation, p. 190.

Marcion really believed in only one ultimate principle, the creator being a mere instrument. Harnack[1] suggests that this is the explanation of the passage in Hippolytus, already referred to, where Hippolytus says that Marcionites, like all the heretics, are reluctantly compelled to recognize ὅτι πᾶν εἰς ἕνα ἀνατρέχει.[2] One thinks also of Apelles, the disciple of Marcion, who definitely returned to the creed of one God, μία ἀρχή, with the creator and Satan as his angels. As has been suggested above, this may have been not so much a modification of his master's teaching, as a fuller expression of what was implicit in it. In this respect Apelles was more logical than Marcion. Marcion's system, as actually taught by himself, was a dualism. Logically, it involved an ultimate Monism, but it was not the logical consequences which Marcion himself emphasized.

If it be claimed that Marcion's creator is really a god (*Certe deum confiteris creatorem? Certe, inquis* (Tertullian 2. 16)), because although not eternal he is not a created being, then it must also be admitted that matter comes in as a third ultimate principle. That there was a place for matter in Marcion's system is implied in two passages of Tertullian. In 1. 15 Tertullian attributes to Marcion the belief that "*creator mundum ex aliqua materia subiacente molitus est, innata et infecta et contemporali deo*" and asks whether this is not tritheism rather than dualism, i.e., is not Marcion going beyond his proper sphere? Here Tertullian is lapsing into the merely facetious. But 5. 19 is more serious in its implication that Marcion did give a place to matter in his teaching, setting it in fact on a par with the creator, "*collocans et cum deo creatore materiam de porticu Stoicorum*". Is this merely an attempt to discredit Marcion by showing that significant parts of his doctrine are copied from other teachers? It may be so, but there remains the implication that Marcion did allow for matter. Hippolytus in one place (*Refutatio* 10. 15) supports Tertullian, and Clement of Alexandria (*Strom.* 3. 3) speaks of Marcion's δίκαιος δημιουργός making the φύσις out of ὕλη κακή. Irenaeus is silent about any third principle.[3] It must have been difficult at that time for any thinker who worked out a theory of the universe to leave out matter altogether.

[1] Harnack, p. 141, n. 1.

[2] *Contra Noetum* 11.

[3] The fourth-century evidence is collected by Harnack, p. 276*. The Esnik reference might be fuller. It is from Schmid's translation of Esnik, pp. 172 ff., where Esnik speaks of three principles in Marcion: The Stranger God, the God of Law, and Matter. Esnik's source is Epiphanius. Elsewhere Esnik attributes to Marcion the three principles of Good, Just, Bad (Schmid, pp. 87, 204). So the Marcionite Megethius in *Adamantius*. The view that Esnik's sources do not take us back earlier than the fourth century is upheld recently in *J.T.S.*, XLV, pp. 65 f.

The idea was the common property of many Gnostics,[1] and has its roots far back in Greek philosophy. Thus it is inherently probable that Marcion had some views about it. That he regarded it as κακή is also probable, seeing that his Demiurge was not himself κακός; for he would be bound to ascribe the origin of evil either to matter, following the philosophic tradition; or to a devil, following the Biblical tradition.[2] The scantiness of our material puts certainty out of reach, but it is probable that Marcion did not develop and lay emphasis on his conception of matter, and Harnack is doubtless right in attributing this to his Biblicist predilection; the Bible makes no use of the idea of matter.

Marcion's isolation of the Redeemer from the World-creator was not difficult to refute.[3] Catholic theology had on its side the strong argument of prophecy to show that Christ was the revealer of the same God who controlled the universe and had brought it into being and who had chosen the Jewish people and inspired their sacred book. It should be remembered that this was a much stronger argument then than it is to the modern mind.[4] It was an immense advantage to be able to say, as evidence of God's actuality, that he had spoken through

[1] E.g., Hermogenes, against whom Tertullian composed a special treatise. Marcion is not mentioned in this, and we infer that Tertullian did not regard him as comparable with Hermogenes as a protagonist for matter as an ultimate principle.

Moffatt (*The First Five Centuries of the Church*, p. 37) connects Hermogenes with Marcion, but on insufficient evidence.

[2] For evidence that Marcion believed in a Devil, see Harnack, p. 271*, and p. 85 below, n. 4. Apelles, a pupil of Marcion, posited a fourth god who was αἴτιος κακῶν.

[3] Cf. Irenaeus, *Haer.* 2. 9; 3. 5–12; 4 *passim*, esp. 2, 9, 20, 40. Cf. also Temple, *Nature, Man and God*, p. 305: "The main field of revelation must be in the history of man rather than in the ample spaces of nature, though it is also true that if nature were severed from God so as to offer no revelation of him at all it would mean that there was no being fitly to be called God."

[4] Cf. Justin, *Apology* 1. 30–60; *Dialogue passim*; Irenaeus, *Haer.* 3. 6; 4. 2, 10 26, 34; Tertullian, *Adv. Marc.* 3 *passim*, *De Carne* 24 (uses O.T. prophecy as referring beforehand to heresies, e.g., refers Isaiah 45. 5 to Marcion), *De Resurrectione* 20, 28–32, *Adv. Praxean* 11–14 (O.T. prophecy about the Trinity), *Adv. Iudaeos* 8–11, *Apology* 18–20, 47.

Origen, *De Principiis, Praefatio* 1; 2. 4 init.; *Contra Celsum* 1. 36, 49–56; 3. 2; 4 passim; 7. 2–8, 14–17 (references to Koetschau's edition in *Die Griechischen Christlichen Schriftsteller*); n.b. especially πολλοὶ προφῆται παντοδαπῶς προεῖπον τὰ περὶ Χριστοῦ, οἱ μὲν δι' αἰνιγμάτων, οἱ δὲ δι' ἀλληγορίας ἢ ἄλλῳ τρόπῳ, τινὲς δὲ καὶ αὐτολεξεὶ (*Contra Celsum* I. 50); ἦλθεν οὐχ ὑπὸ ἑνὸς προφήτου ἀλλ' ὑπὸ πάντων προκηρυχθεὶς Ἰησοῦς Χριστός (*Contra Celsum* II. 79).

Clementine Recognitions 9. 2 ad fin.

For a good discussion of the validity of the argument from prophecy, see Peake, *The Bible: Its Origin, Significance and Abiding Worth*, pp. 362 ff.

a succession of prophets, and that heaven and earth are his handiwork. As for the appearance and work of Christ, so far from being evidence of the existence of another god, it was only God's latest and most wonderful word to man (cf. Hebrews 1. 1); from another point of view it was God's second great act of creation (cf. 2 Cor. 4. 6).

Marcion on his side disclaimed the visible world as a revelation of the highest god, and boldly affirmed that the only revelation worthy of a God of love was the work of redemption. But the Catholic Christian no less than Marcion found in God a redeemer; he would, moreover, inevitably feel that in refusing to see any connection between God and the physical creation Marcion had no claim on the adherence of reasonable men. The Christian's duty, as Origen said, is to worship not a hypothetical deity, but the Creator of all things, including those which are not open to sense-perception; rather than deny the Creator and devote oneself to a supposedly greater one who exists only as a name, and a new-fangled name at that.[1]

We may say that Marcion's doctrine of the two gods reveals at once the strength and the weakness of his system, for it expresses his emphasis on soteriology to the neglect of cosmology. Marcion's soteriological interest was his strength, and he must be given credit for this. Without it there may be a philosophy and perhaps even mysticism, but not true, dynamic religion. But Marcion was too exclusively concerned for redemption. As Burkitt says, "Marcion was only a cosmologist by accident" (as contrasted with, e.g., Mani and Bardaisan).[2] It was all very well for Marcion to assert that it was enough for his god to redeem man "*summa et praecipua bonitate sua*"; but it can fairly be asserted with equal weight on the other side that cosmogony also is God's work and that no theory about God has any title to credence which does not ascribe to his providence the world in which man lives (cf. Tertullian 1. 17).

Moreover, Marcion had nothing convincing to say about the anomalies and terrors of human existence. He makes no attempt to reconcile the redemptive attributes of God, as seen in Christ, with those sterner attributes of his nature, which man learns from the physical

[1] Cf. *Contra Celsum* 8. 16: ἡμῖν μὲν γὰρ τὸ προκείμενόν ἐστιν οὐκ ἐξ ὑποθέσεώς τινα σέβειν θεὸν ἀλλὰ τὸν τοῦδε τοῦ παντὸς καὶ ἄλλου οὑτινοσοῦν μὴ αἰσθητοῦ δημιουργόν· εἴσονται δὲ οἱ . . . τοῦτον μὲν ἀρνούμενοι καινοειδεῖ δὲ ἀναπλάσματι καὶ ὀνόματι μόνον θεοῦ ἑαυτοὺς ὡς μείζονι τοῦ δημιουργοῦ ἐπιδεδωκότες.

[2] Cf. C. W. Mitchell, *St. Ephraim's Prose Refutations of Mani, Marcion and Bardaisan*, vol. ii, p. cxx. The tendency to put soteriology in the foreground and overlook cosmology may be discerned in Ignatius; cf. Preiss in *Revue d'Histoire et de Philosophie religieuses*, 1938, No. 3, p. 240: "Il ne connait qu'un Dieu rédempteur. Le Dieu createur et souverain du monde ne l'interesse pas."

universe and the events of history. Marcion simply turned away from this problem, and he has no real answer to Tertullian's argument (1. 25–26) that God is not *sola bonitas*, but *severitas* and *judiciariae vires* are proper to him.[1] Tertullian's sarcasm is never more effective than when he represents the redemption which Marcion boasted of as a fragmentary, half-and-half affair—" *unde haec dimidiatio salutis nisi ex defectione bonitatis?* "; the very goodness of Marcion's god is defective, because it does not save the whole of man (i.e., not the body), nor embrace the whole of humanity (i.e., not the creator's subjects). (Tertullian 1. 24.) In *De Resurrectione* 2 Tertullian treats Marcion's dualism as derived from his view of the flesh. It was because he regarded the flesh as unworthy of redemption that he inferred the existence of a god who would redeem the essential part of man, i.e., the spirit. It might be granted that the creator-god caused the flesh of his creatures to be raised after death; but that, for Marcion, was not redemption. If there is redemption, therefore, it must be the work of another god: *Per diversitatem promissionum diversitas insinuatur deorum.* For Tertullian, of course (see especially *De Resurrectione* 34: *quam indignum Deo dimidium hominem redigere in salutem!*), redemption included the resurrection of the flesh; and Marcion's inability to accept this was prior to his belief in two gods: " *a quaestionibus resurrectionis incipiunt, quia durius creditur resurrectio carnis quam una divinitas* ". Tertullian argues (*De Resurrectione* 5–9) the illogicality of supposing that God permits the ultimate destruction of that which was originally his own creation, viz., the flesh; such a frustration of purpose is unthinkable for God. Tertullian goes on to expatiate on God's care of human flesh, and sums up " *bonum deum novimus, solum, optimum a Christo eius addiscimus* ". But it was precisely this providence which Marcion found unbelievable, and because of this the *a priori* argument about the impossibility of the Creator's purpose being frustrated would not have convinced him.

[1] So Origen in a famous chapter of the *De Principiis* (2. 5), where with correct Biblical understanding he shows that God's goodness (*bonitas*) is identical with his justice (*justitia*). In the previous chapter Origen had proved that the Bible does not present a clear-cut antithesis of just God in O.T. and good God in N.T. Only a superficial reading could be content with that. The O.T. witnesses to God's mercy as well as to his judgement, and the N.T. to his condemning judgement as well as to his forgiving love: *Quin potius audiant in evangeliis patrem domini nostri Jesu Christi ignem praeparantem diabolo et angelis suis?* (II. 5. 2). Elsewhere (*Comm. in Johannem*, 1. 35, Brooke's edition, p. 47) Origen asserts that the epithet δίκαιος is predicable of Father and Son, not of an imaginary Demiurge.

§ 5. POINTS OF COMPARISON: LUTHER AND KAGAWA

The problem is one which perplexes every generation of Christians. Most solutions that are offered may be suspected of purchasing intellectual tidiness at the expense of religious intensity.

Consider Luther, a much more significant (*pace* Harnack) figure than Marcion, who does, however, bear this comparison with him, that he was not a very systematic thinker. Luther contented himself with a distinction of *Deus revelatus* from *Deus absconditus*. By *Deus absconditus* he understood God as capable of wrath, and this was God as he is in himself, *Deus absolutus*, the creator of all things, before whom men must bow in awe and fear. But for Luther there was no question that this was the same God who had revealed himself in Christ as a God of grace.[1] And yet not very deep below the surface of Luther's thought can be discerned the same dualism which Marcion made no attempt to submerge—the dualism between the grace of God and his justice or righteous anger.

In Pietism and Evangelicalism, in so far as they avoid cosmology and concentrate on the proclamation of God's grace in redeeming man from sin, there is a clear strain of Marcionitism.

The anomalies of Nature—" Nature red in tooth and claw "—and the travesties of justice which often characterize the history of nations and of individuals make it impossible for some to believe in the justice and goodness of God; but men of the deepest piety sometimes do not feel these difficulties at all. Consider, for example, these utterances of that remarkable Japanese Christian, Kagawa:

> " The tempestuous rain—I love it! . . . To men of the common mould and those addicted to indolence and ease the storm is a sort of lash in the hand of God. But to our young souls it is Nature rendering the supremest of symphonies. Blow, tempest, blow! "
>
> " The whole creation is mine. My life penetrates to the heart of every created thing. . . . All things appeal to me. I am merged into everything . . . The earth forms a part of my footstool. I hold the solar system in the palm of my hand. . . . The whole creation is mine. God threw it in when He gave me Christ." [2]

[1] Cf. Tertullian I. 16 where he shows that the antithesis visible–invisible is *within* the Godhead, not a contrast of distinct deities.

[2] Quoted in W. Axling's book, *Kagawa*, pp. 157–159; cf. also pp. 214–216.

The man who could so speak was doubtless a mystic before he became a Christian, and would have enjoyed communion with Mother Nature even if he had not learned to know God as the Father of our Lord Jesus Christ. But note that the words quoted above are those of a confessing Christian who finds no tension between Nature and God or Christ, who sees no problem of evil and needs no dualism to express his deepest thought.

Perhaps Marcion's stumbling over the doctrine that the God of this world is good was due to the fact that his piety was not deep and intense. Was he too matter-of-fact and unimaginative, unable to get beyond the immediate inference, with the result that the deeper insights of faith were hidden from him? His must have been a pedestrian mind, sincere without question, but unfortunately prone to assume that those who were not willing to keep within the confines of his logic must be wrong. If this be a true judgement, it would account for his refusal to allegorize in Biblical interpretation. His narrow rationalism made him apprehensive of the extravagances of the allegorical method. He feared lest it might lead too far away from the truth. But he did not realize that his own rigidly literal exegesis might also miss the truth, and that it was possible to fail to see rightly a whole picture because parts of it were viewed in too great detail.[1]

§ 6. MARCION AND THE GNOSTICS GENERALLY

In his enthusiasm for Marcion and interest in him as a kind of second-century Luther, Harnack claimed for him a special place in the history of the early Church, and lifted him out of the general category of Gnostics. Subsequent study of Gnosticism has tended, however, to reset Marcion in a Gnostic context, and this certainly gives a truer perspective. Marcion's relationship to the Gnostic thinkers of the second century was closer than Harnack allowed. Irenaeus, for example, was not without justification when he classed Marcion with Valentinus and the rest. His second book *Against Heresies* has Valentinus mainly in mind, but he explicitly says (2. 31. 1) that his arguments are also applicable to Marcion. We have already seen reason for insisting on Marcion's indebtedness to the Syrian Cerdo, though Harnack minimizes this.

The terms Gnostic and Gnosticism are here used as general terms for that manifestation of Hellenistic theosophy or religious philosophy which appeared to Christian leaders of the second and early third centuries of our era so dangerous and drew forth so many attempts at

[1] Cf. p. 105 on the insufficiency of Marcion's teaching about sin and salvation.

refutation. This is a modern connotation of the terms, and does not correspond with their usage in early Christian writers.[1] But this connotation has established itself and can hardly be suppressed or emended. Moreover, it is assumed in this section that the ideas so vigorously attacked by Irenaeus and other Christian apologists at that time were not a new growth of their day or even of their century, but a Christian adaptation[2] of a syncretistic religion whose roots go back before the Christian era, and which was characteristic of Hellenistic culture and due to the contact of classical Greek religion and philosophy with the religions and culture of the Orient. The existence of this syncretism cannot be denied. Attention has been called to it by Bousset and notably by Reitzenstein, and to interpret Gnosticism against this background is not to commit oneself to particular theories about the originating cause of the process or the main elements in the compound—Bousset's theory of Persian influence, for example. Casey's denial (op. cit., p. 56) that Oriental religions underwent this modification under the impact of Greek culture is too dogmatic.[3] The view popularized by Harnack that the Gnostics were essentially Christian philosophers needs much modification; the Oriental traits in Gnostic systems are not simply to be classed as evidence of a lower type of Gnosticism.[4] De Faye, whose position is on the whole nearer to that of

[1] This has been pointed out by R. P. Casey in *J.T.S.*, Jan. 1935, pp. 46–60, in an important article on the Study of Gnosticism. "There is no trace in early Christianity of 'Gnosticism' as a broad historical category, and the modern use of Gnostic and Gnosticism to describe a large but ill-defined religious movement . . . is wholly unknown in the early Christian period." See also the article on Gnosticism by Leisegang in *Religion in Geschichte und Gegenwart* (Gnosis, I. Religionsgeschichtlich). This distinguishes a broad sense, according to which any religion of redemption might be called gnostic; and a narrower sense, viz., the specifically Christian Gnosticism with which we are made familiar in the Christian literature of the second and third centuries A.D.

[2] The leading Gnostics claimed to be Christians and were so reckoned by heathen critics like Celsus and Porphyry. Burkitt in *The Church and Gnosis* regards Gnosticism as essentially a Christian product, not a development of Greek philosophy with Oriental elements (op. cit., pp. 9 and 87). It was a series of honest attempts to fill the void left when the eschatological hopes of the primitive Church had become discredited, and it may be said that "without Christianity there would have been no Gnosticism" (op. cit., p. 57).

[3] See the article on Synkretismus in *Religion in Geschichte und Gegenwart*, which contains in its final summary the sentence: "Im Endergebnis mussten die orientalische Elemente die Ueberhand gewinnen".

[4] So Harnack. Lietzmann would emend Harnack's well-known opinion of Gnosticism as "akute Hellenisierung des Christentums" to "akute Rückorientalisierung" (*Geschichte der alten Kirche* i. 317). See also Reitzenstein's Auseinandersetzung with Harnack on this subject in *Historia Monachorum Historia Lausiaca*, pp. 210–

Harnack [1] than that of Reitzenstein, and who holds that Gnosticism does not really begin till *c.* A.D. 120, does allow a period of " gestation " or " fermentation " before that date.[2] He reckons Marcion among the Gnostics, although at the same time he makes the point that the leading Gnostics—Basilides, Valentinus, and Marcion—were highly original thinkers, and protests against using the word Gnosticism as an inclusive term; often it is better to speak of Gnosticisms in the plural. De Faye, nevertheless, bows to prevailing usage and admits that there are certain fundamental ideas underlying the distinctive emphasis of these Gnostic systems. Hence his chapter entitled " L'Unité du Gnosticisme " which enumerates three essential ingredients: (1) Belief in γνῶσις, i.e., knowledge of God, not ordinary knowledge as of natural objects; [3] (2) Desire for salvation; (3) Asceticism. All this, de Faye says, Gnosticism had in common with the culture of the second century A.D., together with the general ideas of God as transcendent, beyond conception (" ce Dieu perdu dans l'abstraction ", p. 437); of the world, over against God, inferior to him, if not positively evil; and of intermediaries between God and the World.

Marcion's supreme God, who is unknown until revealed in Jesus Christ, was not an original conception either with Marcion or with Cerdo. It is attributed by Irenaeus to the Marcosians (1. 19–20) and to Cerinthus (1. 26. 1). It was, in fact, an essential element of the Gnostic dualism. E. Norden in his book *Agnostos Theos* shows how the idea of an unknown god pervades Gnostic thought (pp. 65–73). This god is not the creator and has nothing to do with the world directly; he is known only in Christ. The conception is not at all characteristic of classical literature, nor in the later period of so-called Hellenism does the phrase *agnostos theos* occur in writings that are purely Hellenic, not even in Philo (op. cit., pp. 83–95). " Dieser über alles irdische erhöhte Gott gegenüber den in die Erscheinungswelt hinabgezogenen Mächten " is in origin an Oriental rather than a Greek conception. Norden takes Mt. 11. 27 as evidence of its influence on the Gospel tradition, and suggests that it was rejected as heretical by the

241; and cf. his *Hellenistische Mysterienreligionen* [3], p. 305: " nichts ist irrtümlicher, als wenn man die Gnosis als einen ersten Versuch christlicher Philosophie oder Religions philosophie . . . betrachtet ".

[1] E.g., in his distinction of an original (second-century) " intellectualist " Gnosticism from a later (third-century) " sacramentalist " Gnosticism.

[2] *Gnostiques et Gnosticisme* (1st edition, 1913), p. 452.

[3] On this compare Casey (op. cit., p. 46), and Bultmann's article on γνῶσις in Kittel's *Wörterbuch* (Vol. I, esp. pp. 692–696). Cf. also the quotation from *Corpus Hermeticum* 10. 15 in Reitzenstein: *Hellenistische Mysterienreligionen* [3], p. 295: τοῦτο μόνον σωτήριον ἀνθρώπῳ ἐστίν, ἡ γνῶσις τοῦ θεοῦ.

Church only because of its use by Gnostics to bolster up their anti-judaic dualism (p. 77). The Church both rejected Gnosticism and was influenced by it, e.g., it kept the idea of *agnostos theos*, but identified him with the Creator, and taught that he was made known in the Hebrew prophets as well as in Christ.[1] In the Clementine Literature we find that the creed of Simon Magus comprises many gods and one supreme Unknown God, of whom not only Moses and Jesus, but also the Demiurge are ignorant (*Recognitions* 2. 37 ff.). Mt. 11. 27 is appealed to as a proof text (2. 47). The *Homilies* have a slight variation on this main theme, in that the Demiurge is an emissary of the Supreme Unknown, as is also the god of the Law (a distinct being from the Demiurge). The Unknown is good only, not just, for goodness and justice do not harmonize; in support of this appeal is made to the stock text, Mt. 11. 27; and to Lamentations 3. 38, taken not as a question, but as a statement: ἐκ στόματος ὑψίστου οὐκ ἐξελεύσεται τὰ κακὰ κὰι τὸ ἀγαθόν.

In contrast with Stoic pantheism which identified the world with God and made theology a branch of physics, Gnosticism took up a negative attitude to the world and formulated a theology which set over against this evil world with its evil creator a supreme God who had nothing to do with this world. If this be at all a fair characterization of Gnostic systems taken as a whole, then Marcion is a typical representative of Gnosticism.[2] Certainly this turning away from the world is characteristic of Gnosticism. The dualistic metaphysic (or mythology) to which it gave rise could be modified in a variety of ways and an appearance of Monism could be maintained by the development of theories of æons and emanations mediating between the supreme God and the world of matter[3] (e.g., in the systems of Valentinus and Basilides); but the underlying dualistic scheme can be detected.[4] We

[1] Cf. Irenaeus 1. 19. 2 and 4. 6. On the twofold sense of *agnostos* (unknown and unknowable), see Bultmann in Kittel's N.T. *Wörterbuch*, I, pp. 121 f.

[2] So Hans Jonas, *Gnosis und Spätantiker Geist*, I, pp. 173–176, 243–251.

[3] Leisegang (article "Gnostizismus" in *R.G.G.* II. 1273) describes Gnosticism as both dualist and monist.

[4] Some later Marcionites emended their master's system in the direction of monism. Marcion himself allowed as modifications of dualism in its most rigid form:—

(*a*) the Demiurge is not absolutely evil; he is not simply κακός, but is the O.T. god;

(*b*) the devil is *auctor delicti* (Tertullian 2. 28) although he is *angelus creatoris* (Tertullian 5. 16);

(*c*) the existence of matter.

Bousset maintains (*Hauptprobleme der Gnosis* pp. 109–113) that these qualifications are later, and that Marcion himself held to the dualism most rigidly; but this is not true to the evidence as a whole.

may quote also from Lietzmann's summary at the end of his chapter on Gnosis in his *Geschichte der alten Kirche* (p. 316): "Das Entscheidende ist und bleibt der Gottesbegriff mit allen seinen Konsequenzen. Für das Christentum ist grundlegend die Unbegreiflichkeit, dass derselbe Gott, der fordert und richtet, aus reiner Barmherzigheit die hilflosen Sünder erlöst: das hat Jesus mit schlichten Worten, Paulus in den Formen grübelnder Dialektik zum Ausdruck gebracht. Die Gnosis löst das Rätsel, in dem sie Gott auseinanderbricht." This consideration again puts Marcion on the side of the Gnostics.

Connected with this same dualism, and a further illustration of what Marcion had in common with the Gnostics, was preoccupation with the problem of evil. This, says Tertullian (I. 2), was what started Marcion on his heretical course. According to Epiphanius, Basilides began by obsession with the same question: πόθεν τὸ κακόν.[1]

Beside the fundamental dualism we may mention the docetic Christology and the attitude to the Old Testament and Judaism as further points in common between Marcion and Gnosticism generally. The ascetic way of life which Marcion adopted was common in the second century and long continued to be so, both inside (consider the Apocryphal Acts, for example) and outside the Church, even when not combined with a dualistic metaphysic.

Marcion must be given credit for a deep moral earnestness, and the reproach of having an unethical doctrine of salvation, which Irenaeus levels at the Valentinians (I. 6. 4), does not apply to him. What remains distinctive of Marcion is a lack of speculative interest, such as Irenaeus ridicules in the Marcosians (I. 14–16), and probably a remarkable power of organization, which enabled him to bring into being a body of followers which was not a mere conglomeration of sects, and which proved a more formidable rival to orthodox Christianity than other Gnostic sects because of its discipline and strategy, as it were, and not merely because of its equipment. There must have been something in the man rather than in his doctrines which made him a more dangerous opponent of the Church than other Gnostics. By lack of speculative interest is meant that his interests were practical and religious rather than academic or philosophical. He was a literalist in his treatment of the Scriptures, and averse to any interpretation which avoided what seemed to him the plain sense of a passage. He

[1] Epiphanius *Panarion* 24. 6. As further evidence of the connection between Basilides and Marcion note Basilides's idea of the Archon who is chief of the bad angels and also God of the Jews: Irenaeus I. 24. 4. Cf. also Clement of Alexandria, *Stromateis* 2. 8; *Excerpta Theodoti* 16.

rejected the allegorical method entirely. This led him to textual falsification, as the only way to make Scripture in all places support his theories. Had his bent of mind permitted him to resort to allegory he need not have tampered with the text. His work as a textual critic again marks him out from other Gnostics and explains why to Christians of the second century he appeared the most sacrilegious of their foes.

§ 7. MARCION AND THE APOSTLES' CREED

Do we know of any action taken by the Church to counteract this dualism of Marcion's? We have the writings of protagonists for Catholic doctrine like Hippolytus and Tertullian; but do we also hear of official action prompted by bishops in the more important sees, either unitedly or as individuals? Our knowledge of such official proceedings is regrettably scanty. In the case of the Laodicean Church there is preserved a short credal statement of which the first article is obviously anti-Marcionite: πιστεύομεν εἰς ἕνα θεόν, τουτέστιν εἰς μίαν ἀρχήν, τὸν θεὸν τοῦ νόμου καὶ εὐαγγελίου, δίκαιον καὶ ἀγαθόν.[1] But this belongs to the middle of the fourth century, and all we can say is that Marcionitism was still a danger then to the Syrian Church. The real question is: Can we say of any creed issued or developed in the late second century, when Marcionitism was spreading in its first strength, that it is definitely anti-Marcionite?

It has been suggested[2] that the Old Roman Symbol was formulated against Marcion. In itself this is not improbable, especially when it is remembered that the Marcionite heresy originated in Rome, and grew into a "counter-Church, the only counter-Church, not inferior in compactness and catholicity to the Great Church itself". So Harnack. "But", continues Harnack, "its original nine-clause form (3 × 3) is quite unpolemical and the addition of the historical section concerning Christ is not necessarily polemical. If it is so, however, it is not specifically anti-Marcionite, but in general anti-heretical, just as the *regulae fidei* in Irenaeus and Tertullian are not specifically anti-Marcionite."[3] We may note also the judgement of Kattenbusch:[4] "[The Old Roman Symbol] is not antithetically, but positively conceived (nicht antithetisch, sondern lediglich thetisch). Neither the unity of God, nor His place as Creator are emphasized, however unmistakably they

[1] Harnack, p. 353*. Harnack suggests that the formulation derives from Origen's *Regula Fidei* (*De Principiis* I, *Praefatio*).

[2] By McGiffert (*The Apostles' Creed*, 1902) and by G. Krüger (*Z.N.T.W.*, 1905, pp. 72–79).

[3] P. 316*.

[4] *Das Apostolische Symbol* ii. p. 327.

are included in its conception and even, when the first article is impartially considered, definitely expressed."

By " its original nine-clause form " Harnack means such a form as this :[1]

I. (i) πιστεύω εἰς θεόν. (ii) πατέρα. (iii) παντοκράτορα.
II. (iv) καὶ εἰς Χριστὸν Ἰησοῦν. (v) υἱον αὐτοῦ τὸν μονογενῆ. (vi) τὸν κύριον ἡμῶν.
III. (vii) καὶ εἰς πνεῦμα ἁγίον. (viii) ἁγίαν ἐκκλησίαν. (ix) σαρκὸς ἀνάστασιν.

Certainly this does not give the impression of being worked out as counter-emphasis to false teaching. At this stage in the development of the Creed—if there ever was such a stage—the historical details about Christ had not yet been added. It is widely agreed now that the Roman Symbol is a combination of a confession similar to this—which was probably used as a baptismal formula—and a more detailed confession about Christ.

The Roman form of the Apostles' Creed is first actually found in Marcellus of Ancyra (*c.* A.D. 348),[2] and any reconstruction of earlier editions of the Creed must work backwards from this, using it as a guide in piecing together quotations from various Fathers.

We are concerned most of all to know how this Creed was formulated at the time of Marcion. It was hardly the same then as in the fourth century. Nevertheless, the form attested by Marcellus can be traced back a considerable time. Novatian, *c.* A.D. 260, may be considered a witness for it, and there are quotations in Cyprian, *Epistles* 69 and 70. How much farther back can one go? Tertullian manifests differences and we infer that we must halt before we reach him. Obviously a date between the time of Tertullian and Cyprian is indicated for the origin of this " edition " of the Apostles ' Creed. Seeberg[3] suggests *c.* A.D. 210, and thinks, moreover, that this edition was not only used from that time in Rome, but was actually issued there, by Pope Zephyrinus or Callistus. At the turn of the century Seeberg descries a " general tendency towards hierarchical strengthening of the Church " and he indicates as two of the chief motives which then influenced leaders of the Roman Church " a revision of the Church's armaments ", and the rejection of Montanism and Monarchianism. In accordance with these motives the form of the Creed used by Tertullian and Hippo-

[1] Lietzmann, article " Apostolikon " in *Religion in Geschichte und Gegenwart.*

[2] This is in Greek. Marcellus was exiled from his diocese through Arian intrigues, and was in Rome in A.D. 341. Here he adopted the Roman creed as his own.

[3] *Z.K.G.* xl, p. 30, in an article on " Die Entstehung des Apostolikon ".

lytus will have been revised, and this revised edition seems to have been dominant in the West in the third and fourth centuries.

We now have to enquire what the Creed contained before it underwent this revision; in other words, to ascertain how it was read by Tertullian. A comparison of the four passages,[1] where Tertullian quotes the Creed at some length, enables us to reconstruct it, although we cannot be certain of every word in every clause. It may be assumed that Tertullian quoted from a fixed form of the Creed. Our result will be somewhat as follows:

> I. *Credo in unum (unicum) deum, patrem omnipotentem, mundi conditorem.*
>
> II. *Et in filium eius Jesum Christum, natum de spiritu sancto ex virgine Maria, crucifixum sub Pontio Pilato, mortuum et sepultum, tertia die resuscitatum a mortuis, receptum in caelis (resumptum in caelo), sedentem nunc ad dexteram patris, venturum judicare vivos et mortuos.*
>
> III. *Et in spiritum sanctum, carnis resurrectionem.*[2]

As most relevant to our present purpose, which is to consider this Creed in relation to the teaching of Marcion, we notice *unum* and *mundi conditorem* in the first section, and *receptum* or *resumptum* in the second. The later edition of the Creed omits ἕνα before θεόν, and has the active forms ἀναστάντα, ἀναβάντα, instead of passives, such as ἐγερθέντα, ἀναληφθέντα, which would correspond more exactly with *resurrectum, receptum.* It also has no equivalent for *mundi conditorem.* The omission of ἕνα is easily understood as an attempt to counteract Monarchianism.[3] The question is: How long had ἕνα or *unum* been in the Creed before it was rejected? Was the revised Creed only returning to an older form? In Tertullian's Creed the passive participles emphasize the fact that Christ was raised from the dead by the power of the Father, whereas the later Creed implies that he rose in his own strength. Which was the original emphasis?

As we examine writers earlier than Tertullian for evidence of the existence of the Old Roman Creed the task grows more and more difficult. Probably Tertullian is the first of whom we dare say that he quotes from a fixed form. In the case of Irenaeus we must be content to say that he *teaches* a rule of faith. He describes the faith of the

[1] *De. Virg. Vel.* 1, *De Praescriptione* 13 and 36, *Adv. Praxean* 2. In parallel columns in Burn, *Introduction to the Creeds*, p. 46.

[2] Seeberg would add: *Paracletum* (from *Adv. Praxean* 2, *De Virg. Vel.* 1) and *sanctam ecclesiam* (*de Pud.* 1, *de Bapt.* 15) but NOT *peccatorum remissionem*, which is missing in Hippolytus also.

[3] So Zahn, Burn, Seeberg.

Church as faith εἰς ἕνα θεὸν πατέρα παντοκράτορα, τὸν πεποιηκότα τὸν οὐρανὸν καὶ τὴγ γὴν καὶ τὰς θαλάσσας καὶ πάντα τὰ ἐν αὐτοῖς.[1] In three other places in this work we find εἰς ἕνα θεὸν or *in unum deum*.[2] Evidently, if Irenaeus did know a definite Creed, it had εἰς ἕνα θεόν, and Tertullian is not the only one who attests this reading. τὸν πεποιηκότα κ.τ.λ. also corresponds to Tertullian's *mundi conditorem*. But it must be remembered that Irenaeus's Creed would more probably be the Creed of Asia Minor than of Rome. On the other hand, it is not altogether impossible that Irenaeus used the Roman Creed—if he indeed used a formal Creed at all. He had been sent from Gaul to Rome, and had lectured against heresy in Rome. In the first passage referred to we find τὴν ἔγερσιν ἐκ νεκρῶν καὶ τὴν ἔνσαρκον εἰς τοὺς οὐρανοὺς ἀνάληψιν. But there is not enough to justify the belief that Tertullian's *resuscitatum* and *receptum* are also paralleled in Irenaeus.

With Justin we are on even more uncertain ground. Kattenbusch indeed tries to prove that Justin was acquainted with a form of the Roman Symbol. But this is only possible on the supposition that this Symbol was composed in the first half of the second century. If we had clear evidence of this from other sources we might proceed to search for references to it in Justin's works. All that Justin gives us, however, is teaching about Christ and the confessions demanded from catechumens at baptism. Even in his detailed description of baptism Justin makes no mention of a Creed. The most that can be said is that credal phrases, e.g., σταυρωθέντα καὶ ἀναστάντα καὶ ἀνεληλυθότα εἰς τοὺς οὐρανούς, Ὑιὸν τοῦ Θεοῦ καὶ πρωτότοκον πάσης κτίσεως, were widely known and were used in baptismal formulæ.[3] This is very different from saying that there was one Baptismal Formula in general use, or even that there was a fixed formula for baptism in the usage of the Roman Church. And it is still another question whether such a Roman Baptismal Formula was identical with the Roman Creed, or whether a Roman Creed existed independently of the Baptismal Formula.

These questions are not sufficiently relevant to our theme to be pursued further. It is time to return to Tertullian, and to consider the theory that the Roman Creed was first formulated in opposition to Marcion. Krüger, in advocating this theory, first attempts to make it clear that there is no reason to believe that Christian writers before

[1] I. 10.

[2] I. I. 6; 2. 4; 4. 43. I.

[3] Cf. Krüger, *Z.N.T.W.*, 1905, p. 74. Krüger speaks of Glaubenssätze, which I have translated "credal phrases".

Marcion, e.g., Justin, were acquainted with a fixed Creed. We need suppose neither that when Marcion entered the Roman Church, *c.* A.D. 140, he had to present a confession of his faith, nor that he had to give assent to an already existing Creed of that Church. This is directed against Kattenbusch,[1] who holds that the letter of which Tertullian speaks[2] was a statement made by Marcion accepting the *regula fidei* used by the Roman Church, and declaring that his own views were in accordance with it.[3] With this preliminary assumption Kattenbusch can argue[4] that the *regula* lacked ἕνα before θεὸν in its first article, for otherwise Marcion could not have assented to it. From what we know of Marcion's treatment of the Gospels and Epistles, however, we would hardly suppose him incapable of omitting ἕνα from a creed which did not suit him. Moreover, Kattenbusch admits that Marcion must have expurgated the Virgin Birth and the resurrection of the flesh from the Creed. Kattenbusch surely carries supposition too far here.

Krüger's next main point is that to regard the Baptismal Formula as an entirely uncontroversial Church-confession is to contradict everything we know of the history of Christian Creeds.

Krüger then calls attention to a sentence of Tertullian (at the beginning of ch. 13 of the *De Praescriptione*): *Regula est autem fidei, ut iam hinc quid defendamus profiteamur,* with emphasis on the *ut*-clause. But here Krüger seems to be making much out of nothing. All that Tertullian says is: " We have this *regula*, and will defend it against heretics "; there is no ground for supposing that the Creed was first devised as a method of attack on Marcion.

Krüger goes on to say that the enemies against whom it was to be used might be threefold: heathen, Jews, or heretics. The first article, indeed, suggests that heathen are in mind, but the rest of the Creed is against this. Jews also are excluded by the first article. There remain heretics. The heretics who are intended cannot be dated before A.D. 150 or else the silence of our sources over the existence of a creed cannot be explained (here Krüger is arguing in a veritable circle!). But Marcion exactly meets our requirements. Moreover, if we think of Marcion it becomes clear at once why the Symbol first emerged in Rome: it was in Rome that the Marcionite heresy began.

[1] Op. cit., ii. p. 321.

[2] *De Carne Christi* 2: *Excidisti, rescindendo quod retro credidisti, sicut et ipse confiteris in quadam epistula et tui non negant et nostri probant.* Cf. also *Adv. Marcionem* I, 1: *Non negabunt discipuli eius primam illius fidem nobiscum fuisse, ipsius litteris testibus.*

[3] So Seeberg, i. p. 174.

[4] Op. cit., ii. p. 86.

McGiffert's statement of this theory is much more detailed. He emphasizes again and again the fact that the Old Roman Symbol[1] says very much less than might have been said, and infers that it was only concerned to repudiate certain false views, and that it was therefore justified in omitting what was irrelevant to this purpose (p. 122). So far from being a summary of the primitive Christian faith, this Creed is not even an adequate summary of the faith of the second-century churches. If such were its intention it would contain clauses about the pre-existence of Christ, salvation through Christ, the nature of Christianity, the authority of the Old Testament (pp. 34 f.). All this is conspicuously absent, and there can only be one conclusion: namely, that the Creed was not a calm synopsis made when Christian thinkers had had time to reflect on the implications of their faith, but rather a proclamation called forth unexpectedly because that faith was being misinterpreted. This is McGiffert's main argument.

There is more than one plank in this platform, however. Not only can the Creed be explained as inspired by hostility to the views of Marcion, but there is nothing lacking which an anti-Marcionite Symbol must necessarily contain. Marcion's rejection of the Old Testament is not directly met, it is true, but probably in the eyes of the Church this was not so imperative as to counter his separation of Christ from the Creator (p. 171).[2] All Marcion's views which were offensive to the Church are ruled out by the Old Roman Symbol—how account for this except by the hypothesis that the Symbol is specifically anti-Marcionite? (p. 173).

McGiffert believes that the Symbol was designed as a Baptismal Formula, not as a *regula fidei*, and offers this as a partial explanation of its shortness (p. 173). But hereby his main contention—that the Symbol is primarily a counteraction of heresy, and on this ground leaves some of the fundamental Christian beliefs unmentioned—is weakened. For if the Symbol was a Baptismal Formula, it would have been a full summary, however short, of the Christian faith, not merely an emphasis of those elements which were being questioned.

In view of the crisis precipitated by Marcion the Church was compelled to take some action (p. 174). That may be readily admitted.

[1] Of which he gives a reconstruction, op. cit., p. 100.

[2] Here McGiffert might have strengthened his case by a reference to the only contemporary evidence we have, Justin, *Apology*, I. 58, where the denial that Christ had any relation to the Creator is viewed as the most dangerous part of Marcion's heresy. McGiffert argues that the article about Christ is designed to emphasize that Christ belonged to the Creator, and nothing else: e.g., Why is nothing said of Jesus' baptism and teaching? (McGiffert, op. cit., p. 14).

The Church did take action. But it may be doubted whether it possessed at that time the machinery necessary for the promulgation of an anti-heretical Creed.

McGiffert rightly points out (pp. 10 f.) that the emphasis in the Symbol is entirely on belief, and that not a word is said about conduct. This, he says, is only to be understood if it was made as a defence against wrong belief, i.e., heresy. Marcion was the greatest heretic at that time (*c.* A.D. 150–175); therefore the Symbol was primarily directed against him (p. 13). Here the *apriorism* of McGiffert's logic is manifest.

McGiffert considers each article of the Symbol in detail. He does not attempt to prove that the whole of it as it appears in Marcellus was anti-Marcionite, but distinguishes articles which were framed against Marcion from others which were added later; the clause concerning forgiveness of sins, for example, he assigns to the beginning of the third century. His argument is that the Symbol was essentially anti-Marcionite in origin and conception.

So much for the theory that the Roman Creed was forged as a weapon of counter-attack against Marcion's heresy. Krüger indeed admits that it depends on the argument from silence. What he does not admit, and apparently does not realize, is that, particularly in his own statement of it, it is too *a priori*. It is interesting and may be true. The evidence does not permit us to state definitely that it is wrong, but the very paucity of our knowledge puts the argument beyond the possibility of proof.[1]

The Creed as a whole was not formulated against Marcion: dare we say that its phrasing was altered or that slight additions or omissions were made in face of the new heresy? At first sight it looks probable that *unum* and *mundi conditorem* in the first article of the Creed, as quoted by Tertullian, are specifically anti-Marcionite. A scholar like Kattenbusch can argue that there was no ἕνα in the Creed *c.* A.D. 140 because Marcion accepted it then.[2] But, on the other hand, apart from the fact that Marcion would not have scrupled to excise ἕνα if it did not accord with his own beliefs, there is also the possibility that Marcion found ἕνα in the Roman confession and accepted it because

[1] Seeberg rightly pronounces it undurchführbar (*Dogmengeschichte*[3] i. 216, n. 8). So also Lietzmann, *Geschichte der alten Kirche* ii. 108–110. Moreover, the argument tends to prove too much. For the same method of reasoning could demonstrate that the *Epistle to Diognetus* (particularly ch. 7–10) was put out in anti-Marcionite interest; and why not assume that Diognetus was a Marcionite?

[2] For Tertullian's creed, cf. p. 89 above. Seeberg, *Z.K.G.* xl, p. 26, believes the original formula was εἰς ἕνα θεόν.

his own beliefs had not yet crystallized into the form we are acquainted with. Moreover, we have Tertullian's strong assertion (*De Virg. Vel.* 1): "*Regula fidei una omnino est, sola immobilis et irreformabilis.*" Tertullian evidently regarded the Creed he knew as much older than Marcion, both in substance and phraseology. He believed it to have been handed down from Christ himself; cf. *De Praescriptione*, ch. 13: "*Haec regula a Christo instituta.*" We must not take Tertullian's beliefs, still less his rhetorical statements, as historical facts. But if ἕνα was inserted into the Roman Creed *c.* A.D. 160 it is strange that Tertullian did not know of it; stranger still that he did not mention it in his long work against Marcion. It is unthinkable that Tertullian himself inserted *unum* before *deum*.[1] In some places he gives a paraphrastic quotation of the substance of the Creed, e.g., *De Praescriptione*, ch. 36.[2] Again *De Praescriptione* 13, although a much fuller quotation than ch. 36, does not create the impression that it is a literal transcription. *De Virg. Vel.* 1, however, in view of the emphatic words at the beginning of the chapter, does give this impression. And *unum* is unmistakably there. That the Creed used by Tertullian contained ἕνα is certain; that ἕνα was placed before θεόν as a safeguard against heresy, the Marcionite heresy in particular, is by no means certain until more positive evidence is adduced.[3]

We have next to ask whether the use of passive participles in Tertullian's Creed—*resuscitatum, receptum*—was prompted by Marcion's doctrine that Christ raised himself from the dead. In the interest of this doctrine Marcion avoided ἐγερθείς and preferred ἀναστάς, and actually substituted ἀναστάς for ἐγερθείς in the text of the New Testament, e.g., Rom. 6. 9 (cf. also his omission of καὶ θεοῦ πατρός, Gal. 1. 1). Here again, however, we cannot be certain that the passive participles only appear in the Symbol after the heresy of Marcion was

[1] Tertullian's reverence for the Creed was too great. There is this distinction between Tertullian and Irenaeus, that while Irenaeus regarded Scripture as the rule of faith side by side with the rule of Christian doctrine, the Creed being a sort of digest of the most indispensable articles of Scripture, Tertullian goes further and ranks the Creed above Scripture. He was forced to this by controversy with heretics: cf. *De Praesc.* 17–20, where he complains that appeal to Scripture will never convince heretics. Heretics had their own canon of Scripture.

[2] It professes to be the substance of "*quid Romana ecclesia docuerit*". The phrases *creatorem universitatis*, and *filium Dei creatoris* (after *ex Virgine Maria*), are obviously Tertullian's own variation and emphasis.

[3] McGiffert (pp. 87–89) holds that ἕνα was not in the original form of the Creed, but represents an addition of Irenaeus and Tertullian. Tertullian's varying use of *unum* and *unicum*, according to McGiffert negatives the assumption that either was stereotyped in the Creed.

known. It is likely that in the very earliest formulations of teaching about Christ,[1] He was spoken of indifferently as ἐγερθείς and ἀναστάς, ἀναληφθείς and ἀναβάς; and it would happen that in the creed of one Church ἐγερθείς was used, in the creed of another ἀναστάς, and a travelling Christian who became acquainted with more than one creed would hardly have been surprised at the variation. Seeberg's reconstruction of the original formula of the Apostles' Creed gives ἀναστάντα . . . ἀναληφθέντα.[2] We shall probably be right in supposing that the use of a passive or active verb may be only an accident or a stylistic variation; and we must beware of making too much of Tertullian's *resuscitatum* and *receptum*. Tertullian read his Creed so, and must have rejoiced that no loop-hole was given to Marcionite doctrine; but we can hardly say the words were so chosen expressly to exclude that doctrine. The fact that the later Apostles' Creed read the active participles is to be explained not as an encroachment of Marcionitism, but as an attempt to stress the Son's independence of the Father and so to counteract Monarchianism.

With our scanty evidence there can be no absolute proof that the Old Roman Creed was first stereotyped as an antidote to Marcion's teaching, or even against Gnosticism in general. The hypothesis is in itself probable, but in fact we have no direct information about the origin of the Creed which would justify us in assigning it to a definite occasion or year, as we can in the case of the Nicaean or Chalcedonian Creeds. Of one thing, however, we can be sure: that in the last decades of the second century certain articles of the Creed were reiterated with new emphasis against the Pontic heresiarch. This applies particularly to the first article. Christians were to believe that the God who created the universe is the same being as the Father of the Saviour, Jesus Christ. Christianity was not to become exclusively a religion of redemption. Redemption was to be linked up with

[1] Cf. Mark 8. 31 and its parallel passages in Matthew and Luke. Mark has ἀναστῆναι, but Matthew and Luke have both independently altered to ἐγερθῆναι. Matthew uses ἐγερθῆναι only of the Resurrection, but Luke does use ἀναστῆναι elsewhere. The two words were convertible, and no weight can be laid on a distinction between them.

[2] Kattenbusch (ii. p. 643): "I do not think the Apostolic Symbol *consciously* rejected ἐγερθέντα, ἀναληφθέντα, καθεσθέντα. All these passive forms meet us in later symbols *intentionally or unintentionally* alternating with the actives of the Mother-Symbol. . . . That the Apostolic Symbol fixed on the active verbs was certainly undeliberate, but nevertheless characteristic." Seeberg would disagree with Kattenbusch that the later use of active verbs was undeliberate, for he attributes it rather to the challenge of Monarchianism. But these two scholars are at one in not regarding the use of passive verbs as deliberate defence against Marcionitism.

creation as the concern of the same God—and not of the same God only, but of the same saviour; for Christ, besides being the bringer of the world's salvation, was also believed to have been present at the creation of the world. Herein lies the difference between Christianity and Marcionitism.

McGiffert[1] points out that the earliest Christians paid no special attention to the doctrine of creation; they adopted it from Judaism and believed it as a matter of course. For theologians of the second and third centuries, on the other hand (especially after Marcion's day), the doctrine had a value quite apart from being a part of the Jewish doctrine of God. It served to bring Christianity into a larger setting and connect it with the very structure of the world. So was monotheism rescued. "Had Christ remained only a Saviour while Christianity was made more than a religion of salvation, the new faith would have had two gods. This was prevented not by any new doctrine of the Trinity, but by the ascription to the Saviour Christ of all functions which the religion of creation and judgment demanded of its God." "The functions of Christ were extended to include creation, providence, and judgement. Had it not been for philosophical difficulties, he would himself doubtless have been recognized as the one God of all the earth—as he was by the Modalists—but philosophy made it necessary to distinguish between a god apart and aloof, and a god dying and rising again for our salvation; and so the theologians, while they gave Christ all the functions of the supreme God, refrained from ascribing to the supreme God all the experiences of Christ." [2]

Marcion's supreme God was a god of love only. In other words, Marcion thought of God in exclusively non-physical terms.[3] We may point to another reason why this was unacceptable, and, indeed, incomprehensible, to the majority of Christians. For most Christians salvation had its physical as well as its spiritual aspect. The hope of a speedy return of the Lord to redeem his saints had died out; after death those who had been faithful on earth would see Him and receive their reward—and it was to be a concrete reward, for the σάρξ as well as the πνεῦμα was to rise again. The Creed which began with confession of the God who made heaven and earth ends with confession of the resurrection of the flesh. Only he who created the flesh could cause it to rise again.[4] Marcion denied both the resurrection of the flesh,

[1] *The God of the Early Christians*, 1924, pp. 148 f.

[2] Op. cit., pp. 192, 194 f.

[3] Cf. op. cit., p. 154.

[4] Cf. Tertullian, *De Resurrectione* 14 and 56, where he argues that the flesh must be raised again, in order to be judged at the last day.

and that the God in whom men believed through Christ was the creator of the world and all that is therein. Here was a twofold stumbling-block for Christians.

We can see a further stumbling-block for the men of his day in Marcion's teaching that the Christian God belongs to another realm than this physical one: How can evildoers be punished if God does not wield physical power? What deterrent from sin can there be? Here we touch upon another article in Marcion's faith, namely, that God is not a Judge. Men were quick to object that this would lead to libertinism: "*Quid non in omnem libidinem ebullis? Quid non frequentas tam sollemnes voluptates circi furentis et caveae saevientis et scenae lascivientis? . . . Audite, peccatores, quique nondum hoc estis, ut esse possitis! Deus melior inventus est, qui nec offenditur nec irascitur nec ulciscitur, cui nullus ignis coquitur in gehenna. . . .*"[1] Marcion's reply, "*Absit, absit*", signifies that for him a sufficient deterrent from sin was the horror of it inspired by his vision of the God of Love in Christ.[2] But for most men that was not enough. That was a doctrine for the giants of faith, not for ordinary Christians. Thus the belief that God wielded physical power and would use it to avenge sin received a new stress.

[1] Tertullian I. 27. Cf. also: *hoc est dei optimi et tantum boni, patientiae iniuriam facere, violentiae ianuam pandere, probos non defendere, improbos non coercere.*

[2] Harnack, p. 136, says this "*Absit, absit*" is "a religio-historical document of the first rank".

5

MARCION'S CHRISTOLOGY

THE distinguishing feature of Marcion's Christology is that it coincides with theology proper, i.e., with his doctrine of the supreme God. It is not enough to say that Marcion was a modalist, though the category of modalism does apply to his theory. Marcion would have subscribed to the statement that Christ is a mode of God's manifestation to the world, but he would have added: the only mode; for the supreme God is revealed in no other way than in Christ. "*Deus noster, etsi non ab initio, etsi non per conditionem, sed per semetipsum revelatus est in Christo Jesu.*"[1] For Marcion Christ was the revelation of the Good God, and the guarantee that the God who is solely redeeming love is not a mere creature of fancy.

The familiar categories of modalism and docetism are applicable to Marcion's Christology. Of the former there are indications, apart from Marcion's general conception of Christ, in textual alterations, e.g., Phil. 1. 3, where Χριστῷ is substituted for θεῷ; Gal. 1. 1, Ἰησοῦ Χριστοῦ τοῦ ἐγείραντος αὑτὸν ἐκ νεκρῶν (omitting καὶ θεοῦ πατρὸς after Χριστοῦ and changing αὑτὸν to the reflexive).[2]

But Marcion was not unique in being a modalist, and there is little point in enquiring what influence he had in this respect on Catholic theology. Neither modalism nor docetism had yet been officially defined as heresy.[3] Christians were still for the most part uneducated people, and it is probable that at that time large numbers of them thought of Christ and God interchangeably, without seeing the need for precise distinction.[4] Even the Roman bishop Zephyrinus (*c.* A.D 200) could state his belief in the terms: "I know one God, Jesus

[1] Tertullian, 1. 17.

[2] This was to exclude the inference that the Creator raised Christ from the dead. Christ raised himself. He and his Father are one. Ignatius, too, says that Christ raised himself from the dead (*Smyrn.* 2), but he also says that the Father raised the Son (*Trall.* 9. 2).

[3] Of course it had been denounced, e.g., by Ignatius.

[4] Cf. especially Ignatius at the beginning of the century. His influence was no doubt considerable. Certain statements of the Fourth Gospel also will be recalled in this connection: e.g., "I and the Father are one". Exceptions were those who thought intelligently of Christ as the Logos (though a Logos-Christology may easily become modalist); and the Gnostics, who tended to minimize the historical fact of Christ by their doctrines of æons.

Christ, and apart from him no other, begotten and passible."[1] Marcion is but another example of the same unprecise Christology. An example of modalistic confusion of the Persons of Father and Son is the following expression put into the mouth of the Marcionite Megethius: "The death of the Good became the salvation of men."[2] Later Marcionites were often classed with Sabellians.[3]

Nor was docetism peculiar to Marcion. In an age to which the metaphysical opposition of spirit and matter was orthodox a docetic Christology was more compatible than any other with prevailing thought-forms. Whether it was the best expression of the Christian faith is another question. Many Christians came near to docetic views in their emphasis on the divine aspect of Christ's nature: the author of the *Epistle of Barnabas*, for instance. The Christology of the Gnostics was thoroughly docetic. For example, they distinguished between the divine Christ and the human Jesus with whom he temporarily unites himself. Another main type of docetism is that which denied the material reality of Christ's body. The statement in the Creed: "born of the Virgin Mary" was designed to assert, as against all Docetists and not Marcion alone, the reality rather than the uniqueness of Christ's birth.[4] Some were content with denying the material nature of Christ's body. Some went further and denied the historicity of the Redeemer. We may distinguish a metaphysical type of docetism based on Greek views of the divine nature, e.g., the divine ἀπάθεια; this was attractive to Christians like Clement of Alexandria. With this is contrasted the more practical docetism which recoiled from the flesh as an unclean thing, unworthy to be the vehicle of divinity.[5]

Marcion's docetism was of this latter kind.[6] His hatred of the flesh made the notion of Christ being born and having a human body intolerable to him.[7] In Marcion's view human flesh, being essentially

[1] ἐγὼ οἶδα ἕνα θεὸν Χριστὸν Ἰησοῦν καὶ πλὴν αὐτοῦ ἕτερον οὐδένα γεννητὸν καὶ παθητόν.

[2] ὁ θάνατος τοῦ ἀγαθοῦ σωτηρία ἀνθρώπων ἐγένετο (*Adamantius* 2. 9).

[3] Cf. Socrates, *H.E.* 4. 12; Sozomen H. E. 6. 11, quoted in Harnack, p. 235*.

[4] Cf. McGiffert, *The Apostles' Creed*, p. 14.

[5] For the "best popular exposition" (so M. R. James) of docetism, see the *Apocryphal Acts of John* (M. R. James, *Apocryphal New Testament*, pp. 87–102).

[6] More developed, of course, than the docetism referred to in the N.T. or even Ignatius. The classic answer to it is Tertullian, *De Carne* 9 ff. For Ignatius see *Trall.* 9–10 and *Smyrn.* 2. The docetism here combated extended not to the Passion only, but to the whole earthly activity of the Lord. Lightfoot and Bauer agree that the docetism Ignatius had in view was connected with Judaism. This of itself differentiates it from that of Marcion.

[7] Cf. Chrysostom, *Hom.* 123. 6, quoted in Harnack, p. 368*: Μαρκίων ὅρα τί φησιν· οὐκ ἠδύνατο ὁ θεὸς σάρκα ἀναλαβὼν μεῖναι καθαρός.

earthy, could not be a dwelling-place for the divine; he expressed his contempt for it in gross language.[1] The Redeemer was pure spirit, and the body he assumed at his appearance on this earth was only a phantasm.[2] The invisible substance of the Good God could not be manifested in this world.[3] Christ appeared suddenly as the emissary of that God in the year A.D. 29: "In the 15th year of Tiberius Christ Jesus deigned to descend from heaven, a saving spirit."[4] In this belief Marcion reflects Gnostic theories of the descent of æons or angels from the divine Pleroma to this world. But it is also the distinctive feature of his docetism, for it meant that he gave up altogether belief in the birth of Christ and his growth from a child up to manhood. For most Gnostics it was the passion rather than the birth of Christ which formed the main stumbling-block, since it contravened the doctrine of the divine impassibility; but Marcion was mainly concerned to deny the birth, because to admit that Christ had been born would imply that he really belonged to the Creator.

In support of his theories Marcion could appeal to passages of the New Testament.[5] His opponents were hardly justified in saying that according to him the sufferings of Christ were only apparent,[6] for Marcion in fact attached high value to the reality of the crucifixion.

[1] Cf. Tertullian 3. 10–11 "*stercoribus infusa. . . .*"

[2] Cf. Origen, *Fragm. in Lucam* (Lommatzsch V. 237; the ninth volume of Origen's works in *Die Griechischen Christlichen Schriftsteller*, p. 7): κατὰ φαντασίαν ἐδραματούργει ὁ Ἰησοῦς τὴν ἔνσαρκον αὐτοῦ παρουσίαν.

For Tertullian's mockery of this, see *De Carne* 5 ad fin.

[3] According to Tertullian, *De Carne* 3, Marcion was moved by the argument from the inconvertibility of the divine substance. But, says Tertullian, *periculum status sui deo nullum est*. In this chapter Tertullian argues that if Christ had the mere semblance of a body, it implies deception on the part of God, which is unthinkable; and also that Christ himself could not have been content to have humanity falsely attributed to him, since to create wrong belief about himself must have caused an intolerable tension within him—a sort of divided personality!: "*maluit nasci quam ex aliqua parte mentiri, et quidem in semetipsum*" (ch. 5 ad fin.). Marcion's position was that Christ's self-consciousness made him impervious to hesitation on this score: "*satis erat illi, inquis, conscientia sua*".

[4] Tertullian 1. 19.

[5] E.g., Luke 4. 30; Philippians 2. 7. See also Harnack's notes on p. 188*, where he quotes from an Arian sermon a Marcionite exegesis of Luke 5. 13: Christ could touch a leper, because his body was a phantasmal one and therefore not liable to infection! Further on, p. 310*, Harnack quotes Tertullian 5. 13 to show that Marcion distinguished σῶμα and σάρξ in his interpretation of Romans 7. 4.

[6] Cf. Irenaeus 3. 16. 1: "*putative eum passum dicunt naturaliter impassibilem existentem.*" Tertullian, *De Carne* 5, ridicules Marcion's illogicality in denying the nativity while confessing the crucifixion: "*aufer hoc quoque, Marcion, immo hoc potius. Quid enim indignius deo, nasci an mori?*"

Because Christ's body was not composed of the material elements Christ was not therefore a mere ghost. Marcion found an analogy in the story of the angels who appeared to Abraham: *Et angeli creatoris in phantasmate putativae utique carnis egerunt apud Abraham et Loth, et tamen vere sunt et congressi et pasti et operati quod mandatum eis fuerat.*[1] Tertullian retorts that those angels had human flesh, though they had not been born as men. Elsewhere[2] Tertullian writes as if Marcion agreed that those angels had bodies of flesh, but illogically refused to make the same admission in the case of Christ. Tertullian goes on to mention a quibble of Marcion's concerning the dove which symbolized the presence of the Spirit at the Baptism: *Quaeris corpus columbae ubi sit resumpto spiritu in caelum, aeque et angelorum.* One wonders whether Marcion was the first to raise a similar question about Christ's body in the tomb. Tertullian feels that it is best not to attempt to meet such queries by straightforward reasoning, and contents himself with an emphatic assertion of the inerrancy of the Bible: *non potest non fuisse quod scriptum est!*

We have no evidence that would enable us to reconstruct Marcion's theory of the composition, so to speak, of Christ's Person. Perhaps he did not think out a concise description of it, such as those rebutted by Tertullian in ch. 10, 11 and 14 of the *De Carne*, viz., that Christ's flesh was *animalis*, that Christ's soul (*anima*) was *carnalis*, that Christ had an angelic nature (*angelum gestavit*). Tertullian attributes these theories to heretics generally, and does not mention Marcion by name. He does mention Valentinus, and refutes from Scripture his theory that Christ's flesh was *spiritalis*.

However confident Marcion may have been about this article of his faith, it undoubtedly gave the impression of not attributing full reality to the saving acts of Christ, and it was difficult to defend. Marcion's disciple Apelles was conscious of this difficulty and attempted to safeguard the reality of Christ's acts by his doctrine that, though not born in the ordinary way, Christ nevertheless had a body of real flesh composed of a starry substance.[3]

In its soteriological aspect the death of Christ was regarded by Marcion as in the nature of a purchase. Mankind belonged by right to the Creator, and therefore the Good God could justify himself in

[1] Tertullian 3. 9.

[2] *De Carne* 3.

[3] "*Solidum Christi corpus, sed sine nativitate . . . de sideribus et de substantiis superioris mundi mutuatus est carnem*" (Tertullian, *De Carne* 6). As Tertullian does not fail to remark, this is only to jump out of the frying-pan into the fire! (*de calcaria in carbonariam*).

freeing mankind from allegiance to the Creator only if he had first purchased them in a lawful manner. (The method of wresting them away by superior force was, of course, alien to his nature!) This feature of Marcion's Christology is a corollary to his doctrine that the Good God is a stranger and completely unrelated to this world. Emphasis on the metaphor of purchase prompted the substitution of ἀγοράσαντος for ἀγαπήσαντος in Gal. 2. 20. "*Christus magis adamavit hominem, quando alienum redemit.*"[1] The price paid was the blood of Christ. It is thus clear that for Marcion redemption derived from the death of Christ, not from the Resurrection alone. The significance of the shedding of Christ's blood on this view was not so much to make possible the forgiveness of sins as to cancel the Creator's claims upon his creatures.[2]

The remaining aspects of Marcion's Christology are discussed by Harnack, pp. 126 ff. Here it is sufficient merely to mention the newness of the revelation in Christ, and the fact that his advent was unprophesied;[3] Christ's function as judge at the end of the world; and his redemption of many from the underworld. In the two latter cases Marcion has found a place in his system for ideas that were common to all Christians at that time.[4] Even he, with his conception of the highest divinity as love alone, could not dispense with the idea of an ultimate judgement; though it must be admitted that his was not the material idea of judgement which the majority held. The notion that all the generations of the dead as well as the living must have had the opportunity of redemption was also widespread. The peculiar turn which Marcion gave to it was to proclaim that only those who had been rejected by the Creator, e.g., Cain, were led out by Christ from the lower world, while Abraham and all those who had been "justified" by the Creator must remain unredeemed. This is Marcion's grossest exaggeration of Pauline teaching.

[1] Tertullian, *De Carne* 4.

[2] For further evidence see Harnack, p. 288*. How much Marcion had to say concerning forgiveness is uncertain. Much, says Harnack (p. 133, note). Presumably Marcion gave attention to the references to it in even his truncated text of St. Paul. But his inadequate conception of sin put a truly Christian conception of forgiveness beyond his reach. Von Soden is right in his judgement that "Marcion dem Schuldgedanken völlig verschlossen ist" (in his very thorough review of Harnack's monograph in *Z.K.G.* xl).

[3] *Statim se et filium et missum et dei Christum rebus ipsis esset probaturus per documenta virtutum* (Tertullian 3. 3).

[4] Cf. Hermas, *Similitudes* 9. 16; Origen, *Contra Celsum* 4. 10.

6
MARCION'S PAULINISM

MARCION'S doctrine has been pertinently described as exaggerated Paulinism. Certainly he was, and wished to be, a disciple of Paul. He regarded Paul's proclamation of the Gospel as the only true one, and as identical with the proclamation of it by our Lord himself. But it cannot be forthwith assumed that Marcion fully understood the great Apostle.[1] Christianity as a whole during the second century was turning more and more away from Paul, and becoming less and less capable of appreciating his " gospel ". Marcion, by contrast, rejected the rest of the Apostles as Judaizers, and believed Paul to be the sole safeguarder of the truth of the Gospel. But was his valuation of Paul on that account the correct one ? Whether he had sounded the depths of Paul's experience may be doubted.

Harnack indeed attributes to Marcion a full understanding of Paul's fundamental distinction of Law and Gospel, and asserts that Marcion made this the starting-point of his own teaching. To support this there is Tertullian's statement : *Separatio legis et evangelii proprium et principale opus Marcionis.*[2] The question is whether Marcion was prompted to this distinction by a religious experience as deep and as personal as that of Paul, or whether he was merely in an academic way repeating the Pauline phrases with his own commentary. When Harnack writes (p. 199) : " Not only did (Marcion) take up Paul's struggle and work, but he did so with the Apostle's religious motive (Glaubensgesinnung des Apostels) ; for only Christ Crucified did he wish to know ; in him alone did he behold the face of the Gracious God, and he was conscious of being indissolubly united in faith and love with this God of Goodness and Compassion, because he was conscious of being bought and redeemed through Christ. Behind him lay sin and the world, behind him commandment and law," one scents an over-imaginative reconstruction. It may well be doubted whether Marcion's reverence for Christ and his contrast of the new dispensation of grace with the old legalism are comparable in richness of ethical content with the faith of the Great Apostle of the Gentiles. Von Soden[3] in fact strongly

[1] As even Harnack admits (p. 202, note) : " The Pauline method of thought was absolutely closed to him [Marcion]".

[2] I. 19.

[3] *Z.K.G.* xl, pp. 204 f.

denies this. Harnack is wrong in attributing to Marcion the Pauline–Lutheran antithesis of Law and Grace, Faith and Works. He has not considered that " by Marcion this antithesis is emptied and de-spiritualized, for he transforms it into the mythological antithesis of two gods; and in asceticism a new law is set up ". In contrast with Paul, Augustine, and Luther, Marcion is a stranger to the consciousness of sin.

The plain truth is that the information we possess about Marcion—derived, be it remembered, from the accounts of opponents who were anxious to refute Marcion's system—is not full enough to justify the assertions of either Harnack or von Soden. In order to place Marcion by the side of Paul, Augustine, and Luther without violating the colour-scheme Harnack has to paint him first with the appropriate brush and colour; while von Soden would seem to dip his brush in the paint which best shows up the incompatibility of Marcion with the other three. As an instance of Harnack's colouring of the evidence we may take the quotation he gives from Tertullian on p. 295*: *Marcionitae dicunt hanc esse principalem et perfectam bonitatem, cum sine ullo debito familiaritatis in extraneos voluntaria et libera effundatur, secundum quam inimicos quoque nostros et hoc nomine iam extraneos diligere iubeamur* (Tertullian 1. 23). Harnack remarks that this is the main piece of evidence for Marcion's " frequently attested " contrast of reward for good works with redemption out of pure grace and compassion. But there is not a word in this passage about such a contrast.[1] On p. 296* Harnack quotes Tertullian 4. 25: *Ex dilectione dei consequuntur vitam aeternam Marcionitae*, and by a stroke of the same brush sees in this the distinction of " slavish obedience and faith ". He also quotes from Adamantius a reference to believers being changed " through faith ". It ought to be pointed out, however, that Bakhuyzen in his edition of the treatise omits διὰ τῆς πίστεως after μετέβαλε.[2] Moreover, the context of this passage contains nothing else about faith. The disputants pass directly to the question whether the ψυχή only, or whether the σῶμα, as well, is saved. The general sense is quite compatible with the view that salvation is a rather mechanical transformation to goodness. There is

[1] Elsewhere (p. 263*) Harnack does quote passages which contrast justice and severity with mercy and goodness, in every case except one hypostasized in the doctrine of the two gods. Tertullian (2. 29) avows surprise that Marcion did not give expression to the distinction in an antithesis of Light and Darkness. Making allowances for Tertullian's spleen, we may still point out that Marcion's distinction appeared to Tertullian unethical. Harnack has stronger support in Tertullian 4. 6, where *justum, lex, Judaismus* is set over against *bonum, evangelium, Christianismus*.

[2] P. 70, line 5, of the volume in *Die Griechischen Christlichen Schriftsteller*. But he gives no textual note.

no deep spiritual content in the term "faith" here, and Harnack is making much out of little. His further quotation—τῶν πιστευόντων πατήρ ἐστιν ὁ ἀγαθός—again does not justify the inference which he makes regarding the nature of this faith. The argument simply is that the Good God is rightly called Father, but not in a material sense; he is father only of those who believe.

With regard to sin and salvation, a similar superficiality is apparent in Marcion's doctrine, and we must not be hoodwinked by Harnack's impressive reconstruction. Von Soden asserts that Marcion knew nothing of remorse for sin and that his soteriology is weak in consequence. A consideration of Marcion's asceticism[1] and of his famous "*Absit, absit*" in reply to the question: *Age itaque, qui deum non times quasi bonum, quid non in omnem libidinem ebullis?*[2] may soften this judgement; but in essence it is right, and a necessary corrective to Harnack's more flattering estimate of Marcion's religious significance.

Marcion's belief[3] that salvation extended to Cain and his like, and not to Abel and the righteous according to Old Testament standards, may be taken as an indication of the lack of true ethical and religious depth in Marcion's thought about salvation. This is not a genuine and impressive concern about sin such as we find in an Augustine, a Luther, or a Bunyan (to say nothing of the 7th chapter of Romans). Instead we have in Marcion statements about salvation made as corollaries from his main thesis that there are two gods: if one god saved Abel, then the other must be supposed to save such as are opposites of Abel. This is not high religion. To the troubled conscience longing for forgiveness and solemnized by the thought of judgement upon sin this will appear mere academic trifling. The moral distinction implied in the difference between Cain and Abel or hell and heaven is not one which can be made to do service to a theory. The freeing of mankind which Marcion ascribed to his higher God[4] implied as its antithesis not the bondage

[1] Asceticism may proceed from a quite unethical contempt for the flesh, and there undoubtedly were unethical elements in Marcion's asceticism. But the point to be emphasized is that with Marcion hatred of the flesh did not lead, as in so many cases, to libertinism.

[2] Tertullian I. 27. W. Bauer objected that Marcion knew no experience comparable to that of St. Paul on the road to Damascus. Harnack retorts by quoting the remarkable passage which apparently stood at the beginning of the *Antitheses* (see above, p. 75): O wealth of riches! Folly, power and ecstasy! seeing that there can be nothing to say about it, or to imagine about it, or to compare it to! (*Neue Studien zu Marcion*, pp. 17 f., *Z.K.G.*, 1923).

[3] Harnack, pp. 294* f., 129–131.

[4] "*Sufficit unum hoc opus deo nostro, quod hominem liberavit summa et praecipua bonitate sua*" (Tertullian I. 17).

to sin with which the Bible is concerned, but a different bondage, one might say a physical rather than a spiritual bondage. Evil for Marcion is not so much moral as physical evil; not sin so much as suffering. Marcion was more concerned over the ugliness and misery of man's environment than the ugly passions of man's heart. Contempt of the flesh is more characteristic of his type of piety than a sense of sin as revealed in the Bible—in Psalm 51 or Romans 7, for example.

The passages which Harnack has collected to illustrate Marcion's ideas on this subject do not really permit a more favourable verdict than this. Harnack himself gives Marcion much more credit, but the evidence is not sufficient. "Marcion goes right to the root in his answer to the question: From what has Christ redeemed us—from demons, from death, from sin, from guilt, from the flesh? He has redeemed us from Creation (including ourselves) and its God, in order to make us children of a new, stranger God."[1] That is a fair summary of the matter, and with it we have to be content. So far as the available sources show, Marcion did not go into detail on this subject of sin and salvation, not at least into the kind of detailed exposition which serious people require. The assertion that men are saved from this world so as to be adherents of a new deity in a new order of being remains a bare assertion, boldly enough made, but not arising from the most truly profound religious experience. With all his earnestness, Marcion's thinking is superficial; to the deepest things in religion he is insensitive. He is the slave of dualistic presuppositions, seeing everything antithetically, incapable of perceiving the subtleties which are the very essence of human experience and which cannot be pressed into a rigid classification, dualistic or otherwise. His temperament fitted him to be an organizer and a textual critic, but not to be a prophet or pastor or comforter of sin-sick souls.

There is much in Marcion's teaching as a whole that Paul would have approved. The Apostle would have welcomed his view of religion as being on man's part the acceptance, on God's part the offer, of redemption. The legalism of Christianity in the second century would have forced Paul to admit that his own struggle against the Jewish Christians had been largely in vain, and that the work he had done needed to be done once more; moreover, he must have recognized in Marcion a disciple who was addressing himself to that task. The growing syncretism of Christianity would have alarmed him, but he might have seen in Marcion's system a much needed simplification. For Marcion did stress some of the fundamentals of Christianity and recalled believers to what their religion in essence was.

[1] Harnack, p. 33, n. 1.

But other elements in Marcion's version of the Christian Gospel would have filled the Apostle with horror—Marcion's docetism, dualism, and rejection of the Old Testament. Yet Marcion claimed Paul as his authority for these doctrines. His docetism was founded on Phil. 2. 7, and be it noted that it attributed full reality to Christ's sufferings; it only denied that Christ was born and had a material body. Marcion's attitude to the Old Testament and his doctrine of the two gods belong together, and here again it is not difficult to see how they could be defended by reference to Paul's own teaching.[1] According to Paul the old dispensation of the Law and Prophets was done away, even for Jewish Christians. "Old things are passed away; behold, all things are become new" (2 Cor. 5. 17). "By the deeds of the law shall no flesh be justified" (Rom. 3. 20). "The law entered that the offence might abound" (Rom. 5. 20). "An end was made to our relations with the law"—κατηργήθημεν ἀπὸ τοῦ νόμου (Rom. 7. 6). Further, there are verses in the Pauline Epistles which a Greek could hardly avoid interpreting as references to contrasted deities, e.g., 2 Cor. 4. 4, "The god of this world hath blinded the minds of them which believe not, lest the light of the glorious gospel of Christ, who is the image of God, should shine into them." And how naturally would a dualist interpretation be given to Col. 1. 13: "(God), who hath delivered us from the power of darkness, and hath translated us into the kingdom of his dear Son"! The dualism of flesh and spirit is plainly expressed in Paul's writings, and does not depend on the mind of the interpreter.[2] There are of course in Paul passages which forbid a dualist interpretation, and which assign permanent validity to the Old Testament. But Marcion convinced himself that these were interpolations, and took the simple step of removing them. For Paul there were indeed two covenants or dispensations, but it was the same God who was the author of both. The new era which had been ushered in by Christ, for all the unparalleled Spirit-gifts which accompanied it, was yet a stage in the process of revelation and redemption which had begun with Creation; and this new and more glorious stage was not entirely without relation to previous stages in that process. When Paul set out to describe that relation, however, he must perforce resort to allegorical interpretation and rabbinical theology,

[1] Marcion actually derived the doctrine "of two gods" from Cerdo (see pp. 68 f. above), but would hardly have retained it had it not been compatible in his judgement with Paul's teaching.

[2] Harnack points out (p. 201, note) that Marcion recognized the distinction between this dualism and the one most current in the philosophy of that day—a distinction which many Gnostics apparently did not keep.

e.g., the theory of the first and second Adam in Romans, ch. 5; and often he was content to refer to the unsearchable wisdom of God. Marcion—and many another—was unable to accept this method of preserving the connection between the Old Covenant and the New, between Law and Grace. For Marcion it was unnecessary to attempt to preserve the connection. Others less radical must still have found Paul's dialectic inexplicable.

Alien to the spirit of Christianity as Marcion's dualism was, it nevertheless rested on an interpretation of Paul, and Paul's language in some places gave ground for that interpretation, false though it was. Marcion could more easily find justification for his dualism in Paul's writings than in the recorded teaching of Christ.

About Marcion's conception of faith we are not so well informed as Harnack would lead us to suppose. Paulinist as he was, Marcion must have attributed great importance to πίστις but, unfortunately, the fragments of his teaching upon this point which we can collect give us no idea of the content of πίστις as he saw it. Of course, for Marcion everything depended on faith in Jesus Christ as the emissary and revealer of the Redeemer God; faith meant trusting oneself to the mercy of the Kind Stranger, who, however, had given no evidence of his love or even of his existence except the appearance and work of Christ.

The passages that come into consideration here reduce themselves to three of Tertullian and two of the Pseudo-Origenite dialogues *De recta fide* (*Adamantius*[1]). In his exegesis of Luke 7. 36–50 Marcion seems to have laid stress on the woman's faith;[2] possibly "*paenitentiae stimulus ex fide acciderat*" are his comment. Tertullian retorts that it was nevertheless faith in the same God who declared: *justus ex fide sua vivet* (Habakkuk 2. 4). Marcion also drew attention to the faith of the woman with the issue of blood, and went on to describe it as contempt of the Law: "*At enim, si fidem mulieris invenimus ita meruisse, quis es, ut aemulationem legis interpreteris in isto facto, quod ipse dominus ex fidei remuneratione editum ostendit? sed hanc vis mulieris fidem constituere, qua contempserat legem.*"[3] Here again Tertullian maintained that the woman's faith was faith in the God of the Law. Similarly in the case of the Ten Lepers whom the Lord cleansed Marcion saw faith as the contradiction of the Law, "*Ex fide iam justificandos sine legis ordine remediavit*".[4] Such a view of faith was not the Pauline conception.

[1] Harnack, p. 296*, quotes other passages, but it is hard to see the relevance of all of them.

[2] Tertullian 4. 18 ad fin.

[3] Tertullian 4. 20.

[4] Tertullian 4. 35.

The other passages which should be quoted in this connection are κακοὺς τοὺς ἀνθρώπους ὄντας ῥυσάμενος ἐκ τοῦ πονηροῦ ὁ ἀγαθὸς μετέβαλε διὰ τῆς πίστεως καὶ ἐποίησεν ἀγαθοὺς τοὺς πιστεύοντας αὐτῷ.[1] This gives a more ethical content to the Marcionite faith. It must remain doubtful, however, whether Marcion's conception approached the Pauline in spiritual depth.

The starting-point for Marcion was a conviction of the newness and incomparableness of the revelation given by Christ. Christ had come suddenly from another realm with a wondrous, hitherto unheard, message of deliverance. He was the emissary of an unknown God who with infinite compassion willed to redeem mankind from this world of sorrow and imperfection, and from the stern but not always impartial rule of the God who had created the world. This was a Gospel—good news—if one could only believe it, and Marcion certainly believed it. It seems to have moved him on occasion to rapturous outbursts. "O wonder upon wonder, rapture, power, amazement! that we can say nothing about it [the Gospel], have no thought about it, not even compare it with anything"[2]—these words stood at the beginning of a writing of Marcion's, doubtless the *Antitheses*. This, rather than Law, was the foundation stone of Marcion's faith. One of his most-used proof-texts was not a Pauline saying about grace or faith, but the parable of the new wine and the old wine-skins (Luke 5. 37).[3] The revelation had broken catastrophically into this space–time world on the initiative of a Power beyond Space–Time: had Marcion been a modern man he might have given expression to his belief in some such terms as these. He bowed in awe before a revelation that was unpredicted and utterly new.

The Gospel was not only new, but it created a transvaluation of all values. The new dispensation ushered in by the appearance of Christ was at all points in contrast with the old dispensation of the Creator. "*In lege maledictio est, in fide vero benedictio.*" "*In lege dixit deus: Ego divitem et pauperem facio; hic vero Jesus beatos dicit pauperes.*" Many more such antitheses might be quoted.[4] When Christ descended into the underworld he redeemed and took into his own kingdom Cain and the Sodomites and others who had been rejected by the Creator, while

[1] So speaks the Marcionite Megethius (*Adamantius* 2. 6). The Marcionite Marcus in the same dialogue is made to say (2. 1): ὁ ἀγαθὸς τοὺς πιστεύοντας αὐτῷ σώζει; (2. 19) τῶν πιστευόντων πατήρ ἐστιν ὁ ἀγαθός.

[2] Cf. p. 75 above.

[3] Tertullian 4. 11. *Inflatus es utribus veteribus, et excerebratus es novo vino.* Cf. also Epiphanius, *Panarion* 42. 2.

[4] See Harnack, pp. 292* ff.

Abel and those who had found favour with the Creator remained impervious to his preaching. This was Paulinism run mad!

Marcion may have derived his conviction of the unprecedented newness of the Gospel from his reading of Paul, but more probably it came to him from the Gospel-record itself. Even if he derived it entirely from Paul, however, the form in which he appropriated it was not Pauline. The Pauline antithesis of Law and Gospel was welded on to Marcion's theology, but it was a different metal. Marcion adopted enough Pauline ideas to deserve the title of disciple of Paul, but his fundamental thought was unpauline,[1] or at best depended on a very arbitrary exegesis of Paul. Weight must be allowed to the criticism[2] that Marcion did not find his main thoughts in Paul, but rather assimilated Pauline theology to them.

Marcion studied Paul and saw more deeply into his mind than most Christians at that time. Orthodox Christians of the second century show little appreciation of the teaching of the great Apostle of the Gentiles; for some indeed he might never have existed. It was Marcion and the Gnostics who read Paul with eager interest. It was due to Marcion more than any other single person that the Church during one of the most formative periods of its history did not overlook the significance of Paul. It was largely due to the Pauline content of Marcion's New Testament that the Church received so many of Paul's Epistles into its own Canon.[3] Thus if Marcion did not create a general enthusiasm for Paul in his own generation, he helped to elevate the Apostle's writings to a position from which they could influence later generations. Nevertheless, it was long before Paul came into his own. Tertullian refers to him as "*apostolus Marcionis*", "*apostolus Haereticorum*"; his connection with Marcion was not easily forgotten.[4]

[1] Even Harnack admits (p. 202, n.) that the Pauline *Denkweise* was quite foreign to Marcion.

[2] So W. Bauer, arguing that Harnack overrates the influence of Paul and underestimates the influence of Gnosticism on Marcion. See Harnack's *Neue Studien zu Marcion* 1923, pp. 19–20. The older view classed Marcion with the Gnostics, but when it became clear that in several important respects he was to be distinguished from them the tendency was to place him in a category of his own, and Harnack was very emphatic about this. But Marcion's affinities with Gnosticism must not be overlooked.

[3] Not to be outdone by Marcion, it received three extra epistles (the Pastorals) as Pauline; and in the East a fourth (Hebrews).

[4] Origen could call Paul "the founder, after Jesus, of the churches that are in Christ" (*Contra Celsum* I. 63). But how many shared this regard for the Apostle? There is much truth in T. R. Glover's witticism about Paul: "a man whom it took more genius to explain than the Church had for fifteen centuries" (*The Conflict of Religions in the Early Roman Empire*, p. 156).

On the other hand, the Church asserted against Marcion that Christian theology had a broader basis than Paulinism. It exalted other Apostles beside Paul. It received into its New Testament Gospel-records by Matthew and John, who were among the earliest Apostles, and one by Mark which was believed to contain the reminiscences of no less a man than Peter.[1] It canonized epistles of the Apostles Peter, John, James, Jude. Authority meant apostolicity, and where the Church went beyond Marcion was in refusing to limit the range of authority to the writings of only one Apostle, Paul. The New Testament canon of the Church was catholic in that it found a place for a varied apostolic witness, rather than for the witness of a single Apostle, however eminent. And had the Church been able to trace other writings which had strong claims to be of apostolic authorship, an epistle of Bartholomew, for instance, it would have included them in the canon. Thus the Catholic New Testament is a truer representation than Marcion's New Testament of the most primitive Christian teaching and preaching.

Marcion believed the Pauline to be the one true interpretation of the Gospel. Some to-day would agree with him. Some would argue that it was Paul who made Christianity conscious of its mission to the whole world and sent it along the way to conquer the whole world; and that, moreover, without Paul Christians would have remained a Jewish sect. Such views are Marcion's legacy to later generations. But he is the founder of a richer heritage than historical theories. In his emphasis on the Pauline message as the genuine Gospel he was followed by the Reformers and by much subsequent evangelism. It may be that but for Marcion the Catholic Church might have left Paul's writings out of its canon, and have left the Apostle with no greater authority than the Apostolic Fathers. That is speculation. Beyond all doubt, however, it was good that Marcion drew attention to Paul as he did in the second century. At the same time it must be pointed out that Paulinism is not the Gospel itself, but an interpretation of the Gospel. It may have been the sole adequate interpretation for the third quarter of the first century, but it was not on that account the best interpretation for the following century and for all time. Orthodox theologians, in opposition to Marcion, tried to go further back than Paul, or at least to preserve traditions of Gospel preaching comple-

[1] The Gospel according to Mark was not much used in the second century, probably because all except thirty-one verses was contained in other records, e.g., the Gospels according to Matthew and Luke. Was the reason for its inclusion in the canon a desire to have more writings which could claim the authority of Peter, and so to provide a counterweight to the preponderating amount of Paul's Epistles?

mentary with the Pauline, but no less fundamental for Christianity. A debt is owed to those theologians because they made possible for us a fuller understanding, both of the historical development of Christianity and of the contents of its Gospel, than would have been possible if Marcion had succeeded in stereotyping the tradition.

7
MARCION AND THE OLD TESTAMENT

Quid illi cum Moyse qui deum Moysi rejecit?
TERTULLIAN, *De Carne* 6.

ABOUT A.D. 160 the Valentinian catechumen Flora enquired of her teachers in the faith how the Old Testament was to be understood. She has her counterparts to-day among those who doubt the right of the Old Testament to the dignity of Christian Scripture, and who feel that it ought not to be found within the same covers as the New Testament to make up our Christian Bible. Granted, they say, that the Hebrew prophets are worthy of a place beside the words of our Lord and his Apostles; but what of such books as Leviticus and Esther? In parts the Old Testament is ineradicably Jewish, of significance only for Jews; in parts its ethical presuppositions are far below the Christian standard. In deference to such scruples expurgated editions of the Old Testament are published. The question of the validity of the Old Testament as Christian Scripture would appear to be still not settled; there are still Christians who cannot accept its authority, but prefer to class it in the category of books " good and useful to read ". Here is our point of contact with Marcion. For Marcion had to deal with this question; and although he solved it on the basis of a dualism no longer tenable, it is no less profitable than interesting to study the principles by which he was guided.

Marcion's criticism of the Old Testament proceeded from his conviction that the Gospel was new, utterly new. His bent of mind was literalist and prosaic. He did not deny that the Old Testament had any value at all. It was possibly the only history book he knew, and he accepted it as a reliable account of the past, of the earliest history of mankind, that is, and of the Jewish race in particular, since the time of Moses. Marcion was not concerned to convict it of inaccuracy as a historical record: Abraham was a real figure and so was Solomon. Marcion saw no reason to tamper with the passage which speaks of " Solomon in all his glory ", nor with that which describes a woman as " a daughter of Abraham "—Luke 12. 27 and 13. 16.

Moreover, as a book of ethics the Old Testament was not entirely to be rejected. Here we touch upon the question of Marcion's attitude to the Jewish Law, and the Moral Law in general, which is somewhat baffling. Marcion did not simply say: The Old Testament and all that is in it, is bad, together with the author, the evil Demiurge. His fundamental contrast of the two gods is not as simple as that (so Harnack against Bousset). The creator God has some elements of righteousness in his character, and this is reflected in his book, the Old Testament. Marcion would not speak of the perpetuity of the Law, but he did allow it to have had validity until the Christian era; for example, he retained Luke 16. 16–17 (The law and the prophets were until John . . . it is easier for heaven and earth to pass away than for one tittle of the law to fall) with, however, the significant alteration of "the law" to "my words". Two other passages of the Gospel which Marcion retained show how much positive value he allowed the Mosaic Law as a moral code; 10. 27 approves the summary of duty as love to God and neighbour (quotations from Leviticus 18. 5–19. 18 and Deuteronomy 6. 5); 16. 29 indicates "Moses and the Prophets" as a sufficient guide for men concerning the selfish conduct which they ought to avoid. Marcion made no alteration in Romans 13. 8–10, the Pauline passage parallel to Luke 10. 27. He could also accept Romans 2. 13: not the hearers of the law are just with God, but the doers of the law shall be justified, and 2. 20: "having the form of knowledge and truth in the law". Thus Marcion did think appreciatively of the Mosaic Law. Even in lesser matters, e.g., a church regulation like the prohibition of women speaking, he appeals back to Old Testament precedent (retention of "as the law also says" in 1 Cor. 14. 34). Generally, he seems to have understood and shared the Pauline view, the paradoxical view that though the law essentially belongs to the old order it can be described positively as holy, just, good, spiritual.

Harnack[1] here refers to the doctrine of two gods and works out for Marcion a twofold conception of holiness, righteousness and goodness—one conception of these qualities as they are applied to the God of the law (the creator of this world), and a different conception of them as applied to the supreme God. The subordinate creator God can be called righteous or good only by contrast with absolute evil; compared with the supreme God he is not righteous or good. Harnack admits that as a rule Marcion kept the term righteous for the creator, and reserved good for the higher God who is indeed absolute goodness and love (*summa et praecipua bonitas*). Harnack is surely guilty of an excess of logic when he attributes to Marcion the twofold conceptions above mentioned; it may be doubted whether Marcion drew such inferences, even if they are involved in his premisses.

It is well known that Marcion rejected the allegorical method of

[1] P. 109.

exegesis. This is an aspect of his literal-mindedness.[1] Let us consider it a little further. Marcion not only rejected allegory *in toto*, but he seems to have been blind to any figurative meanings. Tertullian[2] reproaches him for refusing to understand the passage Ps. 72. 10, 15, " The Kings of Arabia and Saba shall offer him gifts. . . . There shall be given to him of the gold of Arabia," except as referring to the military Messiah of Jewish expectation (who, in Marcion's view, was still to come); and not of Christ, who was honoured at his birth by the Wise Men. Clearly such lack of imagination was bound to misinterpret much of the prophetic literature. In one point Marcion—incidentally—anticipates modern criticism of the Old Testament, viz., in his denial that the Old Testament prophesies a suffering Messiah. Tertullian[3] takes the opposite side, of course, and gives interesting examples of early Christian typology: the cross of Christ is predicted in Isaac, Jacob, Joseph, Moses, and in the brazen serpent. Tertullian[4] also uses Psalm 22 (21 LXX) as a prediction of the Passion: " *totam Christi continens passionem, canentis iam tunc gloriam suam* ". In this Tertullian to a much higher degree than Marcion is the forerunner of modern scholarship, as he is also in his reference[5] of Isa. 53 to Christ.

Take two further examples of how Marcion confined himself to the strictly literal or historical sense of Scripture: 2 Sam. 7. 12 and Isa. 16. 4. The first of these passages is part of Nathan's message to David apropos of his desire to build a temple to house the ark: " When thy days be fulfilled and thou shalt sleep with thy fathers, I will set up thy seed after thee, which shall proceed out of thy bowels, and I will establish his kingdom." Tertullian saw here a reference to Christ, but Marcion held that Solomon and Solomon only is intended. Marcion is clearly right, particularly in view of the next verse, " he shall build an house for my name " ; and Tertullian's burst of laughter over Marcion's interpretation (*Hoc si in Salomonem simpliciter edisseres, risum mihi incuties*)[6] is only a revelation of how incapable he was of doing justice in argument to an opposing point of view. Marcion obviously had an idea of the danger of making deductions from verses wrested from their context, a point in which both Tertullian and the other early Christians might have learned from him. Nevertheless, it is patent that with his rigid exegetical rules he was precluded from perceiving some of the deepest truths of Scripture. The second passage, Isa. 16. 4, " Let the outcasts of Moab dwell with thee " (R.V. mg. παροικήσουσί σοι οἱ φυγάδες Μωάβ LXX), is interpreted by Tertul-

[1] As Origen pointed out in an important chapter (*De Principiis* 2. 5).
[2] 3. 13–14. [3] 3. 18. [4] 3. 19.
[5] 3. 7 and 17. [6] 3. 20 ad fin.

lian as a prophecy of Christian conversions.[1] *Ecce, inquit Esaias, proselyti per me accedent ad te, ostendens ipsos quoque proselytos per Christum accessuros ad Deum.* Tertullian connects with this passage other passages of Isaiah, e.g., 2. 2–4, 42. 4, and appeals to the actual fact of the spread of Christianity. Marcion refused to be enticed away from the historical sense by this apparent fulfilment. There is justification for both sides in this exegetical dispute; but who will not say *errare malo cum Tertulliano quam cum istis vera sentire!*

A further word on this question of the use of allegory: Marcion's suspicion of it was a mark of uniqueness in that age. The *Clementine Recognitions* (10. 42), after some exposition of Greek use of allegory, asserts that allegory is particularly dangerous when applied to the Christian Scriptures. The only safeguard against its abuse is a sure knowledge of Christian tradition; otherwise man will read into Scripture "the understanding of their own mind". This is later than Marcion, of course. Tertullian (*De Resurrectione* 20) protests against heretical treatment of the whole Old Testament as allegory. Marcion is beyond the range of Tertullian's attack here! In distinction from Marcion the majority of Christians at that time probably agreed with Tertullian in allowing the allegorical explanation of many passages of Scripture. An example of what Tertullian thought reasonable is to be found in *De Resurrectione* 13, where he discerns in Psalm 91. 12: "δίκαιος ὡς φοῖνιξ ἀνθήσει" a prophecy of the resurrection, taking φοῖνιξ to mean not the palm-tree but the bird phœnix, which was believed to revive miraculously at the moment of death, "*semetipsum libenter funerans renovat natali fine*".[2] For Tertullian's literalism in exegesis, on the other hand, see *De Resurrectione* 35, where he is arguing for eternal punishment. In this of all treatises it was necessary to the whole argument that literal exegesis should be vindicated. Tertullian's strategy, so to speak, is not one of consistency in attack along his whole battle-front, but rather one of vigorous offensive with whatever weapons come to hand against the enemy on any section of the front! The use of allegory was established in Christian exegesis by Origen, who quite properly appealed to the example of Paul.[3] But on the dangers involved the following remark of Windisch in his commentary on the *Epistle of Barnabas*[4] is worth remembering: "Barnabas witnesses

[1] 3. 21.

[2] For the phœnix as a symbol of the Resurrection, cf. *1 Clement* 25. But Clement does not quote Scripture as well in support of this!

[3] *Contra Celsum* 4. 44; cf. also 4. 49–50, 5. 60, and most fully *De Principiis* 4, and, of course, the commentaries themselves.

[4] *Handbuch zum N.T.*, Ergänzungs-Band, p. 375.

to us how the allegorical treatment of the Old Testament almost made the possession of the Gospel superfluous; had this method established itself as early as the Apostolic Age a rich Gospel literature could hardly have arisen." Whatever truth there be in this judgement implies approbation of Marcion for his suspicion of allegory.

Marcion's attitude to prophecy is inconsistent. For, on the one hand, he seems to rank high the office of prophet, and he allowed to stand in his emended Gospel that verse which commends John the Baptist as a prophet and quotes Malachi 3. 1 with reference to him (Luke 7. 26 f.); further, the prophets are classed with Moses as the moral guides of mankind (Luke 16. 29); and in Marcion's " Apostle " the Pauline behest: " Quench not the Spirit, despise not prophesyings" is left untouched (1 Thess. 5. 20). Moreover, Marcion does not invariably strike out Pauline quotations from the Old Testament (e.g., 1 Cor. 1. 19).[1] On the other hand, Marcion did frequently strike out quotations from, and references to, the prophets. He did not believe that all prophecy was destined to be fulfilled (he omitted Luke 18. 31, for example); nor that all prophecy was inspired by God (he omitted Luke 11. 49 f.). Significant, too, is the alteration in Luke 10. 24 of " prophets . . . desired to see " which would have attributed to the prophets a wish accordant with God's will—into the bare statement of fact: " prophets . . . did not see ".

Marcion's views with reference to Messianic prophecy show the same inconsistency. He believed that the prophecies of a Jewish Messiah were to be realized; some, in fact, had already been realized.[2] This Jewish Messiah was not to be identified with Jesus Christ. His task was to bring back the Jews from their dispersion, and was confined to their race, together with those heathen who had become proselytes. According to Ps. 2 other nations will rise against him, but they will be overcome. This event was still in the future and formed the national hope of the Jews; it could be no more than a temporary earthly kingdom like that of David, for this Messiah himself would be only a man, a descendant of David. Apparently Marcion made nothing of the prophecies of a humble Messiah, e.g., Zech. 9. 9, Isaiah 42. 2.

The only Old Testament prophecies which according to Marcion

[1] For a full list of such O.T. quotations which Marcion retained, see Harnack, p. 115.

[2] Isaiah 55. 4 in David, for example; Ps. 132. 11 and 2 Sam. 7. 12 in Solomon—evidence in Tertullian 3. 20. Ps. 110 was referred by the Jews to Ezekiel and possibly Marcion followed Jewish exegesis here, but this is not certain, as Tertullian says simply "*dicunt*"; similarly later in the same chapter (5. 9) Tertullian has the vague "*dicetur*" concerning the reference of Ps. 72 to Solomon, and we cannot be quite sure that Marcion followed this Jewish exegesis.

refer to Jesus Christ are Malachi 3. 1 (Luke 7. 27) and Deut. 21. 23 (Gal. 3. 13), " He that is hanged is the curse of God ", to which we may add the description of Christ as " our passover " in 1 Cor. 5. 7. Tertullian pertinently objects that Marcion ought not to have called his Christ either Jesus or Christ (3. 15–16).

Certainly we have here an illogicality in Marcion's theory that Christ came as the inaugurator of an entirely new order, sweeping away the old and acknowledging no contact with or responsibility for it; as the emissary of a hitherto unknown God whose purpose was to undo the works of the Creator. We must suppose with Harnack (p. 116) that in these three passages the Creator had unwittingly been overruled by the Unknown God to cause the insertion in his book of prophecies of these references to the Mighty One whose advent was to mean his own downfall.[1]

The contrast between the two Christs, i.e., the Jewish and the Christian, is well made by Tertullian:[2] *Iudaicus Christus populo soli ex dispersione redigendo destinetur a creatore, vester vero omni humano generi liberando collatus sit a deo optimo.* Notice the implication that the Jewish Messiah was a merely national hero, while Marcion's Messiah was a universal saviour; this corresponds to the contrast between Marcion's supreme God, who is unbounded compassion, and the creator who is in some sense just, but whose justice is vitiated by his partiality for one people. Although, however, Marcion asserted the universality of his Christ's appeal, he did not expect all to respond and be saved—*non omnes salvi fiunt, sed pauciores omnibus et Iudaeis et Christianis creatoris.* Tertullian makes this the material for some trenchant criticism.[3]

Marcion seems never to have considered the Old Testament as the heritage of Christians, as a body of literature which has a message for future as well as past generations; nor did he consider the peril of cutting loose from the influence of a book which had for so long formed and nourished religious life. How, indeed, could he, starting as he did from the axiom that Christianity had no forerunners, and worshipped a God who entered into no dealings with mankind previous to the fifteenth year of the reign of Tiberius Cæsar? " New wine must not be poured into old bottles ", Christ had said—right enough in theory and genuine as a saying of the Lord, so that no one could quarrel with

[1] For the idea that the prophets may have uttered some of their predictions as prompted by the supreme God, and others as prompted by the Demiurge, cf. Irenaeus 4. 35. Irenaeus attributes this theory to " the Valentinians and the other Gnostics ", not specifically to Marcion. See the previous chapter for Irenaeus's insistence against Marcion that all O.T. prophecy refers forward to Christ.

[2] 3. 21.

[3] 1. 24.

Marcion for setting that up as his major premiss. His minor premiss is also right enough in itself: "The Old Testament is an old bottle"; but one feels the need for some qualifications of this, and one begins to tremble in apprehension of what might be based on these two premisses. The inference which Marcion made justifies that apprehension: "*ergo*, those who have tasted the new wine have no use for the old bottle", i.e., Christians may discard the authority of the Old Testament altogether! This emphasis on the element of newness in the Gospel is wild and exaggerated. Let Marcion be given credit for that insight characteristic of the creative thinker who sees certain truths very clearly. But he can hardly be acquitted of the charge of arbitrariness in refusing to take account of complementary truths.

The Catholic Church at that time was less arbitrary and more appreciative of the wealth of its heritage. It perceived the one-sidedness of Marcion's emphasis on the newness of Christianity. It asserted for its own part that Christianity was the highest development of Judaism.[1] This is a modern mode of expression; what those second-century Christians doubtless said was: Christ is the Messiah for whom the whole Old Testament was looking, the fulfilment of the vision of the prophets of old. The ancient conception corresponding to what we moderns call continuous revelation was belief in prophecy.[2] In the second century, as now, Christianity claimed to be a historical religion. But there can be no history without continuity, and the retention of the Old Testament within the Christian canon served to attest the continuity of Christianity with the past. "The permanent value of the Old Testament consists in the first place in this, that it is a witness to the fact that Christianity is part of the World-Scheme."[3]

In Burkitt's judgement "the real battle of the second century centres around the Old Testament".[4] The point of this is that the underlying issue was whether religion is to be regarded as rooted in philosophy and mythology (so the Gnostics [5]) or in history. The Old Testament is not a book of mythology nor a book of philosophy or systematic theology. It is a book of history, i.e., a record of Divine contacts with

[1] Strictly, it is the prophetic element in the O.T. to which Christian theology points back as its forerunner. Christ was in the succession of the prophets, rather than of the priests or wise men. That Christianity and Christian theology is not the only development from O.T. religion is shown by the existence of Judaism and Rabbinic theology. Cf. Box in *The People and the Book*, p. 466.

[2] Cf. n. 4 on p. 78.

[3] W. E. Barnes in *Cambridge Theological Essays*, p. 362.

[4] *Church and Gnosis*, p. 129.

[5] Cf. Bigg, *Christian Platonists of Alexandria*, p. 30: "O.T. exegesis was the real strength of Gnosticism."

man in and through past events, an interpretation of אותות, σημεῖα, mighty acts of God in history; a witness to the interventions on the plane of this world and in time of him who governs the World and is the Lord of History. The beginning of Christianity was understood by the Church as the crown and climax of those divine interventions, and in the light of this understanding the Church appropriated the Old Testament as its own sacred Scripture. The Jews might limit their faith to the past record of God's mighty acts, and miss the climax; Marcion certainly was committing the error of trying to possess the climax without the antecedents, which alone gave it a setting and made it intelligible. But the Church, illumined with an understanding of the events which brought it into being, was able to discover the golden mean between these two extremes. By appeal to the Old Testament it proclaimed itself the heir of the ages, built upon the foundations of the Israel's prophets, as well as of its own Apostles. Marcion entirely lacked this sense of indebtedness to the past and of the meaning of history, and in consequence the clarity of his logic is really an impossible simplification. He forgot that the stateliest oak must have begun as an acorn, and that even the Kingdom of God moves to its consummation through dim foreshadowings and partial realizations; was it not likened, by one whose authority Marcion professed to acknowledge, to a grain of mustard seed?

The Church then was not deterred by Marcion's impetuous logic from treasuring the Old Testament as a Christian heritage. Let us be clear what this meant. For something more than respect for the Old Testament as a devotional book or as great literature is implied. Such attitudes are far too modern to attribute to Christians of the second century. Perhaps the deepest reason why the Church as against Marcion would not cast itself loose from the Old Testament is that by so doing it would have lost one of its strongest arguments for belief in Christ as the unique Son of God. A divine incarnation was no new idea to that hellenized world. Many had established belief in themselves as sons of some god. And the average Greek or Syrian of the period was prepared to accept Christ as the son of a Jewish god, Jehovah, and thus to place him in the category of these divinely inspired and divinely protected beings. The task of Christian preaching was to convince men that Jesus the Christ was not in that category. One of its most effective methods was to claim that his appearance and work had been foretold hundreds of years before. No pagan son of god could boast such a testimony as that!

A passage of Justin Martyr may be referred to in this connection.[1]

[1] *Apol.* I. 30.

Justin faces the pagan objection that Jesus might have proved himself Son of God simply by resort to magic arts: τί κωλύει καὶ τὸν παρ' ἡμῖν λεγόμενον Χριστὸν ἄνθρωπον ἐξ ἀνθρώπων ὄντα μαγικῇ τέχνῃ ἃς λέγομεν δυνάμεις πεποιηκέναι καὶ δόξαι διὰ τοῦτο υἱὸν Θεοῦ εἶναι; But, replies Justin, you forget prophecy. Outsiders might have some reason to argue that Christ was ἄνθρωπον ἐξ ἀνθρώπων, were it not for the passage in the prophet Isaiah which declares that he is to be born of a virgin. He can have been no mere magician, who had testimony to him 800 years before his birth; nay, more, 5,000 years before![1]

Ignatius also may be cited for evidence of this perception, denied by Marcion, that the Old Testament prophets were inspired by the Father of Jesus Christ and heralded the saving acts of Christ. Two passages are relevant: In the letter to the Magnesians (ch. 8–9) Ignatius speaks of the "most divine" (θειότατοι) prophets living "according to Christ Jesus" (κατὰ Χριστὸν 'Ιησοῦν) and being inspired by his grace. They were already in the spirit Christian disciples, looking forward to the earthly appearance of Christ as their teacher. And in the Philadelphian epistle (ch. 5) Ignatius declares that the prophets proclaimed the Gospel, and are saved by faith in Christ, and "numbered in the gospel of the common hope".[2] This last is written by Ignatius in a context where he explicitly mentions the incompatibility between Christianity and Judaism (ἄτοπόν ἐστι Χριστὸν Ιησοῦν λαλεῖν καὶ ἰουδαΐζειν, *Magn.* 10. 3).

Of course, a large number of Greek-speaking converts had no understanding of the Old Testament and felt no obligation to retain it. It remained for them a book of Jewish fables. These were a field ripe for Gnostic and Marcionite sickles to harvest. Literary evidence of these groups are the *Epistle of Ptolemaeus* to Flora, the *Epistle to Diognetus* and the *Epistle of Barnabas*. Marcion's doctrine of the Old Testament, however, remains *sui generis*. The *Epistle of Barnabas* thinks the ancient Jews were led into error[3] by a too literal understanding of the Old Testament, and vindicates the case of the Old Testament among Christians by astonishing allegorizations. Marcion rejected the Old Testament. He did not resort to the allegorical method, and one wonders whether he was partly influenced by extravagances in the use of this method by Barnabas and those like-minded with him. That Barnabas should depreciate the Old Testament and yet uphold its

[1] Justin apparently put Adam at this date. Or, perhaps more probably, he is referring to Moses. See *Apol.* 1. 31 ad fin.

[2] Christ is called ἡ κοινὴ ἐλπὶς ἡμῶν elsewhere in Ignatius—*Eph.* 21. 2 et passim.

[3] πλάνη, 2. 9–10.

authority for Christians as a book from which they could learn the mysteries of Christ's person and obtain guidance for their daily conduct is an inconsistency with which Marcion cannot be charged.

What, then, is Marcion's real contribution in this matter of the Church's attitude to the Old Testament? Was the Roman Church in the year 144 wrong when it expelled Marcion and anathematized his doctrines? Was the question of the relevance of the Old Testament settled once and for all then? Is it still fair to ask whether the two Covenants which are bound together as our Holy Bible have equal validity and sanctity? Or are we to agree with Harnack's notorious judgement:[1] "The rejection of the Old Testament in the second century was a mistake which the Great Church [die grosse Kirche] rightly refused to make; the retention of it in the sixteenth century was a fatal legacy [Schicksal] which the reformation could not yet avoid; but for Protestantism since the nineteenth century to continue to treasure it as a canonical document is the result of a lameness which affects religion and the Church." Radicalism indeed!—but is there nothing in the Old Testament which should be conserved?

Does modern criticism of the Old Testament, based on the new data provided by archæology and the comparative study of religions, count for nothing as we reflect on this issue? Has it perchance justified that negative attitude to the Old Testament which has its most notable ancient advocate in Marcion, and which finds exponents to-day, among them Harnack as just quoted? It is more than a question of the origins of the various documents, and of historical accuracy, or of the suitability for use in public worship of certain parts of the Old Testament. It is a question of whether the Old Testament is any more than a piece of ancient literature or a collection of historical documents which illustrate the life and ideas of the nation into which Christianity was born; of whether it is by any real *differentia* to be distinguished from other ancient writings, e.g., those of Greece and Rome, which are also very useful as describing the antecedents and environment of early Christianity. Has the Old Testament a quality of revelation which places it in a category apart from other ancient literature, and makes it comparable in quality and authority with the New Testament? Would it be more consistent for the Christian Church to give the Old Testament a place with the Apocrypha as books "good and useful to read", and to cease regarding it as of canonical authority and as on a par with the New Covenant of the Lord and Saviour Jesus Christ? If the authoritative Scriptures of the Church should be that collection of books which reveals what Christianity actually and in practice is—and this is what

[1] Harnack, p. 217.

Marcion strove to teach the men of his generation—then, it may be argued, the Old Testament has no right to be a part of the Bible.

Let Marcion be given credit for his perception of the uniqueness of the revelation in the historic person of Jesus Christ. He thought Christianity could be understood without reference to anything that happened before A.D. 29; the content of the Gospel could be accounted for from within the circle of the Church as it had developed since that date. To this the answer is that he was wrong. The teaching of Christ and its impact on Judaism is not explicable without reference to the history of Judaism. The Church's conception of its place and duty is not explicable without that preparation in earlier centuries. There *was* a *praeparatio evangelica.* And emphasis on the new and creative factor in Christ is quite compatible with appreciation of this past. Newness does not mean unprecedentedness; a new phase of human life does not demand a Melchizedek to inaugurate it. Wiser than Marcion are the following words used about Christ by an anonymous contemporary of his—wiser because avoiding his undue emphasis on the one aspect of the Incarnation: οὗτος ὁ ἀπ' ἀρχῆς ὁ καινὸς φανεὶς καὶ παλαιὸς εὑρεθεὶς καὶ πάντοτε νέος ἐν ἁγίων καρδίαις γεννώμενος.[1]

With regard to the Scriptures, the question of canonicity can only be decided by those who are conscious of their membership among the people of God continuing throughout the centuries since the day when God first spoke to a man and elected a people.

The abiding debt of the Church to the heretic of Pontus in this matter of the Old Testament is his reminder of the pre-eminence of soteriology. Marcion, it is true, exalted soteriology and ignored cosmology, and for this he merits no praise. But his exaggerations may yield one hint useful to others in their approach to the Old Testament. The Old Testament is Christian in so far as it witnesses to God as a saving God. It is more important for men to know that God forgives them and loves them freely, than to know that he created them. Hosea and 2 Isaiah are more indispensable than Genesis 1 and Psalm 104. It is regrettable that Marcion could only put this in

[1] *Ad Diognetum* 11. 4. An interesting passage of Ignatius (*Philad.* 8. 2) maintains the same correct emphasis. Ignatius had come across some who required confirmation in the O.T. before they accepted statements in the Gospel, the O.T. being for them "the archives", i.e., the original deed, the authoritative source of knowledge. Ignatius retorts that Jesus Christ and his Passion and Resurrection are "the archives". Marcion might have felt that Ignatius was on his side. But Ignatius also knew how to hold a balance between the elements of the new and the old in Christianity. Even though the O.T. is not the final court of appeal, its witness is consonant with the Gospel. See 5. 2 of the same epistle, and *Magnesians* 8–9, as quoted above.

the form of an Either—Or. There is no need to follow him in this and to deny that God is a Creator. It is not a question of accepting those passages which reveal God as redeemer and rejecting the rest. Nevertheless, a lesson can be learned from Marcion's mistakes as well as from his wiser statements. The emphasis must be on soteriology, admittedly; but soteriology which has no cosmology as its presupposition is meaningless. This ought we to emphasize—and not to leave the other unemphasized.

Along such lines as these may be sought an answer to those who call in question the canonical authority of the Old Testament. The Old Testament belongs inseparably with the New Testament as the testimony to certain saving acts of God, upon which are based, for the Christian at any rate, knowledge of God and hope of the ultimate redemption of the human race. For the God to whom this witness is borne is no distant President of Immortals and Mortals, but One who is ever active in his concern for the human race. His purpose for mankind was not complete with their creation, but looks forward to a consummation. In prospect of this consummation the Creator is also the moulder of man's destiny, and the events of history are to be understood as the Old Testament understands them, as evidence of his active providence. Marcion degraded the Old Testament because he did not interpret it in this way. But he degraded it for a good reason, viz., because he did not find in it testimony to a redeeming God. This guiding principle of his may be commended, even while his general attitude to the Old Testament is rejected.

SUMMARY

DURING the second century A.D. the Church had to mark out its middle way. On the one hand, it must not allow itself to be so engrossed in its past and its antecedents as to become no more than a sect within Judaism. On the other hand, it had to avoid being assimilated to non-Jewish religious societies which were its rivals for the allegiance of the Roman world. The latter temptation was the more powerful. The Gnostic systems were making a wide appeal. They offered the attraction of novelty and universalism, and many Christians, convinced that Christianity was a new way of redemption and for all men, were inclined to think that the Christian creed and organization should conform to this model. From this direction came the influence of Marcion on orthodox Christianity, even if he is in some respects best considered apart from Gnosticism.

Marcion did well to remind the Church of the newness of its Gospel as compared with the doctrines of Judaism; but his attitude to Judaism was rooted in a repudiation of history which classes him with the Gnostics, and it was a true insight which prompted the Church to designate him a heretic. Orthodoxy realized that even at the risk of remaining entangled with Jewish theology it must not repudiate its origin in Judaism and in those historic events wrought in Jewish history and on Palestinian soil which constituted the life and work of the Lord Jesus. In making this affirmation the Church was guided not only by a sound instinct for its own preservation, but by a sense of the importance of historic beginnings. It was this which determined the survival of the Church through the debates and turmoil of the second century, and has enabled it to maintain its identity in competition with much mysticism and rationalism in later centuries.[1] The Catholic doctrine of Apostolic Succession incidentally witnesses to this, as does also the Protestant emphasis on discovering and conforming

[1] And to bear the reproach of excessive particularity in our own day (*das Aergernis der Einmaligkeit*, as G. Kittel has called it). For the main contention of this paragraph, cf K. S. Latourette, *History of Christianity*, i, p. 344: "The decision on the one hand, between holding to the Jewish roots, to the historic facts of the beginnings and verifiable teachings of the founder as the norm; and on the other hand seeking to integrate and if necessary subordinate this history to a prevailing style in religion and thought . . . determined the character of the forms of Christianity which have since predominated." Burkitt also pointed to its sense of the importance of history as distinguishing orthodox Christianity from Gnosticism in the second century (*Church and Gnosis*, pp. 22 ff., 126 ff.).

to primitive Christian standards of faith, conduct and order. Here we perceive the validity of the argument from tradition. "*Quod ubique*" and "*quod ab omnibus*" are not necessarily the genuine Christian faith; "*quod semper*" may be a surer criterion.

Marcion's chief significance in the history of Christianity was not due to his organization of a church independent of the main body of Christians, nor to any innovations in ecclesiastical practice for which he was responsible. Marcionitism failed to win the whole Mediterranean world and become the dominant, universal Church; it succeeded only in consolidating the Greater Church which was to triumph over it. As compiler of a canon of Scripture—the first New Testament canon—he had a greater influence, though it is extravagant to pronounce him, as Harnack does, the creator of the Catholic canon. His emendations of the New Testament text might have been expected to affect the textual tradition to a far greater extent than was actually the case. We have seen reason to pronounce it limited to the point of negligibility. In any case his work as textual critic and canon-maker, important though it appears, in intention if not in effect, probably seemed to Marcion himself merely incidental to his main work of advocating his theology and organizing his new society on the basis of it. His greatest influence outside the circle of his own followers was probably derived from his emphasis on soteriology and his direction of attention to Paul. Wherever in the history of religion there occurs a revolt of mercy against justice or a rediscovery of Paul, especially if they be in exaggerated forms, we may not inappropriately speak of Marcionitism. "Le Marcionisme est une réaction de la conscience chrétienne qui rappelle que Dieu pourtant est amour. Il est par excellence la religion des pauvres, des persecutés. Il y a beaucoup de Marcionites qui n'ont jamais rien entendu de Marcion."[1]

Marcion's theology, considered as a whole, is too one-sided to be important as a theological system. He had not the sort of mind which could create a worthy intellectual expression for his fundamental convictions. But his insights are important and they recur in many serious Christian (and non-Christian) thinkers. Consider, for example, stress on the divine love, or aversion to the element of Law. Whereever creative imagination wrestles with the central tenets of Christianity it will come upon these factors, and Marcion's reflection upon them will never be irrelevant. It is better that they should be exaggerated than that they should be ignored.

Marcion's faults were on the whole faults of exaggeration rather than of the introduction of alien ideas. It is a pity that his critics—Ter-

[1] H. Strohl in *Revue d'Histoire et de Philosophie Religieuses*, 1923, p. 165.

tullian in particular—in denouncing him have not given him credit for the fact that what he was emphasizing almost beyond recognition was a central element in Christianity. The great merit of Harnack's book is to have appreciated this and to have opened the way to a truer estimate of Marcion's significance. As Harnack points out,[1] the Church overcame Marcion only by accepting the stimulus of his ideas and by developing its own theology so as not merely to controvert them, but to complement them by adding those factors to which Marcion was blind; for example, by insisting on cosmology as well as soteriology; and generally by maintaining that a true theology is of the nature of Both—And rather than Either—Or. The defeat of Marcionitism was mainly due not to Tertullian, but to the Alexandrian school, who took to themselves much for which Marcion had stood and presented a new Christian philosophy which in the end left no room for either Marcionitism or Gnosticism.[2] There is, however, some justice in the remark of McGiffert:[3] "There is much more in the Fathers about the majesty, power and creative activity of God than about His moral character, in spite of their frequent references to divine judgement and God's mercy. On His character they seem to have reflected only as a consequence of Marcion's teaching, and the picture they drew of God was largely determined by the contrast between justice and goodness. Christian theism has not yet recovered from the effects of this situation." Marcion failed indeed of the effect which he himself desired; but he was not altogether ineffectual.

[1] P. 212. Cf. also p. 313*, n. 1, on the need for more thorough study of the progress Catholic theology made in its polemic against Marcion.

[2] So R. S. Wilson, *Marcion*, pp. 182 f.

[3] *The God of the Early Christians*, p. 187.

APPENDIX 7

DID MARCION'S TEXT INFLUENCE THE OLD LATIN?

Did Marcionite readings establish themselves in the text as read by orthodox Latin-speaking Christians? It is *a priori* unlikely that a text emended in the interests of a heresy—and Marcion was the arch-heretic of the second century—should have been allowed by the orthodox to influence their own versions of Holy Scripture. But while this probability must be borne in mind, the question can only be decided by an actual investigation of the available texts. It must be borne in mind that the distinction between heretics and orthodox was not as clear in the second century as it later became. Most of the heretics claimed to be genuine Christians and to be expounding the pure Gospel, and there is no need to doubt the sincerity of such claims. Watchful bishops like Irenaeus, and doubtless the more intelligent Christians, would discern the error of the Marcionite or Valentinian among their congregations, but the average Christian is not likely to have done so, and might even be inclined to admire a heretic's zeal and understanding in the faith. There is also a further point, more definitely related to the treatment of the Scripture by Christians of all types at that time. It is commonly assumed that while pioneers in heresy manipulated the sacred text to suit their own opinions, non-heretical Christians never resorted to the same methods in their defence of the truth. But this assumption ought perhaps to be questioned, as in fact it is by K. and S. Lake in a recent book:[1] "It is not certain that the Catholic text does not contain changes made in opposition to Marcion, and possibly to other heretics . . . . The nature of a Catholic and of a heretic in those days was not so different that the one may be supposed to have emended the text often and the other never." This point cannot be discussed here,[2] but enough has been said to indicate that the possibility of Marcionite influence on the text of Scripture as read outside Marcionite circles must not be disallowed without proper examination. The comparison here set out between the Old Latin versions and Marcion's text of Luke and Paul is an attempt towards such an examination.

Marcion and the Old Latin versions constitute, of course, only part

[1] *An Introduction to the New Testament*, 1938, p. 99. This book is a masterly survey of the field, but spoilt by many inaccuracies in detail.

[2] K. and S. Lake go on to mention the possibility that there was a revision of the Greek text of the Epistles in an anti-Marcionite or anti-Gnostic interest. If of Epistles, why not of Gospels as well?

of the whole material, which includes all the Greek manuscripts and among other versions particularly the Old Syriac.

An obvious and in fact necessary method of working suggests itself, viz., that the comparison be extended first to the Gospel, i.e., Luke, and secondly to the Apostle, i.e., the ten Pauline Epistles which Marcion accepted as genuine, i.e., Galatians, 1 and 2 Corinthians, Romans, 1 and 2 Thessalonians, Laodiceans (= Ephesians), Colossians, Philippians, Philemon. [The order is that of Marcion's New Testament.]

The Marcionite text here quoted is as reconstructed by Harnack.[1] Harnack gives a full *apparatus criticus* based on Tischendorf. It is a relief to find that Harnack did not adopt the new notation of von Soden, but the fact that he contented himself with Tischendorf has caused certain omissions, e.g., there are no citation of readings of *Codex Augiensis* (Ff), *Ussherianus* (r_1r_2) of the Gospels, nor of *Codex Augiensis* (Ff) of Paul. Omissions however are relatively few, and the apparatus is clearly set out and easy to use. The relevant passages of Tertullian are given fully.

For the Old Latin versions the available printed editions have been used. The method followed has been to collate each in turn with the text of Marcion, and to register all similarities of reading. Closer examination of these agreements reveals that the majority of them are of no significance in the present connection, being not original with Marcion, but derived by him and by the Old Latin alike from a widespread Greek text-type (the Western text). There is, however, a number of readings which can only be regarded as innovations of Marcion's in conformity with his peculiar doctrines. If this is allowed we have a clear case of Marcion's tendentious emendations affecting the Latin textual tradition. To what extent, and how widespread geographically, is the task of the following pages to estimate.

To begin with the Gospel. The Old Latin versions of the Gospels which are here compared with Marcion's Luke are the following:

Codex Vercellensis (a), as printed in *Collectanea Biblica Latina* III, ed. A. Gasquet, 1914.

Codex Vindobonensis (b), as printed by Buchanan in *Old Latin Biblical Texts* VI.

[1] Pp. 183*–240* and 67*–127*. Harnack's reconstruction of Marcion's text antiquates those of Zahn (*Geschichte des N.T. Kanons*, 2, pp. 445–529) and all earlier scholars.

Codex Colbertinus (c), as printed by Sabatier, *Bibliorum Sacrorum Latinae Versiones Antiquae*, 1743.

Codex Bezae—the Latin side (d), as printed by Scrivener in his edition of this codex, 1864.

Evangelium Palatinum (e), as printed by Tischendorf in his luxury edition, 1847 (*Evangelium Palatinum ineditum*). The main witness for Luke of the "African" Old Latin text, k not being extant for Luke.

Codex Brixianus (f), as printed by Wordsworth–White in their edition of the Vulgate immediately below the Vulgate text. Wordsworth–White print the edition of Bianchini (*Evangeliarium Quadruplex*, 1749). See also note on q (p. 131, below).

Codex Corbeiensis (ff or ff_2), as printed by Buchanan in *Old Latin Biblical Texts* V.

g^1 = *Codex Sangermanensis* 15 (Sabatier, p. XXXIV, middle para., so describes it, though in his critical apparatus he refers to it as S. Germ. 1). Paris Nat. Lib. 11553, formerly S. Germain 15.

g^2 = "*Sangermanensis cui nulla nota numerica est apposita*" (Sabatier, p. XXV para. 4; in the critical apparatus he quotes it as S. Germ. 2). Paris Nat. Lib. 13169, formerly S. Germain 2. Wordsworth–White say of it "a Sabatier *interdum* citatus" (Novum Testamentum Latine, p. xxxii).

Sabatier gives the readings of these two MSS. only where they differ from the Vulgate. Here only those readings are noted which agree with Marcion, but these include passages where the two MSS. agree with the Vulgate.

Codex Vindobonensis or rather *Fragmenta Vindobonensia* (i) containing only ch. 10. 16–23. 10 of Luke. I have quoted the edition of Belsheim 1885. (It must be admitted that Belsheim's numerous editions of Latin texts, though clearly printed and easy to use, are not free from the suspicion of carelessness, and should probably not be used if another edition is available. Corssen condemns them as "sämtlich wissenschaftlich unbrauchbar".)

Codex Rehdigeranus (l), as printed by F. Haase, Breslau, 1865–1866. "pure Vg. in Mt. Mark; pure b, ff, i in Luke" (Burkitt).

Liber de divinis scripturis sive Speculum quod fertur S. Augustini (m), in *C.S.E.L.*, XII, pp. 287–700. A sort of Biblical Theology or "Christian doctrine proved by quotations from Scripture".

Codex Monacensis (q) in *Old Latin Biblical Texts* III.

q is not very profitable for a comparison with Marcion, because its own character and provenance and grouping are not very clear.

Hort (*New Testament in Greek*, II, p. 79) placed it among the Italian class of MSS.—the third type due to revision of European texts in conformity with Greek texts or for refinement of latinity; i.e., Hort classified it with f as against a b i. Following this Wordsworth-White take f as representing the type of text used by Jerome as the basis of the Vulgate Gospels. Burkitt and Souter protest against this (see Souter, *Text and Canon of New Testament*, p. 44—which implies that f is not of much significance for a comparison with Marcion).

White in his edition of q in *Old Latin Biblical Texts* III puts forward more precise judgement: q may be Italian in its *readings*, but it is European in its *renderings* (p. xxi).

White justifies this judgement by a detailed examination of passages in all four Gospels (pp. xxii–li).

> " q cannot be classed with any one definite branch of the Old Latin family, but has come under the influence of every group in turn . . . we shall find it to have a far stronger resemblance to b than to any other Old Latin MS " (l–li).

See further De Bruyne in *Revue Bénédictine*, 1911, pp. 75–80.

Burkitt (*J.T.S.*, Oct. 1926, p. 96) says q " has an almost unrevised European text akin to b, only the plus of the Byzantine text has been added ".

Codex Usshérianus (r or r_1), as printed by T. K. Abbott: *Evangeliorum Versio Antehieronymiana ex codice Usseriano*, 1884.

Also *Codex Usshérianus alter* (r_2), the readings of which can be ascertained from the appendix of Abbott's book, where we find a collation of r_2 with *Codex Amiatinus* of the Vulgate. Apparently it is to be assumed that where no reading is given r_2 agrees with the Vulgate. With this must be compared the edition of r_2 published by H. C. Hoskier in the *Old Latin Biblical Texts* in 1919. Hoskier strongly impugns the accuracy of Abbott and makes him guilty of neglecting some 700 readings, and misreporting about 300 more.

Nevertheless, Abbott's work is very useful, particularly on r_1, where the Vulgate (according to *Codex Amiatinus*) is printed on the left-hand page and r_1 on the right-hand page, so that the divergences of r_1 from the Vulgate, i.e., its Old-Latin character, can be readily seen. And if bricks are to be thrown, Hoskier must be made a target as well as Abbott, e.g., at Luke 10. 22 even the exact Hoskier has not made clear what the reading of r_2 is.

Neither r nor r_2 is mentioned in Harnack's apparatus.

Fragmenta Curiensia (a_2) [Luke 11. 11–29; 13. 16–34] and *Fragmenta Ambrosiana* (s) [Luke 17. 3–29; 18. 39–19. 47; 20. 46–21. 22] as printed in *Old Latin Biblical Texts* II, pp. 79–88. The date and affinities of these MSS. are so uncertain as to make comparison with

Marcion barely worth while. See *Old Latin Biblical Texts* II, pp. ccxiii–ccxlviii.

The Vulgate. For the comparison of the Vulgate with Marcion I have used the *Editio Minor* prepared by H. J. White (corrected edition 1920).

It is most regrettable that the " African " *Codex Bobbiensis* (k) is not extant for Luke.

The evidence of Latin Fathers is cited according to the *Corpus Scriptorum Ecclesiasticorum Latinorum*, one great merit of which is the Indices with which most volumes are provided. The *Index Locorum* makes the Biblical usage of the author readily available for our present purpose.

No separate comparison is made between Tertullian and Marcion, because Tertullian is the basis of the reconstruction of Marcion's text. In the case of Tertullian there is sometimes uncertainty whether he is quoting Marcion's text, or whether he is quoting an orthodox text, or whether he is repeating more loosely from memory. In view of his professed purpose of refuting Marcion out of his own words we must assume that it is Marcion's text which he quotes ; and this, of course, justifies the reconstruction of Marcion's text out of Tertullian's quotations. After all, Tertullian is our main source for this, and without him the attempt would be almost hopeless. But there is some danger of arguing in a circle, if Marcion's text, reconstructed from Tertullian, is compared with Tertullian himself, for Tertullian's citations of Luke and Paul in his other writings are far less considerable in extent than those in his *Adversus Marcionem.*

H. Rönsch, *Das Neue Testament Tertullians* is indispensable here, in addition to Kroymann's edition and Indices. To take some examples : Tertullian refers to Luke 6. 29 generally (*mandans alterius quoque maxillae oblationem*), and Marcion's reading here could not be reconstructed from Tertullian alone without the help of Megethius and Rufinus. At Luke 6. 25 I should prefer to emend Harnack's reconstruction of Marcion and read πεινάσουσι and πενθήσουσι, in view of Tertullian's *esurient* and *lugebunt* (Rönsch, op. cit., p. 172).

But on the whole we must agree with Harnack, p. 55* : " Tertullian's care and reliability in the matter of quotations should be emphasized . . . . Where we can control him by using the quotations of others he usually stands up to the test, often to the smallest detail, so that initial scepticism disappears during careful study and turns to grateful appreciation."

That Tertullian had Marcion's Scriptures before him in Latin is proved by Harnack. See pp. 48*–55* (for Paul) ; pp. 179*–181* (for the Gospel). So d'Alès in an important article in *Biblica*, 1923, p. 86, n. 2.

The most important Fathers for our purpose are Cyprian and Novatian.

Cyprian. *C.S.E.L.* III. Part III contains the spurious works, referred to as Pseudo-Cyprian.

For *Novatian* reference must be made to the article *Vetus Romana* by A. d'Alès in Biblica IV (1923), pp. 56–90.[1] This is a study of the pre-Vulgate text of Rome; hence the title Vetus *Romana*, not Vetus *Itala.* This meant examination of Novatian. D'Alès considers the *De Trinitate, De Cibis Judaicis* and the two *Epistles to Cyprian* preserved in the Cyprianic correspondence (*Epistles* 30 and 36 in *C.S.E.L.*) alone as genuine works of Novatian. But he also makes cautious use, as being probably of Roman provenance, of the pseudo-Cyprianic *Ad Novatianum* and the *De Spectaculis, De Bono Pudicitiae* and *Adv. Judaeos.* (These are all contained in *C.S.E.L.*, Cyprian, Part III.)

The article brings out the following important points: Novatian has a Bible already fixed—this is clear from the fact that a quotation recurs in identically the same form; but he is not chained to it (p. 71). Novatian's Latin, both of Old Testament and New Testament, differs from the African type, as represented in Cyprian (pp. 71–74). This verdict is supported by the second group of texts (pp. 74–82).

As regards Marcion, d'Alès allows *a priori* that Marcion's Latin may have influenced the Catholic Latin New Testament. That the Marcionite Latin in point of time preceded the Catholic is entirely credible; the Roman Church has never been in a hurry to give its faithful the Scriptures in their own vulgar tongue! But the actual comparison of the available fragments of the third century Roman text with Marcion offers no support to the hypothesis of Marcionite influence. " La Bible marcionite n'a marqué la première Bible romaine d'aucune empreinte pour nous discernable " (cf. pp. 85–90). This judgement is based on a comparison of Novatian's text with Marcion's text not only of Luke, but also of Paul.

Irenaeus. His New Testament text has been pieced together in *Old Latin Biblical Texts* VII (*Novum Testamentum Sancti Irenaei*). It is almost entirely in Latin, of course. Its significance for our purpose would be enhanced if the older view about its date (viz., that it was composed as early as the second century, i.e., before Tertullian, who was thought to have known it) could be established. This view was still upheld by Sanday. But there is powerful support (Hort, Harnack, Souter) for a fourth-century date.

[1] Reprinted in his *Novatien*, 1924, pp. 42–82, with slight additions, e.g., a reference to the Oxford *Novum Testamentum Sancti Irenaei*, 1923, (pp. 75 f.).

See *Novum Testamentum Sancti Irenaei*, pp. lvii–lxiv (Sanday); lxv–cxi (Souter).

Ambrose. C.S.E.L. XXXII, LXII and LXIV. Volume XXXII was planned to be in four parts, but part three has not yet been published, and parts one and two have no *Index Locorum*. I have used the volumes which have Indices. These contain the following works of Ambrose: *Exposition of Luke* (XXXII. 4), *Exposition of Psalm* 119 (LXII), *Exposition of Twelve Selected Psalms* (LXIV).

Victorinus of Pettau. C.S.E.L. XLIX. No influence of Marcion's Gospel text.

Lucifer of Cagliari. C.S.E.L. XIV. Lucifer's Biblical quotations are relatively numerous, for he relied on the Bible alone to confound his Arian opponents, not on general reasoning or his own culture, as, for example, did Arnobius and Lactantius. Nevertheless, the yield for our purpose is practically nil.

Hilary of Poitiers. Part only of his works is available in *C.S.E.L*, i.e., Volume LXV, containing the *Tract on Mysteries*, the *Liber ad Constantium*, *Fragments*, *Hymns* and *Spuria*; and Volume XXII, containing Hilary's exposition of the Psalms, but without an Index. Only Volume LXV has been used in this essay. It reveals no influence of Marcion's text of Luke.

Arnobius in his long treatise *Adversus Nationes* outdoes all the Apologists in paucity of Biblical references. There is a practically complete absence of quotations from Scripture. The explanation is no doubt that Arnobius, having been converted late in life at the age of sixty, was not very familiar with the Bible.

Lactantius. The few Biblical references in his writings show no contacts with the Marcionite text.

For the passages where the Marcionite text of the Gospel offers a variant reading I refer to Harnack, pp. 183*–240*. These variants are not all due to Marcion himself, and most of them were widespread at the time when he compiled his canon, *c.* A.D. 140. Practically speaking, they are readings that are rejected by most editors in our modern critical editions of the New Testament. But some of them have a claim to be regarded as the original text. It is necessary to take account of them all rather than only of those readings which are more definitely Marcionite innovations, because otherwise a very incomplete use would be made of the data available for a study of the influence of Marcion's text.

There follows a report of all Old Latin readings which agree with Marcion in these variants. For this purpose the Old Latin MSS. and

Latin Fathers just mentioned are compared in turn with Marcion. The object of going through them separately, rather than collecting the evidence of all the Old Latin for each passage,[1] is the consideration of the possibility of affinity between Marcion and a particular Old Latin MS. or Latin Father. On the basis of this collection of readings it should be possible to decide whether and to what extent strictly Marcionite, i.e., tendentious and heretical, readings did obtain a place in the Old Latin Bible. The extent of Marcionite influence on the textual tradition as a whole would still remain to be estimated; but the result of the investigation of a limited part of the field would have a certain usefulness as a preliminary.

Agreements between a and Marcion's Luke

4.16 *secundum consuetudinem*, without *suam*, i.e., omits αὐτῷ after εἰωθὸς, cf. d.

5.14 *ut sit in testimonium hoc vobis*, cf. b.
(*hoc* also d D ff q r, *istud* c).

5.24 *tolle lectum tuum.*
tolle = ἆρον > ἄρας, so all Old Latin and Vulgate; also ℵ D.
lectum (= κλινίδιον) is read by a b f ff g^1 l q r_2 and Vulgate.
grabattum (= κράβαττον, so D and Marcion) is read by c d e r.

5.34 *possunt* (= δύνανται Marcion > δύνασθε) so b c d e ff g^1 Ambrose (and also ℵ* D).
quamdiu (= ἐφ' ὅσον Marcion and D > ἐν ᾧ) so b c e r f Ambrose.
The rest read *dum* or *cum*.

5.38 *mittunt* (= βάλλουσι > βλητέον). So all the Old Latin with D and ℵ*.

5.39 omitted, with b c d e ff l r D. It is contained in f g^1 g^2 q r_2 Vulgate.
? Marcionite deliberate omission. So Harnack, p. 190*, arguing from the fact that no ancient evidence actually attributes the verse to Marcion. It is probable that Marcion would have found the verse intolerable, had he known it. But in view of its absence in so many Old Latin authorities and D, it is equally probable that Marcion was not acquainted with it at all.

6.17 Cf. b.

6.22 *cum segregaverint* . . . , cf. b.

6.25 *vae vobis saturis quia esurietis*, i.e., omits νῦν with Marcion after ἐμπεπλησμένοι. So b c d e ff g^2 l q r r_2 Irenaeus, Vulgate.

6.26 *similiter faciebant* = κατὰ τὰ αὐτὰ > Marcion's ταῦτα. c and e read *eadem* and *per eadem*. But see b. Marcion's omission of γάρ is parallelled by the absence of *enim* in all Old Latin except g^2 r r_2 Irenaeus.

6.38 *eadem mensuram* [*sic!*] *qua metitis* . . . so b e f ff g^1 g^2 l q r r_2 Ambrose, Vulgate.
Marcion τῷ αὐτῷ μέτρῳ > ᾧ γὰρ μέτρῳ.
γάρ is omitted, as in Marcion, by a b ff g^1 q r Vulgate.

7.38 *inrigabat*, cf. b.

8.3 *quae et ministrabant illi.* For *illi* cf. b l q pseudo-Cyprian. (Harnack also gives g, wrongly according to Sabatier, who gives *eis* for g^1 and does not quote

[1] Nearly all that is required for this is contained in the *apparatus criticus* of Harnack.

g^2. Sabatier may be nodding here, however; he gives *ei* for Vulgate and Wordsworth–White give *eis*.) Marcion αὐτῷ > αὐτοῖς. The insertion of *et* (Marcion καί) also c d q ff.

8.25 *qui et ventis*, so c r, *qui ventis* ff. Marcion ὅς τοῖς ἀνέμοις > ὅτι καὶ τοῖς ἀνέμοις.

9.20 xpm = τὸν Χριστόν Marcion > τὸν Χριστὸν τοῦ θεοῦ. So Syr^{cur}. But there is no necessity to assume influence of a tendentious alteration of Marcion's. Assimilation to the text of Mark is a safer assumption. So Harnack, p. 201*.

9.22 *Post tertium diem* Marcion μετὰ τρεῖς ἡμέρας. So Syr^{sin}. So all Old Latin except f and r_2 which are conformed to Vulgate *tertia die resurgere*. So all Old Latin and Vulgate, also Marcion ἀναστῆναι > ἐγερθῆναι. But possibility of assimilation to Mark must be taken into account before inferences are made as to Marcionite influence.

9.24b omits οὗτος with Marcion. So c f ff l r_2 Vulgate.

9.54 adds *sicut Helias fecit*.

9.55–6 after *obiurgavit illos* goes on: *dicens nescitis cuius spiritus estis filius hominis non venit animas hominum perdere sed salvare*. These additions in 9.54–6 are also found in Cyprian (v. 56) b c f q r r_2 Ambrose Vulgate as well as Syr. ff unfortunately has lost the two leaves which contain this passage. e and Vulgate contain it all except *sicut Helias fecit* in v. 54. d g^1 g^2 lack *filius hominis . . . salvare*.

Harnack (p. 204*) regards these readings as Marcionite insertions. v. 54 is definitely attested for Marcion by Tertullian. But the additions in vv. 55–6 are not so certainly a part of Marcion's text as is v. 54. The fact that they suit Marcion's belief admirably is not enough, in view of the incomplete certainty as to Marcion's actual reading, to justify Harnack.

10.1 *elegit*, so e. Marcion (Tertullian 4. 24) *adlegit*, which leads Harnack to give ἀπέδειξε as the Greek of Marcion > ἀνέδειξε. D has ἀπέδειξε, d *ostendit*, c *probavit*. The rest of Old Latin and Vulgate have *designavit*, which is probably a rendering of ἀνέδειξε. ff is not extant at this point, and g^1 g^2 are not cited in Sabatier.

10.21 omits πάτερ. So a only among Old Latin, but cf. e. According to Vogels, *Evangelium Palatinum*, p. 80, ε 86 (Soden's notation; generally known as F) also omits πάτερ.

10.22 omits μου after πατρός. So c d l Vulgate and Syr^{sin}.

10.22 *nemo nobit* [*sic!*] *quis est pater nisi filius et cuicumque voluerit filius revelavit* [*sic!*], i.e., omits the clause καὶ τίς ἐστιν ὁ υἱὸς εἰ μὴ ὁ πάτηρ, cf. b.

10.24 omits καὶ βασιλεῖς, so d e ff i l, and the last clause καὶ ἀκοῦσαι . . . ἤκουσαν, so i l.

10.27 omits καὶ ἐν ὅλῃ τῇ διανοίᾳ σου, so b c d ff i l r.

11.11 Cf. b.

11.48 *non consentientes* as b. Marcion μὴ συνευδοκεῖν. There is considerable variety among the Old Latin here. f i c l r r_2 Vulgate have dropped the negative.

12.8 *me* = Marcion's με > ἐν ἐμοι . . . So b c e f ff l Cyprian and Pseudo-Cyprian. The rest of Old Latin and Vulgate are more literal with "*in me*".

12.11 *adducent*. So d, c *perducent*, b q *ducent*. The rest of Old Latin have *inducent*. Marcion προσφέρωσι > εἰσφέρωσι.

12.20 *cuius erunt.* So b c d e f l m q r Vulgate, Cyprian, Irenaeus = Marcion's τινος. ff g^1 g^2 have *cui* (τινι).

13.28 *introeuntes*—so all Old Latin and Lucifer, except d e f g^1 r_2. Some codices of Vulgate have *introire* or *intrare* (so Ambrose), but Wordsworth–White's text does not print this. There is no trace among Old Latin of Marcion's substitution of *justos* for *prophetas,* except in Ambrose.

16.16 *ex quo.* So b c ff i l r. Vulgate g^1 g^2 have *ex eo,* d has *a quo.* These are all agreements with Marcion's ἐξ οὗ > ἀπὸ τότε.

16.25 *hic consolatur.* So all Old Latin and Cyprian, Ambrose. This may support Marcion's ὅδε > ὧδε, but no argument can safely be based on this, because *hic* is both pronoun and adverb. See also note on d.

16.26 *ut hi qui veniunt hoc transire non possint ad vos neque inde hoc transmeare.* There is considerable agreement among Old Latin with this reading. E.g., θέλοντες is omitted also by b ff i l m q r Ambrose, and all Old Latin including m and Vulgate have *hic, huc* or *hoc* (= ὧδε > πρὸς ὑμᾶς) after ἐκεῖθεν. This corresponds largely with Marcion's reading but there is no need to assume that Marcion was the innovator.

16.29 *illi* = Marcion's αὐτῷ: so b c e f ff m q r Vulgate. Also D (not d). But the distinctively Marcionite tampering, viz., omission of Abraham in 29 and 30, finds no correspondence among Old Latin except in e (v. 29 only).

16.30 *ex mortuis.* So all Old Latin except e and Vulgate (d has *de mortuis*). Marcion ἐκ. So D.

16.31 *nec si quis ex mortuis ad illos ierit credent*—so, in the main, a c d e ff i l q r Ambrose, Irenaeus. Marcion οὐδ' ἄν τις ἐκ νεκρῶν ἀπέλθῃ ἀκούσωσιν αὐτοῦ. d ff r have *ierit* with a; the rest have *abierit.* c i l Irenaeus (*credent ei*) and r (*audient eum*) alone reproduce Marcion's αὐτοῦ. d and r have a composite text: *surrexerit et ierit.* r alone uses the verb *audio* (so Marcion).

17.2 *ne nasceretur aut lapis molaris impositus fuisset collo illius et proiectus esset.*
Marcion εἰ οὐκ ἐγεννήθη ἢ . . . περιεκεῖτο . . . καὶ ἔρριπτο (> περικεῖται . . . ἔρριπται).
The insertion of *ne nasceretur* also occurs in b c ff i l q r. These Pluperfects are found in d D also. e has Perfects: *circumjectus sit . . . projectus sit,* which may imply a Pluperfect in the Greek original, as Harnack assumes (he does not give the reading of e). r has Imperfects, and the rest have Presents as b c.

17.10b apparently missing in a. The verse ended "*servi inutiles sumus*" (δοῦλοι ἀχρεῖόι ἐσμεν), although Irico's text adds *facere fecimus,* and Bianchini adds also *quod debuimus.* Gasquet prefers Irico's text and prints it (he says it is more correct "in view of the usual number of lines"). Harnack, p. 223*, suggests tentatively that Marcion omitted 10b because of its harshness.

18.16 *regnum caelorum.* So b c = Marcion's τῶν οὐρανῶν. Cf. Mt. 19. 14.

18.18 omits ἄρχων but has ἐπηρώτησεν (*interrogavit*). So b e ff i l q r.

19.10 *salvum facere et quaerere > quaerere et salvum facere.* S reads exactly as a here, and e has *salvare et quaerere.* Is this due to the influence of Marcion's omission of ζητῆσαι καί? But Marcion's omission may not be deliberate.

20.36 *nec enim iam morituri sunt* = Marcion's μέλλουσι > δύνανται. ff i l q Pseudo-Cyprian have the future *morientur* which seems to imply μέλλουσι. Similarly the reading of e and Cyprian *incipient mori*; and possibly the present *moriuntur* of c.

21.30 *cum florient* = ὅταν προβάλωσιν agrees with Marcion in omission of ἤδη, but not in insertion of τὸν καρπόν. Cf. b.

22.19b–20 omitted. So D d b ff e i l (from *hoc est corpus meum* a goes straight to 21: *attamen ecce manus proditoris*). So b (which has the verses in the order 16, 19a (to *corpus meum*), 17, 18, 21); e is disordered (15, 16, 19a to *corpus meum*) like b. How much of this Marcion had is uncertain.

23.33a *calvariae* as b c d e ff l f Vulgate. Marcion κρανίου.

23.34a omitted (ὁ δὲ Ἰησοῦς . . . τί ποιοῦσιν).
Also omitted in D d (not in b as Harnack, following Tischendorf, says). Harnack thinks it probable (höchst wahrscheinlich) that the words were wholly invented by Marcion and that they found wide acceptance in the textual tradition. It is certainly difficult to explain why the words were dropped out in B D* W Θ Syr[s] sah if they were a part of the original Gospel. But this hardly warrants us giving Marcion credit for their invention.

23.45 *intenebricatus est sol*, Marcion: ἐσκοτίσθη ὁ ἥλιος. So (with similar verb) b c d e f ff l q r Vulgate.

24.6 omits οὐκ ἔστιν ὧδε ἀλλὰ ἠγέρθη. So b c d D e ff r. Marcion omits οὐκ ἔστιν ὧδε. Harnack suggests that Marcion may have deleted the words, because of a reluctance to admit that Christ was not everywhere. But this is not a necessary explanation of the absence of the words from so many MSS. (Harnack does not record the omission of c d ff r.)

24.12 omitted. So b D d e r l and Marcion (not f, as Harnack says). Tendentious omission of Marcion not only because, as Harnack suggests, he did not like to believe Peter was at the tomb, but possibly also because of the implication that clothes provided evidence of the Resurrection.

Sole agreements (i.e., agreements of a alone) with Marcion: 10. 21 and possibly 17. 10.

b and Marcion

5.14 *offer munus pro emundatione tua sicut praecepit moyses ut sit in testimonium vobis.*
This seems to agree with Marcion's τὸ δῶρον ὃ . . . ἵνα ᾖ ὑμῖν εἰς μαρτύριον.
munus: also c.
ut sit in . . . Also a c d e ff q r.
vobis a b c d D ff l q r, but not e f.

5.24 *tolle lectum tuum*, cf. a.

5.34 *possunt*, cf. a; *quamdiu*, cf. a.

5.38 *mittunt*, cf. a.

5.39 omitted, cf. a.

6.3 omits ὁ Ἰησοῦς. So e. Harnack says Marcion reads ὁ Χριστός "with African codices". But he does not set out this African evidence. Von Soden (*Das lateinische Neue Testament in Afrika zur Zeit Cyprians*, p. 462) shows no trace of it either in his printed text or in his apparatus.

6.17 Marcion's reading cannot be reconstructed with any certainty. There is considerable variation among MSS. generally, not among Old Latin only.
b reads *discendit*. So q r. Marcion κατέβη > καταβὰς according to Epiphanius.
ab omni Iudaea et Hierusalem et trans fretum et maritima Tyrii et Sidonis.

trans fretum also a c ff g^1 q r.
g^1 l Vg insert *et* before *Tyrii*; similarly r_2, but with omission of *trans fretum*.
dD c e have also *et aliarum civitatium*. So Marcion.

6.21 Marcion omits νῦν with c l Ambrose.
saturabuntur 3rd person. So e ff g^1 l q r Ambrose; and Marcion. In the next clause b reverts to the 2nd person with ff l q r. Marcion keeps the 3rd plural with e and g^1.

6.22 *beati eritis.* Marcion ἔσεσθε instead of ἐστε. Harnack is wrong to say this *eritis* is otherwise unattested. It is read by b c e ff f g^2 l q r r_2 Vg Cyprian Ambrose.
cum separabunt vos et cum eicient et exprobabunt nomen vestrum Marcion also has *Futures* here; so l and D.
The order of b here, with *exprobabunt* after *eicient*, agrees with a b c ff l q r D Cyprian, but Marcion is on the other side. The Old Latin vary as to the tense, a c e f g^1 g^2 r Vg having Perfect Subjunctive (which is better grammar!), b and l Future Indicative, while ff and q have *oderint* Subjunctive followed by Future Indicatives.

6.25 omits νῦν with Marcion after ἐμπεπλησμένοι.

6.26 *secundum haec faciebant et pseudoprophetis.*
haec also d f ff g^1 q r r_2 Vg Marcion ταῦτα.
et before *pseudoprophetis*: so f q Irenaeus and Marcion.

6.29 *praebe ei.* So c d e f ff g^1 g^2 l q r r_2 Marcion αὐτῷ.
eum qui auferet tibi tunicam et pallium noli prohibere (reading *tunicam* χιτῶνα first, then *pallium* ἱμάτιον). So Marcion and d ff g^1 g^2 l q r Irenaeus.
noli prohibere. So f ff g^1 g^2 q r r_2 Vg. a has *vetare noli*, c *ne prohibeas*, d *ne vetueris.* Marcion's reading προσθὲς αὐτῷ, which Harnack says is otherwise unattested, is apparently supported by e and Irenaeus.

6.31 *et vos.* So c d f g^1 r r_2 Vg. Marcion *ita et vos facite illis.*

6.38 *eadem mensuram*, cf. a. Harnack does not record the agreement of b with Marcion here.

7.38 *rigabat.* So ff g^1 q r. a has *inrigabat.* Marcion ἔβρεξε with D, both Old Syriac, 700.

8.3 *quae ministrabant ei.* So Marcion. Cf. a.

9.22 *post dies tres*, cf. a.

9.35 *dilectus.* So Marcion and d e f q r_2 Ambrose Vg. c has *dilectissimus.*
It is best to regard this agreement simply as assimilation to the text of Matthew and Mark, rather than as due to the influence of Marcionite readings.

9.54f Cf. a.

10.22 inverts the clauses as Marcion does, i.e., has "no one knows the Father" first. This makes a sole agreement of b (among Old Latin) with Marcion; but the disorder is paralleled elsewhere.

10.27 Cf. a.

11.11 implies αὐτοῦ after υἱός. So f ff q and Marcion. b, with Marcion, has the bread-stone clause here, preceding the other two, as also in c d f q r Vg and Gasquet's conjectural restoration of a; and the Curetonian Syriac.

11.42 omits the last clause ταῦτα . . . παρεῖναι. So Marcion and dD. Harnack rightly regards this as a deliberate Marcionite omission: Jesus could not be allowed to concede even a subordinate place to the ethical law.

The more obvious Marcionite emendation (κλῆσιν for κρίσιν) in the previous line has left no effects on non-Marcionite texts.

11.48 *non consentientes*, cf. a.

12.5 *mittere*. So all Old Latin (*a mittendi*) and Vg.
Marcion βαλεῖν (so D) > ἐμβαλεῖν.

12.10 *qui autem in spiritu sancti dixerit*. So c e ff Ambrose. Marcion ὃς ὃ ἄν εἴπῃ εἰς . . . .

12.20 *cuius*, cf. a.

12.38 *vespertina vigilia*. So Marcion ἑσπερίνῃ φυλακῇ instead of ἐν τῇ δευτέρᾳ κἀν ἐν τῇ τρίτῃ. . . .
So c d e ff i l Irenaeus, which, however, have the other two clauses as well.

12.51 *pacem veni mittere in terram*. So Marcion and l q r r_2.

12.59 *quadrantem*. So all Old Latin except g^1 g^2 (not cited in Sabatier) and a (which is missing at this point). Vg has *minutum* (λεπτόν) Marcion κοδράντην, so D.

13.27 *iniquitatis*. So a a_2 c d e ff l q r_2. f i r have *qui operamini iniquitatem*. This use of *iniquitas* may imply ἀνομία in the underlying Greek rather than ἀδικία, and if so we should have a case of correspondence with Marcion. But no argument can be based on this because the Old Latin use *iniquitas* to render ἀδικία as well as ἀνομία.

13.28 *introeuntes*, cf. a.

16.16 *ex quo*, cf. a.

16.25 *hic consolatur*, cf. a.

16.26 Cf. a.

16.31 Cf. a.

17.2 *ne nasceretur aut lapis molaris . . . imponatur . . . et proiciatur*, cf. a.

18.16 *regnum caelorum*, cf. a.

18.18 omits ἄρχων, cf. a.

21.30 *cum producunt iam ex se fructum*. This corresponds with Marcion's καρπόν after προβάλωσιν.
So c d e f ff g^1 g^2 l i q r_2 Ambrose Vg.
Marcion's omission of ἤδη is also found in a d e r and in f (unless *incipient* implies it).

23.2 *hunc invenimus subvertentem gentem nostram et solventem legem nostram et prophetas et prohibentem*. . . .

solventem legem nostram et prophetas is an agreement with Marcion's insertion of καταλύοντα τὸν νόμον καὶ τοὺς προφήτας. It is found also in c e ff i l q r_2. c d have *vetantem* instead of *prohibentem*, which is a further correspondence with Marcion (viz., with his κελεύοντα μὴ > κωλύοντα. Harnack is wrong to say Marcion is alone in reading κελεύοντα. Most probably this is to be regarded as an addition of Marcion's.

23.33 *calvariae*, cf. a.

23.34 διαμεριζόμενοι . . . κλήρους omitted in b alone of Old Latin. So Marcion. Harnack does not mention this agreement of b with Marcion.

23.45 *obscuratus est sol*, cf. a.

24.6 omits οὐκ ἔστιν ὧδε ἀλλὰ ἠγέρθη, cf. a.

24.12 omitted, cf. a.

Sole agreements between b and Marcion: 10. 22; 23. 24.

d and Marcion

4.16 *veniens autem in nazared ubi erat nutricatus introibit* [*sic!*]. *secundum consuetudinem in sabbato in synagogam.* d omits *suam* after *consuetudinem*: this corresponds to Marcion's omission of αὐτῷ. A glance at the parallel Greek of D—ἐλθὼν δὲ εἰς Ναζαρὲδ ὅπου ἦν κατὰ τὸ εἰωθὸς ἐν τῇ ἡμέρᾳ τῶν σαββάτων εἰς τὴν συναγωγήν—suggests the possibility that d may originally have omitted the statement that Jesus was brought up at Nazareth. Certainly D omits this, as Marcion himself must have done. The Marcionite Christ was not brought up at Nazareth; he came down as a "saving spirit" to the Galilean city of Capernaum (cf. Marcion's reading at 4. 31) in the fifteenth year of Tiberius. So Tertullian 1. 19; 4. 7. The exact reading of Marcion here, unfortunately, cannot be discovered from Tertullian 4. 7–8 nor from any other ancient source. The scanty evidence is set out in Zahn's *Geschichte des N.T. Kanons* II 457 more clearly than in Harnack. Harnack is emphatic that Marcion omitted τεθραμμένος and that we have here a case of Marcionite influence on D. One would have expected Marcion to omit κατὰ τὸ εἰωθὸς αὐτῷ, but in view of the statement of Ephraim (quoted in Zahn): *et quaenam erat consuetudo ei, qui tum advenit?* it is clear that the Marcionite text used by Ephraim contained these words. It may be that αὐτῷ was omitted as in D (and also a c d e), and that κατὰ τὸ εἰωθὸς was construed with ἦλθεν εἰς Ναζαρέθ. But we must beware of arguing in a circle, i.e., of assuming that Marcion did influence D, and then using D to reconstruct Marcion's reading.

5.14 Cf. b.

5.24 *tolle grabattum tuum*, cf. a.

5.34 Cf. a.

5.36 *tunica rude* (ablative). d alone of Old Latin seems to use *rudis* rather than *novus* here. Does *novus* in all the others imply that they read νέος with Marcion? Not necessarily. D has καινοῦ.

5.38 *mittent*. D has present tense, cf. a.

5.39 omitted, cf. a.

6.5 comes between 6. 10 and 6. 11 in d and D. So Marcion (see Harnack, p. 190*).

6.17 *ex omni iudaea et aliarum civitatium venientium audire eum*, cf. note on b.

6.22 *quando odierint*. D μισήσουσι, cf. b.

6.25 dD omit νῦν, cf. a.

6.26 dD omit πάντες after εἴπωσι. So Marcion and Old Syriac and Tatian. d is alone among Old Latin in this.
d also (not D) agrees with Marcion in reading *haec*, not *eadem*, cf. b.

6.29 *ei*. Marcion αὐτῷ, cf. b.
d (not D) has *tunicam* first, *pallium* second, cf. b.

6.31 *et vos*, cf. b.

6.34 *recipere*, cf. c.

7.38 *implevit* D ἔβρεξε, cf. b.

8.24 dD alone omit τοῦ ὕδατος after κλύδωνι.

8.28 *fili altissimi*, without *dei*, so D and g^1.

9.22 *post tres dies resurgere*, cf. a.

9.30 *erant autem moyses et helias visi in claritate.* So D and c g^1 g^2 l q r r_2 Vg; and cf. f. Marcion had simply Ἠλίας καὶ Μωυσῆς ἐν δόξῃ αὐτοῦ.

9.35 *dilectus*, cf. b.

9.54–5 cf. a.

10.1 *ostendit*, D ἀπέδειξε, cf. a.

10.22 dD omit μου after πατρός, cf. a.

10.24 dD omit καὶ βασιλεῖς (so a e ff i) and insert ὑμεῖς before ἀκουετε.

10.26 D omits τί before γέγραπται. So Marcion. d inserts the necessary *quid*, but this may be a relic of Marcionite influence in D. For a similar possibility see 11. 2.

10.27 Cf. a.

11.2 *sanctificetur nomen tuum super nos* D ἐφ' ἡμᾶς. Marcion's text probably contained this prepositional phrase, though it is uncertain. It was a prayer for the coming of the Holy Spirit. See Harnack, p. 207*, and cf. note on 10. 26.

11.11 dD contain the bread-stone clause first. So Marcion, cf. a.

11.32 dD omit. ?Marcionite influence. Marcion omitted vv. 30–32.

11.42 Cf. b.

11.48 dD μαρτυρεῖτε μὴ συνευδοκεῖν, cf. a.

12.11 *adducent*, cf. a.

12.20 *cuius*, cf. a.

12.38 *vespertina custodia . . . et si secunda vel tertia*, cf. b.

12.47 Cf. c.

12.59 *quadrantem*, cf. b.

13.27 *iniquitatis* D ἀνομίας, cf. b.

16.16 *a quo*, cf. a.

16.25 *hic consolatur* D ὧδε, cf. a. Is ὅδε a mistranslation back into Greek from Latin *hic*? There is little attestation for ὅδε in Greek MSS., but Tatian had it. See Harnack, p. 221*.

16.26 D has ὧδε after ἐκεῖθεν, d has *hic*, cf. a.

16.29 *dixit autem abraham*, D adds αὐτῷ, cf. a.

16.31 *nec si quis ex mortuis surrexerit et ierit credent*, cf. a.

17.2 *expediebat*, Marcion συνέφερεν e *expedit* (cf. D συνφέρει). The rest of Old Latin have *utilius est* (*utilius fuerat* b) rendering the Greek λυσιτελεῖ.
circumdatus esset . . . proiectus esset. D περιέκειτο . . . ἔρριπτο, cf. a.

18.35 implies ἐπαιτῶν before ἐκάθητο, as actually in D and Marcion. Cf. e.

20.36 *possunt* D μέλλουσι, cf. a.

21.30 *cum produxerint fructum suum*, cf. b.

22.19b–20 omitted in Dd, cf. a.

23.2 *vetantem tributa dare caesari*, cf. b.
D agrees here with the usual text.

23.33 *calvariae*, cf. a.

23.34a omitted, cf. a.

23.45 *obscuratus autem est sol*, cf. a.
dD both omit ἐσχίσθη . . . μέσον.

23.56 dD alone among Old Latin omit κατὰ τὴν ἐντολήν.
Marcion read κατὰ τὸν νόμον.

24.6 Cf. a.
quanta, D ὅσα, cf. c.

24.12 omitted in both dD, cf. a.

24.37 *fantasma videre*, so D. According to Harnack, p. 239*, Apelles is the only other witness for this reading beside Marcion himself.

24.39 The order of words here is worth noticing:—

spiritus ossa non habet nec carnes
τὸ πνεῦμα ὀστᾶ οὐκ ἔχει καὶ σάρκας.

This might be explained on the hypothesis that Marcion's deletion of σάρκα καὶ at first had some effect on the general textual tradition; but that later the words were re-inserted.

Possible Marcionite influence in 5. 39; 24. 37; 24. 39.
Less probable Marcionite influence in 4. 16; 8. 28; 54–5.
Sole agreements: 4. 16?; 6. 26; 8. 24; 17. 2? (*expediebat*).

c and Marcion

4.16 *secundum consuetudinem*, cf. d.
5.14 *offer munus pro emundatione tua sicut praecepit Moyses ut sit in testimonium vobis istud*, cf. b.
5.24 *tolle grabatum tuum*, cf. a.
5.34 *possunt*, cf. a.
quandiu, cf. a.
5.38 *mittunt*, cf. a.
5.39 omitted, cf. a.
6.17 *de tota Iudaea et Ierusalem et trans fretum et maritimi Tyri et Sidonis et aliarum civitatum*, cf. b.
6.21 omits νῦν after πεινῶντες. So Marcion and l.
6.22 *eritis* cf. b.
quando separaverint . . ., cf. b.
6.25 without νῦν after ἐμπεπλησμένοι, cf. a.
6.29 *praebe illi*, cf. b.
6.31 *et vos*, cf. b.
6.34 *recipere*. So d f ff l q r.
6.38 *bonam cumulatam superfundentem*. I.e., apparently omits σεσαλευμένον with Marcion. Cf. r and Old Syriac (not noted by Harnack). e appears to omit πεπιεσμένον. There is considerable divergence among Old Latin in the Latin words used here, but all except c e r have four adjectives. Marcion's καὶ linking πεπιεσμένον and ὑπερεκχυννόμενον occurs between the second, third and fourth adjectives in f and Vulgate.
qualem mensuram . . ., cf. a.
8.3 *quae **et** ministrabant **eis**,* cf. a.
8.25 *qui et ventis*, cf. a.
mari. So f ff g^1 g^2 q r r_2 Vulgate; and Old Syriac.
9.22 *post tridum*, cf. a.
9.24 omits οὗτος, cf. a.
9.30 *erant autem Moyses et Helias visi in claritate*, cf. d D.
9.35 *dilectissimus*, cf. b.
9.54 + *sicut fecit Helias*, cf. a.
9.55–6 + *et dixit nescitis quali spiritu sitis. Filius enim hominis non venit animas perdere, sed salvas facere*, cf. a.
10.1 *probavit*, cf. a.
10.21 *Domine pater*, cf. e.

10.22 omits μου, cf. a.

10.27 omits ἐν ὅλῃ τῇ διανοίᾳ σου, cf. a.

11.11 contains the bread-stone clause, cf. b.

11.48 = i l, cf. a.

12.10 *si quis autem in spiritu sancto dixerit*, cf. b for this parallelism with Marcion. But the addition of *neque in hoc saeculo neque in futuro* at the end of this verse in c (so d) shows that the text is assimilated to Mt. 12. 32.

12.11 *perducent*, cf. a.

12.20 *cuius*, cf. a.

12.38 *et si venerit vespertina vigilia . . . et si in secunda et si in tertia*, cf. b.

12.47 omits ἑτοιμάσας ἢ with Marcion. So d e g^1 l q r Irenaeus; i ff r_2 omit ἢ ποιήσας.
g^2 omits the words καὶ μὴ ἑτοιμάσας . . . θέλημα αὐτοῦ.

13.28 *introeuntes*, cf. a.

16.16 *ex quo*, cf. a.

16.31 Cf. a.

17.2 *ne nasceretur aut lapis molae imponatur . . . et projiciatur . . .*, cf. a.

18.16 *regnum caelorum*, cf. a.

20.19 *principes sacerdotum et scribae*. So f ff g^1 i l q r Vulgate. Marcion omits.

20.36 *moriuntur*, cf. a.

21.8 *ego sum Christus*. This insertion of *Christus* with Marcion is also found in e ff g^1 i l q r_2 s.

21.27 *venientem de caelo* = Marcion's ἀπὸ τῶν οὐρανῶν (de caelis Tertullian). So c only among Old Latin, but cf. l.

21.30 *cum producunt iam ex se fructum*, cf. b.

22.19–20 in full.

23.2 Cf. b. c has *evertentem* instead of *subvertentem*; a also had *evertentem*, though this has now become illegible (see Gasquet).

23.5 *et filios nostros et uxores avertit a nobis: non enim baptizatur sicut nos*. This includes the words καὶ ἀποστρέφοντα τὰς γυναίκας καὶ τὰ τέκνα, which Marcion had in verse 2 after φόρους μὴ δοῦναι. e exactly agrees with c in this insertion (except that e has: *sicut et nos*, and goes on: *nec se mundant*). c and e alone of all ancient texts support Marcion here, and it is very probable that this is a case of a tendentious insertion of Marcion's finding a place in the Western textual tradition.

23.33 *calvariae*, cf. a.

23.45 *tenebricavit sol*, cf. a.

24.6 Omits οὐκ ἔστιν ὧδε καί. So Marcion, cf. a. *quae* so Marcion. All other Old Latin except d read *qualiter* (*sicut* a). d reads *quanta*, which is probably a conformation with D ὅσα.

24.38 *in cor vestrum*. So d e. a b ff read *in corde vestro*. f has *in cordibus vestris*. Vg *in corda vestra*. Harnack prints εἰς τὴν καρδίαν for Marcion tentatively.

e and Marcion

Lacunae 8. 30–48 and 11. 4–24.

4.16 *cum venisset autem in nazara ubi fuit nutritus introivit sabbato in synagogam et surrexit legere*. Omits *secundum consuetudinem suam*. For the possibility that this is not accidental, but a trace of Marcionite emendation, cf. note on d.

5.14 *offert* [*sic!*] *illi pro emundatione tua quod praecepit moyses ut in testimonio sit illis*, cf. b.

5.24 *surge et vade* (i.e., omits καὶ ἄρας τὸ κλινίδιον).

5.25 *grabattum*, cf. a.

5.34 *non possunt . . . quamdiu*, cf. a.

5.38 *mittunt*, cf. a.

5.39 omitted, cf. a.

6.2 *Pharisaei*. So Marcion apparently (*accusant Pharisaei*, says Tertullian, not *quidam Pharisaeorum*. Presumably, therefore, Marcion read φαρισαῖοι rather than τινες τῶν φ).

6.3 simply *dixit*, cf. b.

6.17 *de tota iudea et hierusalem et de transmarinis tyro et sidone et aliarum civitatium*, cf. note on b.

6.21 *saturabuntur*, cf. b.
ridebunt. So Marcion and g[1].

6.22 *beati eritis*, cf. b.

6.25 omits νῦν after ἐμπεπλησμένοι, cf. a.

6.29 *praebe ei*, cf. b.
ei qui a te auferet palleum tuum, remitte tunicam. The reading *remitte* seems to correspond to Marcion's προσθὲς αὐτῷ καὶ > μὴ κωλύσῃς. e and Irenaeus are alone among Old Latin in this agreement with Marcion, cf. note on b.

6.35 *altissimi dei*. e only. Harnack makes no remark, but surely this is a possible case of the influence of the Marcionite substitution of θεοῦ for an original ὑψίστου alone. But cf. 8. 28, where e has *dii altissimi* and original text was θεοῦ ὑψίστου. Marcion always deleted ὑψίστου.

6.38 *mensura bona commota superfundens dabitur* . . . i.e., apparently omits πεπιεσμένον, cf. c *qua enim mensura mensuraveritis eadem et metietur vobis*, cf. a.

7.9 *talem fidem*, so r and Syriac, Tatian. Harnack is wrong to say there is no other evidence for this reading of Marcion's.

7.38 The whole verse reads: *et stetit retro ad pedes eius flens et lacrimis suis lababat* [*sic!*] *pedes eius et unguebat unguento*; i.e., omits more than Marcion.

8.3 e reads *eis* before *ministrabant*. Hans von Soden (*Das Lateinische Neue Testament in Afrika*, p. 468) prints *ei* in the text and relegates *eis* to the apparatus—with what authority is not clear, cf. a.

9.18 *homines* = οἱ ἄνθρωποι. Marcion.
Probably not tendentious but assimilation to Mt. 16. 13. Tatian read similarly, according to Ephraim.

9.22 *post triduum resurgere*, cf. a.

9.24 *illam* = αὐτὴν rather than the second τὴν ψυχὴν αὐτοῦ. e only of Old Latin agrees with Marcion in this.

9.35 *dilectus*, cf. b.

9.41 omits καὶ διεστραμμένη. e alone of Old Latin agrees with Marcion here. But Syr^{cur} and Syr^{sin} $Tat.^{eph}$ also support Marcion.

9.55–6 Cf. a.

10.1 *elegit*, cf. a.

10.9 omits ἐφ' ὑμᾶς. Only e of Old Latin agrees with Marcion in this. Harnack's apparatus, following Tischendorf, attributes the omission also to one scribe of f. Bianchini does not note this, and Wordsworth–White's apparatus says nothing of it.

10.21 *Domine pater* (> *pater Domine*) so c f ff i r_2. Is this alteration of the place of *pater* due to Marcion's omission of it?
Omits et prudentibus (καὶ συνετῶν). So r_2.

10.24 Omits καὶ βασιλεῖς, cf. a.

11.46 omits ὑμῶν after δακτύλῳ. So c Marcion.

11.48 *nempe consentitis non placere vobis facta patrum vestorum* . . . , cf. a. *non placere* corresponds to the μὴ συνευδοκεῖν of Marcion and D. But for the verse as a whole in e the scribe allowed himself a free hand! So Buchanan *J.T.S.*, Jan. 1906, p. 250.

12.10 *qui autem dixerit in spiritu sancto*, cf. b.

12.38 *et si venerit vespertina vigilia*, cf. b.

12.47 *et non paruerit ad voluntatem ejus* for καὶ μὴ ἑτοιμάσας ἢ ποιήσας πρὸς τὸ θέλημα αὐτοῦ, cf. c

12.59 *quadrantem*, cf. b.

16.12 *quod meum est.* τὸ ἐμόν Marcion. So i l (also 157).

16.25 *hic consolabitur*, cf. a.
Abraham autem dixit > *dixit autem Abraham.* So Marcion.

16.26 Cf. a.

16.29 *dicit illi* (omits *Abraham*), cf. a.

16.31 Cf. a.

17.2 *expedit*, cf. d.

18.18 omits ἄρχων, cf. a.

18.35 *quidam mendicus sedebat*, cf. d.

19.10 *salvare et quaerere*, cf. a.

20.19 omits ἐν αὐτῇ τῇ ὥρᾳ. So only e and Marcion.

20.36 *neque enim incipient mori.* So Cyprian, cf. a.

21.8 *ego sum xps*, cf. c.

21.30 *cum coeperint mittere fructus suos*, cf. b.

21.32 *non transiet caelum istud doneque omnia perficiantur. caelum istud*—only e and Marcion. For *perficiantur* cf. Marcion *peragantur* (Tertullian) > γένηται. "Dieser Vers ist eine Schöpfung Marcions" (Harnack, p. 232*).

22.68 omits ἐὰν δὲ ἐρωτήσω οὐ μὴ ἀποκριθῆτε. These words may have been omitted by Marcion; there is no ancient attestation of their rejection by him.

23.2 Cf. b.

23.5 Cf. c.

23.33 *calbariae* [sic!], cf. a.

23.45 *obscuratus est sol*, cf. a.

24.6 omits οὐκ ἔστιν ὧδε ἀλλὰ ἠγέρθη, cf. a.

24.12 omitted, cf. a.

24.38 Cf. c.

Sole agreements: 6. 2; 9. 24; 9. 41; 10. 9; 20. 19; 21. 32; ?22. 68.

f and Marcion

5.24 *tolle lectum tuum* . . . , cf. a.

5.34 *quamdiu*, cf. a.

5.38 *mittunt*, cf. a.

6.22 *beati* ***eritis***, cf. b.

6.26 has *et* before *prophetis*, cf. b. [f has here the reading *prophetis* > *pseudoprophetis*.

g1 and l also read *prophetis* and some codices of Vulgate (see Sabatier), but Wordsworth–White print *prophetis* as the Vulgate reading.]
secundum haec, cf. b.

6.29 *praebe illi*, cf. b.
6.31 *et vos*, cf. b.
6.34 *recipere*, cf. c.
6.38 *eadem* ***enim*** *mensura* . . . , cf. a.
8.24 *tempestati* ***maris***. Conformity with Mt. and Mark as in Marcion.
8.25 *mari*, cf. c.
9.24 omits οὗτος, cf. a.
9.30 *erant autem* M et H ***qui*** *visi sunt in gloria* . . . , cf. d., but note that f is translating οἱ ὀφθέντες, and agreement with Marcion is only partial, compared with d etc.
9.35 *dilectus* cf. b.
9.54 *sicut et Helias fecit*, cf. a.
9.55 *nescitis cuius spiritus estis*, cf. a.
10.9 Cf. e.
10.21 *domine pater*, cf. e.
11.11 αὐτοῦ after υἱός, and also the bread-stone clause, cf. b.
11.48 *testimonium perhibetis consentientes* . . . , cf. a.
12.20 *cu**ius***, cf. a.
12.50 *quadrantem*, cf. b.
16.25 *hic consolatur*, cf. a.
16.26 Cf. a.
16.29 Cf. a.
20.19 *principes sacerdotum et scribae*, cf. c.
20.36 *neque enim ultra mori poterunt* = Vg only, cf. a.
21.30 *cum incipient ostendere fructum* . . . , cf. b.
22.19–20 in full.
23.33 *calvari**ae***, cf. a.
23.45 *et obscuratus est sol*, cf. a.

ff and Marcion

Lacuna 9. 48–10. 20, 11. 45–12. 6.

5.14 *ut sit in testimonium hoc vobis*. So Marcion, cf. b.
5.24 ***tolle*** *lectum tuum et vade* . . . , cf. a.
5.34 *possum* (corrected to *possunt*) . . . *dum*. For *possunt*, cf. a.
5.38 *mittunt*, cf. a.
ff has after *mittunt*: ***et utraque conservantur***, cf. d.
5.39 Omitted, cf. a.
6.17 Cf. b.
6.20 ***ipsorum***, cf. *illorum* Marcion. Influence of Mt.—but ff is the only Old Latin which has 3rd person here.
6.21 *saturab**untur***, cf. b. ff has 2nd plural in next clause *Setis* . . . *ridebitis*. So b.
6.22 *beati* ***eritis***, cf. b. For order of following words see b.
6.25 *vae vobis qui saturati estis*—without *nunc*, cf. a.
6.26 *secundum haec*, cf. b.

6.29 ***prebe* [*sic!*] *ei* *alteram***, cf. b.
rest of verse = b.
6.34 ***re**cipere*, cf. c.
6.38 *eadem mensuram quam*, cf. a.
7.26 *sed quid existis videre prophetam*, i.e., omits ναὶ . . . προφητοῦ, which is partly absent from Marcion.
7.38 *rigabat* = b.
8.25b *quisnam est hic* ***qui*** *ventis imperat* ***et mari***, *et obaudiunt ei*. For *qui*, cf. a. For *mari*, cf. c.
9.22 *post tres dies resurgere*, cf. a.
9.24b omits οὗτος. So a.
10.21 ***domine pater***, cf. e.
10.24 omits καὶ βασιλεῖς, cf. a.
10.27 omits ἐν ὅλῃ τῇ διανοίᾳ σου, cf. a.
11.11 implies αὐτοῦ after υἱός, cf. b.
12.10 *in spiritu autem sancto qui dixerit*, cf. b.
12.38 *et si venerit vespertina vigilia* . . . , cf. b.
12.47 omits ἢ ποιήσας, cf. c.
12.59 *quadrantem*, cf. b.
13.28 *introeuntes*, cf. a.
16.16 *ex quo*, cf. a.
16.25 *hic consolatur*, cf. a.
16.26 Cf. a.
16.29 Cf. a.
16.31 Cf. a.
17.2 *ne nasceretur*, cf. a.
18.18 omits ἄρχων, cf. a.
20.36 *neque enim morientur*, cf. a.
21.8 adds *christus*, cf. c.
21.30 *cum producunt iam ex se fructum*, cf. b.
22.19b–20 omitted, cf. a.
23.2 = b.
23.33 *ad locum qui* **dicitur** *calvariae*, cf. a. ff is alone in reading *dicitur* which corresponds to Marcion's λεγέμενον.
23.45 *et obscuratus est sol*, cf. a.
24.6 omits οὐκ ἔστιν ὧδε ἀλλὰ ἠγέρθη, cf. a.

Sole agreements: 6. 20; 7. 26; 23. 33 (*dicitur*), but these are not significant.

g¹ and Marcion

5.24 *tolle lectum tuum*, cf. a.
5.34 *possunt*, cf. a.
5.38 *mittunt*, cf. a.
et utrique conservabuntur (after *mittunt*), cf. d.
6.17 Cf. b.
6.21 *saturabuntur*, cf. b.
ridebunt, cf. e.
6.26 *secundum haec*, cf. b.

6.29 *praebe illi*, cf. b.
tunicam . . . pallium, cf. b.
6.31 *et vos*, cf. b.
6.38 *eadem mensura*, cf. a.
7.38 *rigabat*, cf. b.
8.25 *mari*, cf. c.
8.28 *altissimi* without *Dei*, as dD.
9.18 *homines* instead of *turbae*. So Marcion, but no significance attaches to this sole concurrence of g^1 (among Old Latin) with Marcion, as the reading is best explained as a case of assimilation to Matthew.
9.30 = Vulgate and d.
12.47 (apparently from Sabatier) omits ἑτοιμάσας ἤ, cf. c.
16.16 *ex eo*, cf. a.
21.30 Cf. b.

g^2 and Marcion

6.22 *eritis* = Vulgate, cf. b.
6.25 without νῦν after ἐμπεπλησμένοι, cf. a.
6.29 *praebe illi*, cf. b.
tunicam . . . pallium, cf. b.
6.38 *eadem mensura*, cf. a.
8.25 *mari*, cf. c.
9.30 = Vulgate and d.
10.25 omits *aeternam*. So Marcion. Harnack's apparatus does not record this correspondence with Marcion. Tertullian (quoted fully in Harnack, pp. 206* f.) makes it clear that Marcion struck out αἰώνιον under the influence of his theory that eternal life could only be given by the Stranger God, and that the Creator neither had the power to confer it, nor made any claim to do so in his Law. We have therefore a clear case of Marcionite influence on g^2.
12.47 omits καὶ μὴ ἑτοιμάσας . . . θέλημα αὐτοῦ, cf. c.
16.16 *ex eo*, cf. a.
21.8 *ego sum Christus*, cf. c.
21.30 Cf. b.

Sole agreement: 10. 25.

i and Marcion

Contains only Luke 10. 6–23. 10.

10.21 *domine pater*, cf. e.
10.24 omits καὶ βασιλεῖς, cf. a.
and the last clause καὶ ἀκοῦσαι . . . ἤκουσαν, cf. a.
10.27 omits ἐν ὅλῃ τῇ διανοίᾳ σου, cf. a.
11.48 *testificamini consentire operibus . . . ?* omits μή. So. cl, cf. a.
12.11 omits συναγώγας, so i only among Old Latin, but it looks as if *synagogas* may have dropped out accidentally.
12.38 *vespertina hora vigilia . . . et si secunda et tertia*, cf. b.
12.47 omits ἢ ποιήσας, cf. c.
12.59 *quadrantem*, cf. b.
13.28 *introeuntes*, cf. a.

16.12 *quod meum est.* So Marcion, cf. e.
16.16 *ex quo,* cf. a.
16.25 *hic consolatur,* cf. a.
16.26 Cf. a.
16.31 Cf. a.
17.2 *ne nasceretur,* cf. a.
18.18 omits ἄρχων. So a.
20.36 *neque enim morientur.* So ff q l, cf. a.
21.8 adds *Christus,* cf. c.
21.30 Cf. b.
22.19b–20 omitted.
22.70 *vos dicitis* = Marcion's ὑμεῖς λέγετε without ὅτι ἐγώ εἰμι.
23.2 = b.

Sole agreement: ? 12. 11; 22. 70.

l and Marcion

5.14 *in testimonium* ***vobis*** (without *ut sit* . . . as b, etc. Harnack, p. 189*, is wrong to say l reads ***ut sit*** *in testimonium vobis.*
5.24 *tolle lectum,* cf. a.
5.38 *mittunt,* cf. a.
5.39 omitted, cf. a.
6.17 Cf. b.
6.21 omits νῦν after πεινῶντες, cf. c.
saturabuntur, cf. b.
6.22 *eritis,* cf. b.
cum separabunt . . . nomen vestrum = b.
6.25 omits νῦν after ἐμπεπλησμένοι, cf. a.
6.29 *praebe ei.* So b.
tunicam . . . palleum, cf. b.
6.34 *recipere,* cf. c.
6.38 Cf. a.
8.3 *illi,* cf. a.
8.25 *et mari,* cf. c.
9.22 *post tres dies,* cf. a.
9.24 omits οὗτος, cf. a.
9.30 So Dd.
10.1 *designavit,* cf. a.
10.22 omits μου after πατρός, cf. a.
10.24 omits καὶ βασιλεῖς, and καὶ ἀκοῦσαι . . . ἤκουσαν. So a i.
10.27 omits ἐν ὅλῃ τῇ διανοίᾳ, cf. a.
11.48 *testificamini* ***consentire*** *operibus* . . . . So f i c r r_2, cf. a. (? Marcion's (Dd) reading with μή dropped).
12.20 *cuius,* cf. a.
12.38 *et si venerit* ***vespertina vigilia*** . . . ***Etsi secunda et si tertia beati sunt,*** cf. b.
12.47 omits ἑτοιμάσας ἤ, cf. c.
12.51 *mittere,* cf. b.
12.59 *quadrantem,* cf. b.
13.28 *introeuntes,* cf. a.

16.12 *meum*, cf. e.
16.26 Cf. a.
16.31 Cf. a.
17.2 *ut non nasceretur aut*, cf. a.
18.18 omits ἄρχων. So a.
20.36 *neque enim morientur*. So ff i q, cf. a.
21.8 adds *Christus*, cf. c.
21.27 *in nubibus* **caeli** seems to show influence of Marcion's reading ἀπὸ τῶν οὐρανῶν which Harnack regards as tendentious (mit irdischem Nebel sollte Christus nichts zu tun haben, p. 231*).
21.28 *adpropiavit*, cf. r. Cf. Old Syriac (cur and sin).
21.30 *cum producunt iam ex se fructum*, cf. b.
22.19b–20 omitted.
23.2 b (except *plebem* for *gentem*).
23.33 *calvariae*, cf. a.
23.45 Cf. a.
24.12 omitted, cf. a.

Sole agreement: 21. 27.

m and Marcion

p. 308 quotes Luke 1. 35, p. 322 quotes Luke 1. 34–5.
pp. 341–2 quote Luke 14. 16–20, 24.
p. 381 quotes Luke 17, 3–4.
p. 412 ,, Luke 11. 41.
,, 21. 1–4 (again p. 584).
,, 12. 33–4.
p. 415 ,, Luke 11. 5–10.
21. 36.
p. 571 Luke 10. 16.
p. 583 Luke 2. 36–7.
p. 618 Luke 16. 19–31. v. 26, cf. a.
v. 29 αὐτῷ, cf. a.
p. 620 Luke 12. 13–21 v. 20 *cuius erunt*.

The quotations are mostly from the Old Testament and of the Gospels mostly from Matthew. The few noted above from Luke reveal divergences from the Vulgate, justifying its classification as pre-Vulgate (or at least, not conformed to Vulgate); but no agreement with Marcion.

q and Marcion

5.14 *ut sit in testimonium* **hoc** *vobis*, cf. b.
5.24 **tolle** *lectum* . . . , cf. a.
5.38 *mittunt*, cf. a.
6.17 *et descendit*, etc., cf. b.
6.21 *saturab***untur**, cf. b.
6.22 *eritis*, cf. b.
6.25 omits νῦν after ἐμπεπλησμένοι, cf. a.
6.26 *secundum haec*, cf. b.
et speoprofetis [*sic!*] Marcion's καὶ τοῖς ψευδοπροφήταις; so b.

6.29 *prebe* **ei**, cf. b.
tunicam first, then *pallium*. So Marcion, cf. b.

6.30 omitted.
The second half of the verse (καὶ ἀπὸ τοῦ αἴροντος τὰ σὰ μὴ ἀπαίτει) is not mentioned by Tertullian as being in Marcion's text. It does not necessarily follow that Marcion omitted the words, however.

6.34 *recipere*, cf. c.

6.38 *eadem mensura qua* . . . , cf. a.

7.38 *rigabat*, cf. b.

8.3 *illi*, cf. a.

8.25 *mari*, cf. c.

9.22 *post tres dies resurgere*, cf. a.

9.30 *erant autem Moses et Elias visi in maiestate* = dD.

9.35 *dilectus*, cf. b.

9.54–6 Cf. a.

10.24 *et iusti* instead of καὶ βασιλεῖς. So r, cf. a.

11.11 αὐτοῦ after υἱός, and also the bread-stone clause, cf. b.

11.28 *qui audiunt verbum dei* ***et facient***: Marcion's ποιοῦντες. q alone of Old Latin agrees with Marcion here.

11.48 *non consentientes operibus* . . . , cf. a.

12.20 *cuius*, cf. a.

12.47 *et non paruerit ad voluntatem illius*, i.e., omits ἑτοιμάσας ἤ, cf. c.

12.51 *mittere*, cf. b.

12.59 *quadrantem*, cf. b.

13.28 ***introeuntes***, cf. a.

16.25 *hic consolatur*, cf. a.

16.26 Cf. a.

16.31 Cf. a.

17.2 *ne nasceretur*, cf. a.

18.18 omits ἄρχων. So a.

20.34 *respondens* = Marcion's ἀποκριθείς. So only q among Old Latin.

20.36 *morientur* = ff i l, cf. a.

21.8 adds *Christus*, cf. c.

21.30 *cum producunt iam ex se fructum*, cf. b.

22.19–20 full text.

23.2 = b (except that q has *plebem* > *gentem*).

23.45 Cf. a.

Sole agreements: ? 6. 30; 11. 28; 20. 34.

r and Marcion

5.14 *ut sit in testimonium hoc vobis*, cf. b.

5.24 *surge* ***et tolle grabattum***. . . . See note on a.

5.34 *quamdiu dum*, cf. a.

5.38 *mittunt*, cf. a.

5.39 omitted, cf. a.

6.17 *et descendit*, etc., cf. b.

6.21 *satura**buntur***, cf. b.

6.22 *eritis*, cf. b.

6.25 omits νῦν, cf. a.
6.26 *secundum haec*, cf. b.
6.29 *praebe illi*, cf. b.
pallium second, cf. b.
6.31 *et vos*, cf. b.
6.34 ***recipere***, cf. c.
6.38 *bonam cumulatam supereffluentem . . .*
? = omission of σεσαλευμένον with Marcion, cf. c.
eadem mensura qua . . ., cf. a.
7.9 *talem* = Marcion's τοιαύτην > τοσαύτην, so e.
7.38 ***coepit plorare et lacrimis*** *rigabat*, cf. b.
8.25 *qui et*, cf. a.
mari, cf. c.
9.22 *post diem tertium resurgere*, cf. a.
9.30 *erant autem Moses et Elias visi in maiestate*= dD.
9.54–6 Cf. a.
10.24 *et iusti* instead of καὶ βασιλεῖς = q, cf. a.
10.27 omits ἐν ὅλῃ τῇ διανοίᾳ, cf. a.
11.11 has the bread-stone clause, cf. b.
11.48 ***quia*** *consentitis operibus patrum*, cf. a.
12.20 *cuius*, cf. a.
12.38 *vespertina vigilia* = b.
12.47 *et non paruerit ad (volun) tatem eius*, i.e., omits ἑτοιμάσας ἤ, cf. c.
12.51 *mittere*, cf. b.
12.59 *quadrantem*, cf. b.
13.28 ***introeuntes***, cf. a.
16.16 *ex quo*, cf. a.
16.25 *hic consolatur*, cf. a.
16.26 Cf. a.
16.31 *nec si quis ex mortuis surrexerit et ierit ad eos audient eum*, cf. a. r seems to be the only Old Latin which agrees with Marcion's ἀκούσωσιν.
71.2 *ut non nasceretur*, cf. a.
18.18 omits ἄρχων. So a.
21.28 *adpropiavit* =? Marcion's ἤγγικε > ἐγγίζει. So also l and the Old Syriac.
21.30 *cum producunt ex se* ***folia***, cf. b.
22.19–20 full text.
23.45 Cf. a.
24.6 omits οὐκ ἔστιν ὧδε ἀλλὰ ἠγέρθη (though the words are inserted, by a later hand?, above the line). Cf. a.
24.12 omitted, cf. a.

Sole agreement: 16. 31.

r_2 and Marcion

It is clear that r_2 *is nearly always conformed to the Vulgate* (much more so than r). E.g., it has *lectum* > *grabattum* in 5. 24.
dum > *quamdiu* in 5. 34.
mittendus [*sic!*] [= βλητέον, i.e., *mittendum*] > *mittunt*, 5. 38.
saturabimini > *saturabuntur*, 6. 21.

but not entirely:

E.g., 6.29 *praebe ei* r_2: *praebe* Vg.
12.47 r_2 omits *et non fecit.*
10.21 r_2 omits *et prudentibus*, and has *domine pater* > *pater domine.*
12.59 r_2 *quadrantem*: Vg *minutum.*
21.8 r_2 + *Christus sum.*
23.2

The readings of r_2 which are worth recording as showing coincidence with Marcion are:

5.24 *surge et tolle lectum tuum*, cf. a.
6.17 Cf. b.
6.22 *eritis*, cf. b.
6.25 r_2 (and Vg) omit νῦν, but contain *vobis* (= ὑμῖν), cf. a.
6.26 *secundum haec*, cf. b.
6.29 *praebe ei*, cf. b.
6.31 *et vos*, cf. b.
6.38 *eadem mensura qua . . .*, cf. a.
8.25 *mari*, cf. c.
9.24 omit οὗτος with Marcion, cf. a.
9.30 = dD.
9.35 *dilectus*, cf. b.
9.54–6 Cf. a.
10.21 *domine, pater*, cf. e; omits *et prudentibus* (καὶ συνετῶν), cf. e.
12.47 omits *et non fecit*, cf. c.
12.51 *mittere*, cf. b.
20.36 Cf. Vulgate.
21.8 inserts *Christus*, cf. c.
21.30 *cum producunt iam ex se fructum*, cf. b.
22.19–20 full text.
23.2 = b.
24.12 omits. So r.

Marcion and $\left\{\begin{matrix} a_2 \\ s \end{matrix}\right.$

a_2

11.11–29 no agreements with Marcion.
11.13 has *bona data* > *spiritum sanctum*, cf. b.
13.16–34 13.28 **introeuntes** *in regnum Dei*, cf. a.

s

17.3–29 no agreements.
18.39–19.47 19.10 *salvum facere et quaerere*, cf. a.
20.46–21.22 21.8 *ego sum xps*, cf. c.

Vulgate and Marcion

5.24 *tolle lectum tuum*, cf. a.
6.22 *beati* **eritis**, cf. b.
6.25 omits νῦν after ἐμπεπλησμένοι, cf. a.

6.26 *secundum haec*, cf. b.
6.31 *et vos*, cf. b.
6.34 *recipere*, cf. c.
6.38 *eadem quippe mensura* . . . , cf. a.
8.25 *mari* = Marcion's θαλάσσῃ, cf. c—assimilation to Mt. and Mark.
9.22 *resurgere*, cf. a.
9.24 omits οὗτος, cf. a.
9.30 *erant autem Moses et Helias visi in maiestate* = dD.
9.35 *dilectus*, cf. b.
9.55–6 Cf. a.
10.22 omits μου after πατρός, cf. a.
11.48 *testificamini quod consentitis*, cf. a.
12.20 *cuius*, cf. a.
12.59 *minutum*, cf. b.
16.16 *ex eo*, cf. a.
16.25 *hic consolatur*, cf. a.
16.26 Cf. a.
20.19 *principes sacerdotum et scribae*, cf. c.
20.36 *neque enim ultra mori poterunt* = f r_2, cf. a.
21.30 *cum producunt iam ex se fructum*, cf. b.
22.19–20 in full.
23.33 *calvariae*, cf. a.
23.45 *et obscuratus est sol*, cf. a.

Cyprian and Marcion

6.22 *beati eritis*, cf. b.
9.56 *filius hominis non venit animas hominum perdere sed salvare*, cf. a.
12.8 *qui confessus me fuerit* . . . *et ego confitebor*, cf. a.
12.20 *cuius erunt*, cf. a.
16.25 *hic consolatur*, cf. a.
20.36 *neque enim incipiunt* (elsewhere *incipient*) *mori*, so e, cf. a.

Irenaeus (the Latin New Testament quotations) and Marcion

6.25 omits νῦν, cf. a.
also omits καὶ κλαύσετε.
6.26 has *et* before *pseudoprophetis*, cf. b.
6.29 has *tunicam* first, *pallium* second, cf. b.
remitte ei et pallium, cf. e.
12.20 *cuius*, cf. a.
12.38 *vespertina vigilia*, cf. b.
12.47 omits ἑτοιμάσας ἢ and πρὸς τὸ θέλημα αὐτοῦ, cf. c.
12.59 *quadrantem*, cf. b.
16.31 *nec si quis a mortuis resurgens ad illos eat credent ei*, cf. a.

Ambrose of Milan and Marcion

5.14 *ut sit in testimonium hoc vobis*, cf. b.
5.24 *tolle*, cf. a.

5.34 *possunt . . . quamdiu*, cf. a.
6.21 *saturabuntur*, cf. b.
omits νῦν after κλαίοντες, cf. b.
6.22 *beati eritis*, cf. b.
6.38 *eadem mensura*, cf. a.
9.35 *dilectus*, cf. b.
9.55–6 has the addition as in Marcion, cf. a.
12.10 in spiritum *autem sanctum qui dixerit*, cf. b.
12.59 *quadrantem*, cf. b.
13.28 *cum videritis iustos intrare in regnum caelorum*, cf. a. (Ambrose has also the other reading: *Abraham et Isaac et Iacob*), cf. *C.S.E.L.*, vol. XXXII, par. 4, pp., 188, 400.
16.25–6 agrees with Marcion, cf. a. (*C.S.E.L.*, vol. LXII, p. 398).
16.31 *nec si quis ex mortuis ad illos abierit credent*, cf. a.
17.4 seems to omit τῆς ἡμέρας.
18.35 seems to omit ἐπαιτῶν, cf. d, e.
21.30 *fructum*, cf. b.

Sole agreements: 13. 28 (N.B.); 17. 4; 18. 35 (?).

Pseudo-Cyprian (Hartel's Appendix) **and Marcion**

8.3 *ministrabant illi* (*De Singularitate Clericorum*, ch. 25 ad fin), cf. a.
12.8 *qui me confessus fuerit . . . et ego confitebor* (*De Laude Martyrii*, ch. 11), cf. a.
20.36 *neque enim morientur* (*De Singularitate Clericorum*, ch. 40), cf. a.

Lucifer of Cagliari and Marcion

11.48 *non consentientes*, cf. a.
13.28 *introeuntes*, cf. a.

On the basis of the foregoing detailed evidence the following conclusions would seem justified :—

(1) The majority of the agreements between Marcion and the Old Latin are not tendentious and did not originate with Marcion, but were drawn by him from the Greek text of his day with which he was most familiar (i.e., a form of the " Western " text-group).

To this category belong the coincidences of reading between Marcion and Old Latin MSS. in

5.14 5.24 5.34 5.38 6.2 (e only) 6.3 (b e) 6.17 6.21 (*saturabuntur videbunt* e g[1]) 6.22 (*eritis*) 6.25 6.26 6.29 6.31 6.34 6.38 7.9 (e r) 7.38 8.3 8.25 9.30 (d) 9.35 9.41 (e only) 9.54–6 10.1 10.9 (e only) 10.21 (e r_2) 10.22 (b only) 10.24 (a i) 10.27 11.11 (d) 11.48 12.5 12.8 12.11 (a) 12.20 12.38 12.47 12.51 12.59 13.28 16.16 16.26 (cf. a) 16.30 16.31b 17.2 17.4 (Ambrose only) 18.18 18.35 (d e Ambrose) 20.23 (q) 20.36 21.30 23.2 23.34b 23.45 24.37 (d).

(2) There is, however, a small class of tendentious alterations by Marcion which crept into the Old Latin tradition at certain points.

Decision must be somewhat tentative here, but the following passages may be listed:

? 5.39 (cf. note on a).
? 6.35 (cf. note on e) e only.
10.21 (cf. note on a) a only.
10.25 (cf. note on g^2) g^2 only.
11.29–32 see Lagrange below.
11.42 (cf. note on b) b d.
13.28 (*iustos*) Ambrose only.
16.12 (cf. note on e) e i l.
?? 17.10b (cf. note on a).
21.27 (cf. note on l) c l.
21.32 (cf. note on e) e only.
23.2 (cf. note on b) b c e ff i l q r_2.
23.5 (cf. note on c) c e.
? 23.34a (cf. note on a) a d.
? 24.6 (cf. note on a) a b c d e ff r.
24.12 (cf. note on a) a b d e l r.

Harnack would add 9. 54–6, but reasons have been given (cf. note on a) for assigning these verses to the former class.

M. J. Lagrange[1] would go further than Harnack in allowing Marcionite influence on Catholic texts.

His list of passages in evidence of this would be:

9.54 9.55 23.2 24.40 (so far in agreement with Harnack), but also 11.2 11.29–32 (omitted by Marcion; 30 is lacking in C, 32 in D), 11.49 12.10 16.12 24.37.

W. Bauer[2] also goes beyond Harnack with regard to one important passage in allowing Marcionite influence. Bauer dares to suggest that Luke 22. 19b–20 is an addition of Marcion's. Assuming himself that the so-called shorter text of Luke (which proceeds straight from verse 19a to verse 21) is the original, Bauer argues that Marcion found this in his text of the Gospel, but ventured to expand it by the addition of 19b–20, which he derived from 1 Cor. 11, because he needed some authority for the continued observance of the Eucharist by his own adherents. Later scribes—so runs the theory—combined the Marcionite text with the genuine Lucan text. Tertullian says nothing of vv. 16–18 and probably Marcion had omitted them; though one might have expected the omission to draw forth a Tertullianite sting.

Having thus established the fact that the influence of distinctively Marcionite readings was felt outside Marcionite circles, we must also report that this influence was very limited. Of palpable Marcionite

[1] In his review of Harnack's *Marcion* (1st edition) in *Revue Biblique*, 1921, p. 611.

[2] *Göttingische Gelehrter Anzeigen*, 1923, pp. 13–14.

emendations like the substitution of *iustos* for *prophetas* (13. 28) or the omission of 24. 27 there is practically no trace in non-Marcionite texts. (Cf. also the alteration of κρίσιν to κλῆσιν 11. 42 and the omission of Abraham 16. 29.)

On the whole, however, the influence of Marcion on Catholic texts was greater than Harnack allowed. Possibly not the whole of the passages catalogued in Group (1) above need be assigned to the Western text which was the common source of Marcion and the Old Latin. Some of them, though dogmatically harmless, may still be Marcionite alterations, for it is possible that Marcion tampered with the text on stylistic grounds, and not merely in the interests of his peculiar doctrines.[1] It must be remembered, too, that Christians in the second century probably did not share our regard for the precise letter of Scripture: cf. p. 128 (K. and S. Lake). In favour of taking some even of the dogmatically indifferent readings shared by Marcion and Old Latin as Marcionite in origin, Vogels[2] argues that it is difficult on the other hypothesis—that they originate in a type of text current *c.* 140—to explain why these readings maintained themselves only in a limited number of MSS. or a single MS.—e.g., 9. 24; 10. 9; 12. 10; 14. 16, where there are readings found only in Marcion and e. It is not, of course, impossible to explain them on the latter hypothesis: they may for a time actually have been much more widely spread than MSS. now extant show, but have been gradually brought into conformity with the dominant text, until their attestation in the limited number of MSS. which now agree with Marcion. Vogels's argument, however, must be given due weight as a general consideration. It does not, of course, attempt to measure the amount of Marcionite influence.

(3) No connection of Marcion's text with any Old Latin MS. or group of Old Latin can be established.

Vogels has pointed out[3] (following Harnack and Pott) that e stands nearer to Marcion than any other Old Latin. This raises the possibility of connection between Marcion and the African type of Old Latin Gospels, for e is an "African" MS., and as it happens the other extant MSS. which witness to this type of Old Latin—k and h—are not extant for Luke (or for Paul). Vogels gives a list of seventy-four passages where e and Marcion concur and twenty-two passages where e and Marcion are practically alone in agreement. These twenty-two passages are not all significant, however. Only fifteen seem to me to bear the weight of an argument based upon them. Even so, it remains

[1] Harnack (p. 44) thinks this improbable. There is no direct evidence.

[2] *Evangelium Palatinum*, pp. 97–98.

[3] In *Evangelium Palatinum*.

true that no other Old Latin MS. stands so often alone in agreement with Marcion as does e.[1] Vogels is inclined to give the priority to Marcion in these cases, and he certainly maintains that Marcion's text in a Latin form preceded and influenced the Catholic Latin.

But before too many inferences are based on these agreements between e and Marcion it must be noted that, as Vogels himself shows,[2] e is closer to D than any other Old Latin. We must also compare 16. 30 where—in a context where mere counting of agreements would suggest the influence of Marcion on e—e is the only Old Latin which agrees with the Greek against Marcion in having a *mortuis* > *ex mortuis*. The safest conclusion is that a special influence of Marcion on the African text of the Gospels is not definitely established; and in view of von Soden's examination of Tertullian's and Marcion's texts of Paul we should assume the contrary (pp. 58 f. above). This is also the refutation of Lietzmann's suggestion (p. 58).

The Pauline Epistles

The available Old Latin versions are:

Claromontanus (d), ed. Tischendorf, 1852.
Augiensis (f), ed. Scrivener, 1859.
Boernerianus (g), ed. Matthaei, 1791.[3]

With regard to f Gregory says: "Ziegler: Italafragmenta der paulinischen Briefe 28 n. 2 bezeugt, dass diese Handschrift nur in Rom. und 1 Kor. einen Text bietet, der nicht mit Vulgata übereinstimmt. . . . Hort dachte, dass sie einen Vulgatatext biete, der mit Lesarten aus dem altlateinischen Text vermischt wurde." With regard to g: "Hort meinte, dass g aus zwei Quellen fliesse, einer des reinen altlateinischen Textes, einer des veränderten Textes."

Sangermanensis (e), ed. Belsheim, 1885. A bilingual MS. like d_1 f_1 g. The Greek side (E) is dependent on the Greek of d, according to most scholars (cf. Belsheim, p. VI). The Latin is probably more useful. It is not necessarily a translation of the

[1] The sole agreements of other Old Latin are as follows:

a 10.21 and ?? 17.10b.
b 10.22 and 23.34b.
d 6.26; ? 4.16; ? 17.2.
ff 23.33 (also 6.20; 7.26, but these have no significance).
g 10.25.
i ? 12.11; 22.70.
l 21.27.
q 11.28; ? 6.30; 20.34.
r 16.31.

Ambrose 13.28; 17.4.

[2] op. cit. p. 92.

[3] Corssen believed in a common original of d f g. See C. R. Gregory, *Textkritik des Neuen Testaments* II, p. 612.

Greek side; Belsheim thought that its scribe was ignorant of Greek. It is very close to the Vulgate. In Gregory's opinion (*Textkritik* I, pp. 109–110) it was altered according to a text distinct from D and mostly identical with the Vulgate.

The Freising Fragments ($r_1 r_2 r_3$), ed. de Bruyne, 1921.[1]

The sixth-century Latin fragment attached to Ulfilas' Gothic version of St. Paul (gue), ed. Tischendorf in *Anecdota Sacra*, 1855, pp. 153–158. This contains only Romans 11. 33–12. 5, 12. 17–13.1, 14. 9–20, 15. 3–13, and even within that small compass offers nothing for comparison with the text of Marcion.

We have also for comparison the New Testament quotations of the following Fathers: Irenaeus, Cyprian, Novatian, Lucifer, Hilary, Ambrose and Victorinus of Pettau, as cited from the editions used in our Gospel comparisons. In addition, there are also available for the Pauline material, Victorinus Afer's commentary on Galatians, Ephesians and Philippians,[2] and Ambrosiaster's commentary on all the Pauline Epistles.[3]

dD (Claromontanus) and Marcion

Galatians

2.5 dD omit οἷς οὐδέ with e, Irenaeus, Victorinus Afer, Ambrosiaster, Pelagius. Marcion omits οἷς.

2.9 *Petrus et Iacobus et Johannes* dD. So Marcion and e fF gG Victorinus Afer and Ambrosiaster. r has *petrus*, but in second place.

3.14 dD εὐλογίαν τοῦ πνεύματος > ἐπαγγελίαν.
So gG F (not f) Ambrosiaster. Harnack, p. 73*, also cites Vigilantius as attesting this reading.

5.1 *qua libertate*. So e Ff Gg Ambrosiaster, Vulgate and many Latin Fathers as well as Marcion.

5.14 dD *omnis enim lex in vobis uno sermone impletur*. So gG and F (not f). Also Ee Victorinus Afer, Ambrosiaster. Marcion seems to have known this reading, and deliberately dropped ἐν ἑνὶ λόγῳ, leaving ἐν ὑμῖν isolated and making possible the interpretation: in you Christians and not in the Jews!

There is no real reason to assume, as Harnack, pp. 78*, 153*, is inclined to do, that Marcion himself inserted ἐν ὑμῖν, and that, therefore, this is a case of a deliberate Marcionite falsification influencing the Latin tradition.

5.24 omits Ἰησοῦ, with many Greek MSS. and versions.

6.17 *stigmata domini Iesu Christi* dD. So e and Marcion.

1 Corinthians

10.9 See Irenaeus.

---

[1] *Collectanea Biblica Latina*, V. In de Bruyne's opinion, shared by C. H. Turner (*J.T.S.* XXIV, pp. 218–221), r is, roughly speaking, the text used by Augustine. See also *J.T.S.* XXXII, p. 333.

[2] Text printed by Mai in Vol. III of *Scriptorum Veterum Nova Collectio*. There is no critical text in *C.S.E.L.*, in spite of the mention of one by Brandt in von Soden's article "Victorinus" in *Religion in Geschichte und Gegenwart*.

[3] Text as printed in Migne, *P.L.* XVII. There is no critical edition yet.

15.51 πάντες ἀναστησόμεθα *omnes resurgimus.*
οὐ πάντες δὲ ἀλλαγησόμεθα *non omnes autem immutavimur* [*sic!*]. So e f F (but F has κοιμηθησώμεθα > ἀναστησόμεθα, so Gg) m Vulgate has: *omnes quidem resurgemus, sed non omnes immutabimur.* So Ambrosiaster and Ambrose.

No ground for assuming that Marcion innovated here; but this is a case of Marcion sharing the specifically Latin reading.

Tischendorf does not quote any Syriac evidence. Syriac (peshitta) evidence is given in Lietzmann's commentary on 1 Cor. in *H.N.T.* It agrees with B and the Greek text.

2 Corinthians

4.11 *vita Iesu Christi* (not simply *vita Iesu*). Marcion had *Christi.*

5.10 (ἵνα κομίσηται ἕκαστος) ἃ διὰ τοῦ σώματος ἔπραξεν εἴτε. . . . So FG (*ut ferat unusquisque*) *propria corporis secundum quod gessit sive* . . . (i.e., d read:, ἴδια σώματος πρὸς ἃ . . .), cf. f g.
Vulgate agrees with f.

Romans

5.21 *in mortem*, so f g r Ambrosiaster and Marcion (though this cannot be regarded with certainty as Marcion's reading, cf. Harnack, p. 105*).
> *in morte* ἐν (τῷ) θανάτῳ, which is read by D F G and all Greek MSS.

6.9 *surgens.* So m e r and Vg. f g Irenaeus, Ambrosiaster, Ambrose *resurgens.* D F G ἐγερθείς. Victorinus of Pettau *resurrexit.* Tertullian *suscitatus.* Marcion ἀναστάς > ἐγερθείς.
No Greek MS. has ἀναστάς and this is a Marcionite alteration (cf. Harnack, pp. 67* f). But too much must not be made of the agreement of d f g with Marcion, as even Vg. has *surgens.* Also, Marcion did not alter Rom. 7. 4; 8. 11.

13.8 *proximum*, so e f g Ambrosiaster, Lucifer, Ambrose, Vulgate. Does this at all explain Marcion's πλήσιον > ἕτερον? Harnack bases this on Epiphanius only. Tertullian gives nothing here.

1 Thessalonians

4.16–17 The peculiarities of Marcion's text (according to Adamantius, Tertullian is only fragmentary here) are: (1) πρῶτοι > πρῶτον in 16, (2) ? θεοῦ with κελεύσματι > σάλπιγγι, (3) ἐσχάτῃ inserted before σάλπιγγι, (4) κύριος between καταβήσεται and ἀπ' οὐρανοῦ, (5) omission of ἐν Χριστῷ after νεκροί, (6) ἐγερθήσονται > ἀναστήσονται, (7) τῷ Χριστῷ > τοῦ κυρίου after ἀπάντησιν.

Of these (1) and (7) are shared with Marcion by d f g and Vg (also D F G). See Harnack, p. 112*.

Ephesians

1.6 Addition of υἱῷ αὐτοῦ after ἠγαπημένῳ.
So Dd Ee Ff Gg r Victorinus Afer and Marcion
Also some MSS. of Vulgate.

1.13 *in quo credentes* (not: *et credentes*).
So D e Gg F (not f) r Irenaeus and Marcion. Ambrosiaster omits ἐν ᾧ as well.

2.11 μνημονεύοντες implied by d. > μνημονεύετε. Cf. Ambrosiaster, e.

2.15 *in se ipso reflexive.* So Ee Gg Ffm Victorinus Afer, Ambrosiaster, Vg and Marcion.

3.9 + πάντας with Marcion. So Ee Ff Gg Ambrosiaster, Victorinus Afer and also X^{c} B Vg.

4.6 adds *nobis* at end. So Ee Ff Gg Victorinus Afer m Irenaeus Cyprian and also K L Vg.

5.28 τὸ ἑαυτῶν σῶμα Dd (also Ambrosiaster).
? "Rest aus einer tendenziösen Umarbeitung Marcions, wie Zahn richtig gegen Harnack (p. 120*) gesehen hat." (Vogels in *Amicitiae Corolla*, p. 296.)

Sole agreements of d and Marcion: Eph. 2. 11 (not f g, but F G).

fF (Augiensis) and Marcion

Galatians

2.4 f (not F) omits δέ after διά (not noted by Harnack or by Tischendorf, who, however, quotes the opinion of Theodoret and Jerome that this δέ is superfluous).

2.9 *Petrus et Iacobus et Iohannes*, cf. d.

3.14 F has εὐλογίαν τοῦ πνεύματος, cf. Dd, but f has *pollicitationem* (ἐπαγγελίαν); so Vulgate; Harnack does not note this reading of F.

5.1 Cf. d.

5.14 Cf. dD.

1 Corinthians

10.9 See Irenaeus.

15.51 Cf. dD.

2 Corinthians

5.10 *ut referat unusquisque propria corporis prout gessit sive* . . . = Vulgate. Cf. Dd.

Romans [Lacuna in Ff to 3. 19]

6.9 *resurgens*, cf. d.

1 Thessalonians

4.16–17 cf. d.

Ephesians

1.6 cf. Dd.

1.13 cf. Dd.

2.15 cf. Dd.

3.9 cf. Dd.

4.6 cf. Dd.

2.11 μνημονεύοντες > μνημονεύετε, so Gg.

Sole agreements of f and Marcion: Gal. 2. 4.

gG (Boernerianus) and Marcion

Galatians

1.6 omits Χριστοῦ. So G Cyprian Lucifer and Victorinus Afer.

2.9 cf. dD.

3.14 cf. dD.
5.1 cf. d.
5.14 cf. dD.

1 Corinthians

10.9 cf. Irenaeus.
15.51 cf. dD.

2 Corinthians

4.11 *vita Iesu Christi*, cf. d.
5.10 *ut recipiat* / *reportet.* } *unusquisque propria corporis prout gessit sive . . .*
cf. Dd.

Romans

1.16 Ἰουδαίῳ τε καὶ ἕλληνι / *Iudaeo et graeco* } i.e., omits πρῶτον.
So Marcion. Also B (Tischendorf).
6.9 *resurgens*, cf. d.

1 Thessalonians

4.16–17 cf. d.

Ephesians

1.6 cf. Dd.
1.13 cf. Dd.
2.11 μνημονεύοντες > μνημονεύετε, so Ff.
2.15 cf. Dd.
3.9 cf. Dd.
4.6 cf. Dd.

Sole agreements of g and Marcion: Rom. 1. 16 (but lacuna in Ff here).

e and Marcion

Romans

6.9 *surgens*, cf. d.
8.2 *me*. So Vg and several Greek MSS. Marcion ἡμᾶς.
13.8 *proximum*, cf. d.

1 Corinthians

10.9 *Christum*, cf. Irenaeus.
15.51 *resurgimus*, cf. d.

2 Corinthians

4.11 *vita Iesu Christi*, cf. d.
5.10 *ut ferat unusquisque propria corporis secundum dominum quod gessit sive . . .*, cf. d.

Galatians

2.5 *ad horam cessimus*, i.e., omits οἷς οὐδὲ, cf. d.
2.9 *Petrus et Iacobus et Iohannes*, cf. d.
5.1 *qua libertate*, cf. d.

5.14 *in vobis uno sermone*, cf. d.
5.24 = d.
6.17 *domini Iesu Christi*, cf. d.

Ephesians

1.6 adds *filio suo*, cf. d.
1.13 *in quo credentes*, cf. d.
2.2 *omnes*, cf. d.
2.11 *memoriam habentes*, cf. d.
2.15 *in se ipso*, cf. d.
3.9 *omnes*, cf. d.
4.6 *nobis*, cf. d.

No sole agreements.

r and Marcion

Romans

5.21 *in mortem*, cf. d.
6.9 *surgens*, cf. d.
14.10 *xpi* = Marcion's Χριστοῦ. So Ambrosiaster, and also ℵ[c] CLP, etc.

2 Corinthians

5.10 *ut ferat unusquisque secundum ea quae per corpus gessit sive . . .*, cf. d.

Galatians

2.9 *iacobus et* **petrus** *et iohannes*, cf. d.
5.1 *(qual)i libertate*, cf. d.

Ephesians

1.6 + *filio suo*, cf. d.
1.13 Cf. d.

Philippians

1.12 omits ἐλήλυθεν with Marcion. Tischendorf gives no further evidence of this omission.
1.14 omits τοῦ θεοῦ with Marcion. So D[c] K, etc.

No sole agreements with Marcion except Phil. 1. 12, which is not significant.

Irenaeus and Marcion

Galatians

2.5 omits οἷς οὐδέ, cf. d.

Romans

6.9 *resurgens*, cf. d.

1 Corinthians

10.9 *Christum* > *Dominum*. So d e f g Ambrosiaster Vulgate. r is missing here. Tischendorf gives as witnesses for Χριστὸν > Κύριον D E F G K L al pler it vg syr[sch] et p[txt] sah cop[wi] Irenaeus Ambrosiaster, etc.

There is a possibility of this being a Marcionite alteration as Epiphanius says, because Κύριον in this context refers to the Creator, and if Marcion was going to make any use of the passage at all he had to alter Κύριον here, as he could have no object in exhorting his followers not to tempt the Demiurge.

15. 3 *tradidi enim vobis in primis quoniam* . . . , i.e., apparently omits ὃ καὶ παρέλαβον with Marcion.
So Tertullian, Hilary, Ambrose, Ambrosiaster.
" wohl Einfluss des Marciontextes " (Harnack, p. 91*).

Ephesians

1. 13 omits καὶ before πιστεύσαντες, cf. d.
2. 14 *inimicitias.* So Ambrosiaster, Ambrose and Victorinus Afer. d g m r have the singular *inimicitiam.*
4. 6 + *nobis,* cf. d.

No sole agreements, but cf. 1 Cor. 10. 9, 15. 3.

Cyprian and Marcion

Galatians

1. 6 omits Χριστοῦ, cf. g.
1. 8 ***aliter** adnuntiet.* This agreement of Cyprian with Marcion's ἄλλως is not noted by Harnack (it is not in Tischendorf) who, however, notes that Rufinus has it.
5. 24 omits Ἰησοῦ, cf. d. Harnack and Tischendorf do not explicitly mention Cyprian's reading here.
6. 9 seems to omit μὴ ἐκλυόμενοι with Marcion.

Ephesians

4. 6 + *nobis,* cf. d.

Philippians

2. 7 *hominis* = Marcion's ἀνθρώπου > ἀνθρώπων. So also Origen, Hilary and Victorinus according to Harnack (p. 125*) and Tischendorf.

No agreements with Marcion in Pseudo-Cyprian.
Sole agreements of Cyprian and Marcion: Gal. 6. 9 a bare possibility.

Lucifer of Cagliari and Marcion

Galatians

1. 6 omits Χριστοῦ, cf. g.

Romans

13. 8 *proximum,* cf. d.

Ambrose and Marcion

Romans

6. 9 *resurgens,* cf. d.
10. 3 *ignorantes deum,* i.e., reads with Marcion θεὸν > τὴν τοῦ θεοῦ δικαιοσύνην.
13. 8 *proximum,* cf. d.

1 Corinthians

15. 3 omits ὃ καὶ παρέλαβον, cf. Irenaeus.
15. 51 *omnes quidem resurgemus, sed non omnes immutabimur,* cf. d.

2 Corinthians

5.18 Cf. Ambrosiaster.

Ephesians

2.14 *inimicitias*, cf. Irenaeus.

Sole agreement: Rom. 10. 3.

Hilary and Marcion

Galatians

1.8 *aliter* = Marcion's ἄλλως (*C.S.E.L.*, LXV, p. 50).

Philippians

2.7 Cf. Cyprian.

Victorinus of Pettau and Marcion

Romans

6.9 *resurrexit*, cf. d (*C.S.E.L.*, XLIX, p. 18).

Victorinus Afer and Marcion

Galatians

1.6 omits Χριστοῦ, cf. g.
2.5 omits οἷς οὐδὲ, cf. d.
2.9 *Petrus* first, and either *Johannes et Jacobus* or *Jacobus et Johannes*, cf. d (the rest of the comment makes the order uncertain).
5.1 *qua libertate*, cf. d.
5.14 *universa enim lex* **in vobis** *uno sermone impletur*, cf. d.

Philippians

No agreements with Marcion (except omission of καὶ εἴδετε 4. 9, which has no significance). At Phil. 2. 7 Tischendorf states that Victorinus has the reading *hominis* (= Marcion) as well as *hominum*. Cf. Cyprian.

Ephesians

1.6 *filio suo*, cf. d.
2.2 omits νῦν.
2.14 *inimicitias*, cf. Irenaeus and Ambrosiaster.
2.15 *in semet ipso*, cf. d.
2.16 seems to omit διὰ τοῦ σταυροῦ. Marcion has it at end of verse.
3.9 *omnes*, cf. d.
4.6 Cf. d.
5.28 Cf. d.

Sole agreements of Victorinus Afer and Marcion: Eph. 2. 2; 2. 16. No argument can be based on this because we have only three epistles in Victorinus' text to compare with Marcion.

Ambrosiaster and Marcion

Romans

5.21 *in mortem*, cf. d.
6.9 *resurgens*, cf. d.

13.8 *proximum*, cf. d.
14.10 *tribunal* ***Christi***, cf. r.

Galatians

2.5 omits οἷς οὐδὲ, cf. d.
2.9 *Petrus et Jacobus et Johannes*, cf. d.
3.14 *et benedictionem Spiritus accipiamus per fidem*, cf. d.
5.1 *qua libertate*, cf. d.
5,14 ***in vobis*** *in uno verbo*, cf. d.
5.24 = d.

1 Corinthians

10.9 *Christum*, cf. Irenaeus.
14.19 *per legem* = Marcion's διὰ τὸν νόμον. Paulinus of Nola has *in lege*.

See Harnack, p. 90*: "nicht eine tendenziöse Korrektur sondern ein uralter Fehler."

15.3 omits ὃ καὶ παρέλαβον, cf. Irenaeus.
15.51 *omnes quidem resurgemus, sed non omnes immutabimur*. So Vulgate, cf. d.

2 Corinthians

5.10 *ut recipiat unusquisque propria corporis prout gessit* = g. Cf. d.
5.18 *ecce* ***omnia*** *facta sunt nova*. So Ambrose, Epistle 46, according to Tischendorf *ad loc*. See Harnack, p. 100*. Apart from Ambrose this is a sole agreement between Ambrosiaster and Marcion, as far as the Latin MSS. are concerned. D^{bc} have it, also K L P.

Ephesians

1.6 *filio suo*, cf. d.
1.13 omits ἐν ᾧ καὶ, cf. d.
2.11 *memoria retinentes*, cf. d.
2.14 *inimicitias*, cf. Victorinus Afer and Irenaeus.
2.15 *in se ipso*, cf. d.
3.9 *omnes*, cf. d.
4.6 + *nobis*, cf. d.
5.28 *suum corpus diligit qui uxorem suam diligit*, cf. d.

Sole agreement: 1 Cor. 14. 19.

m and Marcion

The page numbers given below are those of Weihrich's edition (Vol. XII of *C.S.E.L.*).

p. 311	2 Cor. 1. 3	1 MS. (codex Theodulfi Aniciensis (8th cent.)) omits καὶ πατὴρ
p. 313	Eph. 4. 6	+ *nobis*, cf. d.
p. 325	Phil. 1. 19	Ἰησοῦ Χριστοῦ omitted in five MSS.
p. 429	1 Cor. 15. 51	*omnes quidem resurgemus, sed non omnes immutabimur* = Vg (some MSS. read *resurgimus*), cf. d.
p. 627	Romans 6. 9	*surgens*, cf. d.
p. 668	Eph. 2. 15	*sententiis* = δόγμασιν without ἐν Vg *decretis*. *in semet ipso*, cf. d.

Sole agreement: Phil. 1. 19.

Vulgate and Marcion

Romans

6.9 *surgens*, cf. d.
8.2 *me*, cf. e.
13.8 *proximum*, cf. d.

1 Corinthians

10.9 *Christum*, cf. Irenaeus.
15.51 *resurgemus*, cf. d.

2 Corinthians

5.10 Cf. f.

Galatians

5.1 *qua libertate*, cf. d.
5.24 = d.

Ephesians

2.15 *in semet ipsum*, cf. d.
3.9 *omnes*, cf. d.
4.6 *nobis*, cf. d.

Colossians

1.5 *audistis*. So the citation of Marcion's reading by Tertullian 5. 19. All the Greek MSS. have προηκούσατε and the Latins agree with *ante audistis*. Harnack does not note this apparent sole agreement of Vulgate with Marcion.

No sole agreements.

The results of the foregoing comparison are:

(1) The majority of concurrences of reading between Marcion and the Old Latin are taken from the Greek text dominant in Rome in the middle of the second century, e.g., 2 Cor. 5. 10; Eph. 1. 6.

(2) The question of Marcionite tendentious emendations affecting non-Marcionite texts arises only concerning the following passages: Rom. 1. 16 (g only), 6. 9; 1 Cor. 10. 9, 15. 3; Eph. 5. 28 (Harnack, p. 153*, would add: Gal. 5. 14, Eph. 4. 6, and probably Gal. 1. 6).

(3) In no case are there sufficient agreements between a single version and Marcion to suggest the probability of a special connection between that version and Marcion's text, e.g., Phil. 1. 12 is probably a mere coincidental agreement between r and Marcion. So 2 Cor. 1. 3 (m and Marcion).

(4) Marcion's reading διὰ τὸν νόμον, 1 Cor. 14. 19, is of some interest as an example of Marcion mediating a curious reading (not a Marcionite tendentious alteration) to one or two other texts.

These results concur in the main with those obtained from examination of the Gospels.

APPENDIX 8

DID MARCION'S TEXT INFLUENCE THE OLD SYRIAC?

The following comparison of Marcion's text with the Old Syriac Gospels and Diatessaron only corroborates the inferences drawn from our examination of Marcion and the Old Latin. There is no case of a tendentious Marcionite alteration affecting these Syriac texts. The agreements between them and Marcion are to be explained as originating from the "Western" type of text; among them we may indicate as the most notable: 7. 9 (τοιαύτην), 9. 54, 12. 38, 12. 51 (βαλεῖν), 16. 12 (εὑρέθητε), 16. 31, 21. 30, 23. 45. This must also be the explanation of the two sole agreements which occur: viz., at 13. 19 Tatian and Marcion alone read ἔσπειρεν (neither Old Latin nor Old Syriac agree with Marcion in this, and no other occurrence of the reading is given by Tischendorf or von Soden); at 21. 18 no other MS. agrees with Marcion in omitting this verse except Syr^{c}.

The Old Syriac Gospels

(In Burkitt's *Evangelion da Mepharreshe.*) Burkitt prints C (Curetonian) in text, and gives readings of S (Sinaitic) in apparatus. 3. 16–7. 33 and 16. 12–17. 1 are missing from C; and 5. 28–6. 12 missing from S (Souter, p. 57).

Luke

5.24S — ἆρον. Also all Old Latin Vg א D Tatian.

5.28–6.11 — missing in Syr^{s} as well as Syr^{c}.

6.21–2S — Syriac has 3rd plural with Marcion and b, etc.

6.26S — omits πάντες; so Marcion and D, and d alone among Old Latin Tatian.

6.38S — reads only καλὸν καὶ ὑπερεκχυννόμενον. Cf. e.

7.9S — "(aught) like this faith" (Burkitt)? implies τοιαύτην as Marcion, cf. e note. So Tatian.

7.38SC — ἔβρεξε > ἤρξατο βρέχειν.

8.25SC — τῇ θαλάσσῃ > τῷ ὕδατι. So c, etc., and Marcion.

9.20C — τὸν Χριστὸν (without τοῦ θεοῦ). S is illegible here. So a and Marcion.

9.22S — μετὰ τρεῖς ἡμέρας, cf. a.

9.24SC — omit οὗτος, cf. a.

9.35C — ἀγαπητός. So Marcion; cf. b. S has ἐκλελεγμένος.

9.55 — S has simply: He rebuked them, and they went to another village. C has the additions to vv. 55 and 56 as in Marcion. Cf. a.

10.22S — omits μου. So Marcion, cf. a, etc.

11.11C — has the bread-stone clause inserted here before the other two. So Tatian, cf. b.

12.38C " and if in the first watch he come and find them watching, happy is it for them, whom he will make sit down to meat and will serve; or if in the second watch . . . ." Cf. b, etc.

12.51 C has a verb which Burkitt translates " make "; and S has " lay ". Marcion βαλεῖν > δοῦναι. von Soden gives βαλεῖν as reading of S, and also Peschitta.

16.12S εὑρέθητε, so Marcion and Tatian; but no Old Latin. Tischendorf does not note the reading εὑρέθητε. According to von Soden it is found also in Peschitta.

16.31S (ἀπ)έλθῃ πεισθήσονται αὐτῷ, cf. a.

18.16SC τῶν οὐρανῶν, so Marcion, and a, etc.

19.26C δοκεῖ ἔχειν. So Marcion. No Old Latin agrees with Marcion here, but a few Greek MSS. do, also Cyril of Alexandria.

21.18C omits. So Marcion. No other MS. beside C agrees with Marcion in this omission.

21.28CS ἤγγικε (?). So Marcion and l r, m also according to Tischendorf. Tischendorf and von Soden do not give the perfect as the reading of Old Syriac.

21.30CS " what time they have begun putting forth (their leaves) and giving their fruit ye understand that the summer hath drawn nigh ", i.e., agrees with Marcion in addition of τὸν καρπὸν and ἤγγικε > ἐγγύς ἐστί, and in omission of ἤδη and ἐγγύς. Cf. b.

22.15CS omit τοῦτο. So *probably* Marcion.

22.17–20CS have the order vv. 19, 17, 18 and omit 20, cf. a.

23.45CS καὶ ἐσκοτίσθη ὁ ἥλιος. So Tatian and nearly all Old Latin, cf. a.

Tatian's *Diatessaron*

J. Hamlyn Hill's translation in *The Earliest Life of Christ*, 1894.

H. W. Hogg's translation in Ante-Nicene Christian Library (Additional Volume), 1897.

Preuschen's translation in *Tatian's Diatessaron*, ed. Pott, 1926.

Marmardji's translation in *Le Diatessaron de Tatian*, 1935.

5.24 ἄρον. So Old Latin ℵ D Old Syriac.

5.38 βάλλουσι > βλητέον.

6.17 κατέβη > καταβάς. So Marcion and b q r.

6.25 omits νῦν. So most Old Latin and Marcion.

6.26 omits πάντες. So d, Old Syriac.

6.38 omits σεσαλευμένον. So Old Syriac, cf. c.

Hill's translation " With the *same* measure . . ." suggests that Tatian read with Marcion τῷ αὐτῷ. . . . But Hogg and Preuschen and Marmardji suggest the opposite. So von Soden.

7.9 τοιαύτην, cf. Old Syriac.

8.25 " who commandeth also the wind and the waves and the sea ", i.e., agrees with Marcion in reading ὅς > ὅτι, and in θαλάσσῃ.

9.18 reads οἱ ἄνθρωποι > ὄχλοι, and adds τὸν υἱὸν τοῦ ἀνθρώπου. (This is assimilation to Mt.)

9.24 omits οὗτος. So Old Syriac.

9.54–56 Has the Marcionite additions in 55–6 (so Syr^c) and also in 54.

11.11 Has the bread-stone clause first. So Syr^c.

12.51 Probably read βαλεῖν with Marcion ("send" Hill; "cast" Hogg; "senden" Preuschen). So b l q r r_2 and Syr^s.

13.19 ἔσπειρε. So Marcion.

16.12 εὑρέθητε. So Marcion and Syr^s and Peschitta.

21.28 ? ἤγγικε (Marcion) or ἐγγίζει "draweth nigh" Hill, "is come near" Hogg, "ist herangekommen" Preuschen.

23.45 καὶ ἐσκοτίσθη ὁ ἥλιος. So Old Syriac and most Old Latin.

24.12 apparently not known to Tatian.

24.21 seems to have read ἐνομίζομεν, although von Soden does not note this reading as Tatian's: "we thought" Hill, "we supposed" Hogg. Marmardji gives "nous avons cru" as translation of the Arabic in the Vatican codex and of Ciasca's edition; and "nous espérions" as the translation of an Arabic correction.

BIBLIOGRAPHY

The list which follows makes no pretence to be exhaustive, but enumerates books which have been used and found useful in the study of Marcion. Commentaries and editions of the Fathers are omitted from this bibliography.

A. The one indispensable work, apart from the ancient authors, is Harnack's *Marcion : Das Evangelium vom fremden Gott* (1st edition 1921, 2nd edition 1924), with which should also be read his *Neue Studien zu Marcion*, 1923 ; and the following reviews :

By Lietzmann in the *Zeitschrift für die N.T. Wissenschaft*, 1921, pp. 94 f.
By Hans von Soden in the *Zeitschrift für die Kirchengeschichte*, Vol. XL, pp. 191 ff.
By W. Bauer in the *Göttingische Gelehrter Anzeigen*, 1923, pp. 1 ff.
By M. J. Lagrange in *Revue Biblique*, 1921, pp. 602 ff.
By Amann in *Revue des Sciences Religieuses*, 1923, pp. 111 ff.
By H. Strohl in *Revue d'Histoire et de Philosophie Religieuses*, 1923, pp. 156 ff.
By Moffatt in the *Hibbert Journal*, Vol. XIX, p. 772.
By Lowther Clarke in *Theology*, 1921, pp. 297 ff.
By A. d'Alès in *Recherhes de Science Religieuse*, 1922, pp. 137 ff.

B. General books on the history of the Church during the first two centuries :

Harnack, *Mission und Ausbreitung des Christentums* (4th edition, 1924).
The Constitution and Law of the Church, 1910.
Die Geschichte der altchristlichen Literatur, 1893–1904.
Sohm, *Kirchenrecht*, 1892.
Heiler, *Urkirche und Ostkirche*, 1937.
Lietzmann, *Geschichte der alten Kirche*, 1936.
Dill, *Roman Society from Nero to Marcus Aurelius*, 1905.
Glover, *The Conflict of Religions in the Early Roman Empire*, 1909.
Loofs, *Theophilus von Antiochien und die anderen theologischen Quellen bei Irenaeus* (*Texte und Untersuchungen*, XLVI, 1930).
Dix, *The Egyptian Church Order* (*The Apostolic Tradition of St. Hippolytus*), 1937.
Wilson, *Marcion, a Study of a Second-Century Heretic*, 1933.
La Piana, *The Roman Church at the End of the Second Century* (*Harvard Theological Review*, 1925).
McGiffert, *The Apostles' Creed*, 1902.
The God of the Early Christians, 1924.
Krüger, *Das Taufbekenntnis der Römischen Gemeinde als Niederschlag des Kampfes gegen Marcion* (*Z.N.T.W.*, 1905, pp. 72–79).
Lietzmann, Article " Apostolikon " in *Religion in Geschichte und Gegenwart*.
Lietzmann, *Symbolstudien* in *Z.N.T.W.*, 1922–.
Kattenbusch, *Das Apostolische Symbol*, 1894–1900.
Burn, *Introduction to the Creeds*, 1899.
James, *The Apocryphal New Testament*, 1924.

Burkitt, *The Gospel History and its Transmission*, 1907.
Church and Gnosis, 1932.
Religion of the Manichees, 1924.
Bauer, *Rechtglaübigkeit und Ketzerei in ältesten Christentum*, 1934.
Hitchcock, *Irenaeus of Lugdunum*, 1914.
Tollinton, *Clement of Alexandria*, 1914.
Werner, *Der Paulinismus des Irenaeus*, 1889.
Barnikol, *Die Entstehung der Kirche im zweiten Jahrhundert und die Zeit Marcions*, 1933.
Philipper 2: Der Marcionitische Ursprung des Mythos-Satzes Phil. 2. 6–7, 1932.

C. On the Canon and Text:

Zahn, *Geschichte des Kanons*, 1888–92.
Forschungen zur Geschichte des N.T. Kanons, 1881–1929.
Westcott, *Canon of the New Testament*, 1855.
Souter, *Text and Canon of the New Testament*, 1912.
The New Testament in the Apostolic Fathers, by a Committee of the Oxford Society of Historical Theology, 1905.
P. N. Harrison, *Polycarp's Two Epistles to the Philippians*, 1936.
Pott, *Marcions Evangelientext*, in *Zeitschrift für Kirchengeschichte*, Vol. XLII, pp. 202 ff.
De Textu Evangeliorum in saeculo secundo (Mnemosyne, 1920, pp. 267–309).
Harnack, *Die Entstehung des N.Ts*, 1914.
Die Briefsammlung des Apostels Paulus, 1926.
A. Bill, *Zur Erklärung und Textkritik des ersten Buch adv. Marcionem*, 1911.
E. Bosshardt, *L'Originalité et la probité de Tertullien dans son Traité contre Marcion*, 1921.
Lake, *Introduction to the New Testament*, 1938.
Tischendorf, *Novum Testamentum Graece*.
Gregory, *Textkritik des Neuen Testaments*, 1900.
Canon and Text of the New Testament, 1907.
Wordsworth–White, *Novum Testamentum Latine*, 1889–1905.
Sanday, *The Gospels in the Second Century*, 1876.
J. Knox, *Marcion and the New Testament*, 1942.

On the Prologues:

De Bruyne, *Revue Bénédictine*, 1907, pp. 1–16, 257 ff.; 1928, pp. 193–214.
Harnack, *Z.N.T.W.*, 1926, pp. 160–163.
Sitzungsberichte der preussischen Akademie, 1928, pp. 322–341.
De Bruyne, *Bulletin d'ancienne Littérature chrétienne latine*, Oct. 1921, pp. 13–15.
Corssen, *Z.N.T.W.*, 1909, pp. 36 ff and 97 ff.
Mundle, *Z.N.T.W.*, 1925, pp. 56 ff. and 83 ff.
R. P. Lagrange, *Revue Biblique*, 1926, pp. 161–173.
W. F. Howard, *Expository Times*, 1936, pp. 534 ff.
B. W. Bacon, *Journal of Biblical Literature*, XLIX, pp. 43 ff.

D. On the Old Latin:

Sabatier, *Bibliorum Sacrorum Latinae Versiones Antiquae*, 1743.
Corssen, *Bericht über die lateinischen Bibelubersetzungen* in the *Jahresbericht über die Fortschritte der classischen Altertumswissenschaft*, 1899, pp. 1–83. Also Burkitt's review of this article in *J.T.S.*, July 1900.

Vogels, Survey of research on O.L. in *Biblische Zeitschrift*, 1914, pp. 251–268.
Evangelium Palatinum, in *N.T. Abhandlungen*, ed. by Meinertz, Vol. XII, 1926.
Vulgatastudien, 1928; with Burkitt's review in *J.T.S.*, July 1929.
The seven volumes of Old Latin Biblical texts (Oxford 1883–1923).
Wordsworth–White: *Novum Testamentum Latine*, 1889–1905.
Rönsch, *Das N.T. Tertullians*, 1871.
Itala und Vulgata, 1875.
Burkitt, *The Old Latin and the Itala* (Cambridge Texts and Studies, IV. 3), 1896.
The Rules of Tychonius (Cambridge Texts and Studies, III. 1), 1894.
Monceaux, *Histoire Littéraire de l'Afrique Chrétienne*, I, pp. 97–173.
Zimmer, *Ein Blick in die Entwicklungsgeschichte der Itala* (*Studien und Kritiken*, 1889, pp. 331–355).
De Bruyne, *Étude sur les Origines de notre texte latin de S. Paul* (*Revue Biblique*, 1915, pp. 358–392).
Diehl, *Zur Textgeschichte des lateinischen Paulus* (*Z.N.T.W.*, 1921, pp. 97–132).
von Soden, *Das Lateinische N.T. in Afrika zur Zeit Cyprians*, 1907.
Der Lateinische Paulustext bei Marcion und Tertullian (*Jülicher Festgabe*, 1927, pp. 228–276).
Haussleiter, *Zwanzig Predigten Novatians* (*Theologisches Literaturblatt*, April 6, 13 and 20, 1900, three articles).
d'Alès, *Novatien*, 1924.
Vetus Romana (*Biblica*, 1923, pp. 56–90).
Souter, *A Study of Ambrosiaster*, 1905.
The Earliest Latin Commentaries on the Epistles of St. Paul, 1927.

E. On the general thought-background of the second century:

Bousset, *Hauptprobleme der Gnosis*, 1907.
Norden, *Agnostos Theos*, 1913.
Wendland, *Die Hellenistisch Römische Kultur*, 1912.
de Faye, *Gnostiques et Gnosticisme*, 1913 (2nd edition, 1925).
Casey, *The Study of Gnosticism* (*J.T.S.*, Jan. 1935).
Jonas, *Gnosis und Spätantiker Geist*, 1934.
Cumont, *Les Religions Orientales dans le Paganisme romain* (4th edition, 1929).
Nock, *Conversion*, 1933.
Tollinton, *The Two Elements in Marcion's Dualism* (*J.T.S.*, 1914, pp. 263 ff.).
Angus, *The Mystery Religions and Christianity*, 1925.
The Religious Quests of the Greco-Roman World, 1929.
Dodd, *The Bible and the Greeks*, 1935.
W. L. Knox, *St. Paul and the Church of the Gentiles*, 1939.
Some Hellenistic Elements in Primitive Christianity, 1944.
Reitzenstein, *Das Iranische Erlösungsmysterium*, 1921.
Die Hellenistischen Mysterienreligionen (3rd edition, 1927).
Mitchell, *St. Ephraim's Prose Refutations of Mani, Marcion and Bardaisan*, 1914 and 1921.
Harris, *On the Trail of Marcion* (*Deissmann Festgabe*), 1927.
Marcion's Book of Contradictions.

SUBJECT INDEX

INDEX OF AUTHORS

INCLUDING THE FATHERS

REFERENCES TO SCRIPTURE

OLD TESTAMENT

GOSPELS

(apart from the citations on pp. 135–157, 169–171.)

LATIN CODICES